YOUR
SECONDARY
SCHOOL PLACEMENT
TOOLKIT

YOUR
SECONDARY
SCHOOL PLACEMENT
TOOLKIT

JOHN KEENAN & ANDY HIND

1 Oliver's Yard
55 City Road
London EC1Y 1SP

2455 Teller Road
Thousand Oaks
California 91320

Unit No 323-333, Third Floor, F-Block
International Trade Tower
Nehru Place, New Delhi 110 019

8 Marina View Suite 43-053
Asia Square Tower 1
Singapore 018960

British Library Cataloguing in Publication data

A catalogue record for this book is available from the British Library

Editor: James Clark
Assistant editor: Esosa Otabor
Production editor: Victoria Nicholas
Marketing manager: Maria Omena-Neale
Cover design: Sheila Tong
Typeset by: TNQ Tech Pvt. Ltd.
Printed in the UK

ISBN 978-1-5296-8457-5
ISBN 978-1-5296-8456-8 (pbk)

Contents

About the Authors

John Keenan taught English in secondary schools, sixth form and Further Education before moving to Higher Education, teaching at Leicester University, Coventry University, Worcester University and now Birmingham Newman University, where he is Senior Lecturer in Education. Previous roles included lead tutor of **Teach First** English for the West Midlands, coordinator of an Advertising and Media degree and lead tutor of Post Graduate Certificate of Education (**PGCE**) English. John has a research focus on teacher education and Further Education and supervises doctoral students researching these areas. He has published journal articles and book chapters in the field of education, co-edited a book on *College-based Higher Education* and co-written *Your Secondary School Direct Toolkit* with Andy.

Andy Hind worked as a science teacher in Leeds and Bradford before moving to the University of Leeds as a researcher of science education. Andy then returned to secondary teaching as Head of Science in a secondary school in Leeds. He moved on to work in Initial Teacher Education as a science tutor for both the Open University and Manchester University. Andy moved to Birmingham Newman University in 2010 where he taught on both undergraduate and postgraduate programmes before his current role as Head of the Centre for Teacher Education at Warwick University. Andy is a member of the Universities Council for the Education of Teachers and sits on national steering committees, helping to define the future direction of teacher training.

Acknowledgements

As ever, with love and thanks to Rebecca and Blossom – John.

To Sarah, Rebecca and Rory, for your unfailing love, support and kindness – Andy.

We would like to thank the following contributors for allowing us to publish their work: Dan Bevan, Lewis Hyde, Elizabeth Lawson, Karen Teasdale, Melisa Watkins, Luke Amos, Alex Harden, Gabriel Zanovello, Arte Artemiou, Sam McDonough, Naima Begum, Evie Booton-Ford and Barwago Ismail. Special thanks also to Rebecca Moden for proofreading and expertise. We would also like to thank our colleague Upkar Singh for his words of wisdom.

We extend these thanks to all of our former trainee teachers as this book contains your experiences. We learned so much from being part of your lives during your year of ups, downs and a deep desire to just get some more sleep.

Introduction

One of our colleagues, on being told that we were about to write this guide to surviving a secondary teacher training school placement, said: 'A whole book! They only need one word: doasyertold'. We cannot really disagree with this, because if you 'do as you're told' by those running your **Training Provider** and your school mentors, then you are likely to survive your placement. If 'do as you're told' was all that you read from this book, and you thought, 'That will do, that's good advice' and it helped you to succeed, then the book would have served its purpose. This book is not designed to be explored and analysed like a Shakespeare play but used like a dishcloth (not literally – it wouldn't be very good) to be picked up and put down when needed.

We have tried to make this book resemble a 'toolkit' as far as possible – though we are not really 'toolkit' kind of people ourselves. For one thing, give either of us a bag of DIY tools and we are likely to say, 'Thank you' (for we are always polite) and put it in a shed, if we can find a part that is dark and inaccessible enough. We would be the same, we suspect, if our 'toolkit' was a make-up bag; we have shown little aptitude for appearance-making so far in our lives, as evidenced when we both turned up for a meeting to discuss plans for this book wearing the same jumper, in both cases given as a gift and not liked very much. Much like this jumper, simplistic views of education do not suit us. We do not think there are easy answers to anything, but in this 'toolkit' of a book, we try to rein in our natural woolly-mindedness so that it does not obscure our key messages which will help you survive your placement. We have, between us, over 50 years of experience to share, working in schools, sixth forms, further education colleges and six universities. We have been guides for hundreds of trainees, and in every chapter of this book we distil what we have told them. We select the best of what we have witnessed from the evidence-base – the writing on, about or around education – and add our own interpretations, experience and advice.

The book is conversational in style (albeit, inevitably, a little one-way) because we know that there is no certainty in teaching. The answer to most questions about whether this or that approach will work is, 'it depends'. Should you be strict at the start? It depends – on the class, on who you are, the school, the time of day, the needs of the pupils in the room, etcetera. Teaching is, in the end, the dynamic that you, the teacher, create in a particular room at a particular time with a particular group of pupils. We cannot be in there with you nor do it for you, but we can advise you to put all of your energy and focus on the precious hour or so that you have with these pupils at this time – because it will never occur in exactly the same way again. This book cannot protect you from the often difficult realities of teaching (unless you take it into lessons with you and hold it in front of your body to bat away the projectiles the pupils are firing). We think in terms of 'surviving' the school placement but of course this might not be how you experience it, as all placements are different: essentially, what we want is for you to thrive, excel, show the experienced teachers a thing or two and 'wow' them all!

One central message of this book is that schools are unique places. Each school has responded to the macro government requirements mixed with the meso-level of the social expectations of the geographical area, formed into a microcosm into which you, as a trainee teacher, will enter. You may become part of this microcosm, or find that your 'face doesn't fit'. If the latter, you may fail that particular placement in that particular school. If you get to another school and it happens again, then you may just be unlucky; if it happens in yet another school that might be the time to start considering whether teaching is the job for you.

We offer 'practice-informing research and theory' (Goodson, 2003: 123). There is some reluctance, we often find, on this vocational course, for trainee teachers to read about their profession. It is as if teaching is something you should just 'do' rather than learn about. We want you not only to read, but also to question what you read – including everything we write ourselves. The theory we present is just that: theory. As Jean Baudrillard wisely noted, if there is debate, then there cannot be a single correct answer: 'The secret of theory is that truth does not exist' (2007: 120). In place of 'truth' comes insight; greater understanding of a topic. An education theory is, essentially, an idea someone believes and as much as governments might want to claim that some theories are 'evidence-led' and others not, nothing is proven and no approach is a panacea. The theory of education is like the ancient story of a group of blind men who came across an elephant, each man grabbing hold of part of it. The one who had taken hold of the leg was convinced he had found a trunk of a tree, the one who held the tusk was convinced he had found a spear and the one who had held the tail, a rope. As the poet John Godfrey-Saxe (1872), retelling this story, observed: 'each was partly in the right, And all were in the wrong!' Someone gets hold of an aspect of education and develops an approach or a theory, but may not see the whole system or circumstances, so their approach or theory is likely only to be relevant in certain cases. The ideas we present will both be right and wrong: they will work in some circumstances and not in others; they will work for another teacher but not for you. As training teachers you are trying to make sense of what is new. We hope to widen your experience to let you see more of the whole elephant – if this is not too strange an idea.

While we very much hope the contents of this book are applicable to all those who are training to teach in school and interested in education, the United Kingdom is a devolved nation, meaning that each part of it has its own education system and rules. England, Scotland, Wales and Northern Ireland have differing curricula. If you live in Scotland, for example you get the benefit of a free Post Graduate Certificate of Education (PGCE) course and, if you qualify, even a **maintenance loan** (Teach in Scotland, 2024; TGTCS, 2024) Northern Ireland, and Wales (Gov.Wales, 2024) but we are both English (with a bit of Irish in one of us) and we work in England, so this dominant focus on the English system is one of the book's biases. Another bias is that we are both male. Education theory has a tendency to privilege this sex and is particularly fond of the ideas of Dead White Males. This book, being written by two non-dead ones (at the time of writing), inevitably contributes somewhat to this privileged position and cannot avoid coming out of it. We are particularly aware of the attribution of, and praise for, often pretty common-sense ideas to males who were accorded their status by a patriarchal power-base and a hierarchical academic system. We try to recognise that when we are attributing, for example, the common-sense idea that given the choice of a chocolate bar or being hit with a stick most would prefer the former to Burrhus Frederick Skinner, what we are doing is replicating the idea that only white, middle-aged males, who worked in universities have the wisdom and insight to take collective thought forwards. As white, middle-aged, middle-income males who work in universities, we are very much set against this idea. We have tried to include a variety of theories – in terms of historical time period, geography, culture, ethnicity, as well as sex – and also to give the floor to a diverse range of voices and lived experiences in the case studies of this book. In this book, we have mostly used gendered pronouns but occasionally not, when we were unsure of the preferred form.

This book was written at a time of change in teacher education. The phrase 'a time of change in teacher education' could actually reference any year over the past forty – but the current situation is particularly momentous, because the recent change of government will bring change in education policy. We were made painfully aware of this when just after our last book, *Your Secondary School Direct Toolkit*, was published the government decided that 'School Direct' was no longer the compulsory term for school-led training! We hope that you will forgive the out-of-dateness of some of the details and find our underlying messages still relevant and useful.

Despite all of the tried and tested educational approaches and theory we present in this book, we recognise that they do not have the ultimate answers – you do. You are the master of your fate, the 'captain of your soul' as it were, which is a satisfying position to be in. We present the 'kit' (this book) with the 'tools' (approaches to education, information about the system, and advice about how to make sense of it) and invite you to use them to make something purposeful, beautiful and life-changing. With these tools, in this kit, are you a 'craftsperson'? An artisan? A 'bodger of the job'? At times, we all are 'bodgers'; this book is partly here to tell you that sometimes this is okay. It is not that you are just 'allowed' to make mistakes: you must. It's how you learn. The car bumper sticker: 'I have learnt so much from my mistakes, I am thinking of making a few more' should be given out free with this book.

The book addresses key issues which you will face while training to be a teacher. Chapter 1 focuses on how you can become part of the teaching profession. It explores the likely teaching curriculum in your training year and advises you to give self-care. Chapter 2 considers how schools work. It describes types of schools and the management system which might be employed there alongside giving advice in how to manage the typical and untypical school day. Your mentor will guide you through a placement, so Chapter 3 discusses how to work best with them. Chapter 4 stresses the importance of you as a subject expert. Chapter 5 informs you of the law and regulation of schools, with a focus on safeguarding children.

Once this central role is considered, we move you onto the most important aspect of what you do in school in Chapters 6 and 7, which focus on learning theory, and explore what you will need to plan and run a lesson. All pupils must be able to access your lesson and be challenged by it, so Chapter 8 examines how to adapt it for all. The learning in the lessons will need to be known, recorded, and fed back to parents/carers; this is discussed in Chapter 9. The complexity of learning is considered in Chapter 10. Chapters 11 to 13 look forward, beyond your placement, to consideration of your future as a teaching professional. Chapter 11 considers how you can create a professional identity and explores some of the issues about seeing yourself as a 'teacher'. Chapter 12 advises you on interviews and first jobs and Chapter 13 recommends ways in which you can keep learning about your profession.

In each chapter, we present the reflections of a former trainee teacher so that you can not only learn about what might happen career-wise after achieving **Qualified Teacher Status** (QTS), but also learn from their experience. Each chapter also contains a personal **reflection** point, suggested actions and recommended reading, giving you more places to access tools for your toolkit.

The placement will develop you; toughen you up, probably. You earn your medals in this business, and wear your scars with pride. This is likely to be a year when the worst days are the best ones for you because you learn most from the worst days. Remember that all you can do, on those worst days, is your best.

References

Baudrillard, J. (2007) *Forget Foucault*. Los Angeles, CA: Semiotext(e).

Godfrey-Saxe, J. (1872) *The Blind Men and the Elephant*. Available from: https://www.poem hunter.com/poem/the-blind-man-and-the-elephant/

Goodson, I. (2003) *Professional Knowledge, Professional Lives*. Maidenhead: Open University Press.

Gov.wales (2024) *Curriculum for Wales*. Available from: https://hwb.gov.wales/curriculum-for-wales/summary-of-legislation/

TGTCS (2024). *The General Teaching Council for Scotland*. Available from: https://www.gtcs.org.uk/

Teach in Scotland (2024) *Become a Teacher*. Available from: https://teachinscotland.scot/become-a-teacher/funding-and-fees/

1

Becoming Part of the Teaching Profession

What this chapter will cover

- Welcome to the world of teaching
- Your training curriculum
- Resilience
- Well-being
- The emotional teacher

Introduction

Imagine a spring – perhaps the one you took out of your pen because you were bored in a lesson, or so that you could use the pen stem to shoot a chewed-up paper pellet at the teacher. There is a rule about this spring called Hooke's Law which tells us about the way a spring will behave until it reaches its limit, after which point it no longer springs. Now imagine that you are that spring. At what amount of being stretched by life, school, your Training Provider and your bank manager would you no longer be able to reshape yourself? It is worth remembering that there is a breaking point for even the thickest steel. This chapter discusses what you are expected to be able to do, prepares you for school and gives you some tools to cope. This chapter is also here to help acculturate you into a proud professional community: one that has written, unwritten, spoken and unspoken ways of working, habits, words and practices that, as a trainee teacher, you are expected quickly to understand. The nature of being a professional is explored, in terms of being someone who is both able to act within the school system and conform to the institution and act autonomously from an informed and moral standpoint. A key message of this book is in this chapter: your school is a place with certain rules and you are new to it, so you will need to learn about and accept the institution as it is, with all of its flaws, for the short time you are there. The chapter also introduces you to the **Initial Teacher Training and Early Career Framework** (ITTECF) which sets out what trainee teachers need to know and practise.

Welcome to the World of Teaching

We would like to start by congratulating you on an excellent choice of course. We think it is a course you will never regret doing however long you teach: six months, a year, five years or 30 years. You should never regret having been engaged with young people's learning and their lives: it is a real privilege. You will affect the children you meet for the rest of their lives. Teachers are rarely forgotten – and even if they are, their effects are not.

There is no single type of school in which to train. Having visited hundreds of schools, we have observed that each school has its own culture and each school contains people who think that everything taking place within its walls is perfectly normal – no matter how crazy it might seem to us (and our trainee teachers). A school is its own unique world. We've come across doors we cannot get into or out of, and ones plastered in signs about what you cannot do, including: 'Do not open this door'. We've been in schools which have silent pupils in corridors and lessons, and others where dodging the footballs on the way in is a real achievement; if the pupils' aim had been better they would have got us. There are many different types of schools including grammar, mainstream comprehensive, faith, independent and character. One **character education** school (designed to instil in its pupils a positive attitude to learning and life) exhausted one of us when about 75 pupils walked past in reception, each offering the cheery greeting, 'Good Morning, Sir!' to which we felt obliged to reply, about 75 times. Schools have similarities and differences but, in the end, it is best to think of the school you're undertaking your placement in as unique.

What if this school does not suit you? We have conducted 'exit interviews' in which the trainee teacher explained that their reason for quitting was that they were being overly directed despite wanting a career in which they could make their own decisions; other trainee teachers stated that they were quitting because they did not get told what to do and could not cope. If only the right school could be matched to the right person and personality but then, how can you know what is right for you until you have actually experienced the school? If only there was such a thing as speed-dating schools, then you might be able to find your perfect match. You will be placed in two schools during your trainee year and they should be contrasting in type. We often find that trainee teachers on their first school placement have little to compare it with until the second. When the second placement starts, the scenario can begin to resemble the first boy/girlfriend you 'dumped' but now desperately want back because you ended up with someone who suits you less. Or, worse, you accepted a job at the first school and are now in love with the second. In terms of taking jobs, we advise you to never say a 'yes' you do not mean – and this is not bad advice for other areas of life as well.

Whatever school you happen to be in, you will undergo some similar experiences to other trainee teachers in other schools. One is that the day runs quickly. If you have five spare minutes in school, for example, you will find yourself hopefully thinking: 'I could phone three parents and mark five books'. The teacher's never-ending list of tasks means that speed is necessary and this, we find, sometimes gets misinterpreted by trainee teachers who think that teachers and mentors in school have been 'short' with them, are barking orders or have no time to speak. Everyone has time in school – time is, arguably, infinite – but there are hundreds of things that teachers need to do with that time. We notice that time pressures can cause body language and verbal indications to change. Teachers and mentors might ask a trainee teacher how they think the lesson went, but sometimes their body language shouts: 'Hurry up and tell me!' The vast majority of teachers are good people and the vast majority of schools are good places but school culture can be stressful. If you want nourishment, realistically, we suggest that you buy some spinach. Teachers' shortness of time – sometimes resulting in shortness of temper – is a cultural change we have experienced within our lifetimes. While we were not of the generation where ample time to read a newspaper and smoke a pipe in the staffroom was the norm, invariably we would go to the staffroom (there were staffrooms in every school in those days) and have a cup of coffee at morning break time; it was rude not to. The pace and the amount of sheer 'stuff' we had to do in those days were not the same as today, for three reasons:

- Emails and the **Virtual Learning Environment** (Moodle, Blackboard, etc.) have brought an enormous workload which is currently unrecognised by many schools' work allocation methods.
- Datafication and datwith veillance – at some point, everything got turned into numbers, from attendance to learning, and these numbers are used to check on teachers in a form of surveillance to monitor whether targets (often unrealistic ones) are being met.
- Responsibility – at some point in the last 20 years the learning moved from being the responsibility of the pupils to the responsibility of the teacher.

You will have to work quickly, in a fast-moving environment, where everyone is busy and trying to meet several deadlines. You might learn, as we have done, that as much as you try to complete everything on time, you can relate to Douglas Adams (2002: xxv) who said: 'I love deadlines. I love the whooshing noise they make as they go by.' You certainly have to learn to prioritise if you are going to survive. What needs to be done right now is what matters first. What can wait until later on (or, rather, until it becomes absolutely necessary) . . . can wait.

From the very beginning of your course you, as a trainee teacher, are expected to act and behave like a 'real' teacher even though you are not being paid; even though no-one is giving you any status or a contract. That is, unless you are one of the few trainee teachers who are on a '**salaried**' route. If not, you are the most dispensable person in the building, because you do not run the classes on your own and your removal from the school causes no gaps in the function of the organisation; if you are 'not very good', your removal will make it easier. Like an understudy actor, you are expected to demonstrate that you could be playing this role properly; the only way of demonstrating that you could be a teacher is to be one for a short while.

Prior qualities, skills and knowledge expected of a trainee teacher include:

- Dependability. You need to turn up (sounds odd, but some of our trainee teachers had a series of reasons why they did not do so and they did not last long on a placement) and you need to do so on time.
- Open-mindedness. You need to act as a learner, not someone who knows everything (or why would you be a trainee?)
- Adaptability. You will be given lots of differing (and sometimes contradictory) advice and will be expected to be open to changing your approach to teaching; it is important to realise that there are many ways to teach well.
- Self-care. Try not to not end up weeping on your mentor's shoulder every night (and remember to use antiperspirant, which will help if you do).
- Subject knowledge – although everyone knows this will develop over time.
- The desire to work with children – because if you do not take pleasure with working with young people, it is a tough job!

Prior skills and knowledge not expected of a trainee teacher include:

- Class control. This is something you will be expected to learn on the placement.
- Knowledge about how to adapt lessons for the class. This will be expected to develop through the year.
- Pedagogical Content Knowledge (PCK) – it is the Training Provider and subject mentor's job to give you the subject-specific theoretical domains of professional knowledge for teaching.
- Assessment. You will learn how to evaluate learning and to mark and give feedback from having it modelled from moderation sessions and good old-fashioned trial and error.
- Knowledge of the **Teachers' Standards**, against which you are assessed (these will be included in your Training Provider's curriculum and assessment criteria).

Your Training Curriculum

In 2019, the **Core Content Framework** (CCF) (DfE, 2019a) was put in place alongside an **Early Career Framework** (ECF) (DfE, 2019b) which had similar content for teachers in the first two years of employment. It made sense to amalgamate the two; so in 2024, the CCF and ECF were replaced by the Initial Teacher Training and Early Career Framework (ITTECF) which contains a selection of 'evidence-based' education theory and insists that this theory is included on teacher training courses and during a teacher's first two years in school. Before the CCF, ECF and ITTECF, there was always shared practice and a common sense about what should be taught and which education theories were useful. These frameworks explicitly challenged Training Providers to remove learning theory that was not 'evidence-led'. Out went, for example, Benjamin Bloom's Taxonomy of Learning, and out went the idea that pupils had different styles of learning such as the visual, auditory and kinaesthetic about which the ITTECF states:

> There is a common misconception that pupils have distinct and identifiable learning styles. This is not supported by evidence and attempting to tailor lessons to learning styles is unlikely to be beneficial. (DfE, 2024a: 21)

We had been very sceptical of both ideas before the frameworks, and suspect most teacher trainers were, but now we were told that they were 'neuromyths' and we were definitely not to teach them as truths.

In terms of the messages it gives about teaching, the ITTECF is not contentious. While we do not like the limited and limiting nature of it, there is nothing in it we would explicitly disagree with in terms of the messages about teaching. To give you a 'flavour' of what the ITTECF advises:

- Children cannot cope with too much information.
- Memorisation is important.
- Children need clear rules.
- Teachers need to support positive behaviour.
- Assessment is integral to learning.
- Good teaching adapts to specific challenges experienced by learners.
- Subject knowledge of teachers is very important.

The ITTECF gives Training Providers such compulsory messages and related reading matter which, they claim, is 'evidence-led'. To borrow the language of the ITTECF, you will need to 'learn that' (i.e. you will be given knowledge) and 'learn how to' (i.e. you will be expected to put this knowledge into practice). It is a two-pronged framework meant to ensure that you not only learn in theory but act on it.

Resilience

You cannot prevent life carrying on - it does not just stop when you start to train to teach - but you can work on your strengths and therefore your springiness, and therefore your resilience. Some of our trainees have painful relationship break-ups, others have parents die, some end up in hospital and yet, having been in tears with us on Friday, there they are back in school on the next Monday: often we do not understand how they manage to do it. We recall one trainee teacher passing out on a school playing field, coming round three days later in hospital, and on being asked if he was okay cheerfully shrugging, saying: 'I was fine as I had no idea anything went on. It was everyone who had to deal with me I felt sorry for'. Like the Japanese folk tale of the tree and the reed – the smaller, lighter reed is more able to bend than the great tree when the storms come.

The governmental, mediated and cultural definitions of the job can be problematic for a trainee teacher. You may not always get the respect the position deserves – not only from busy teachers and mentors but from central government and cultural expectations. Teaching is, strangely, simultaneously denigrated and revered in the United Kingdom. There is the widely quoted saying, based on a line from George Bernard Shaw's *Man and Superman* that: 'Those who cannot do, teach'. Government rhetoric often claims that these people who supposedly cannot 'do' are not 'not-doing' it enough. Take this instance, witnessed by one of us in a coffee shop: a barista told some customers he was going to be a teacher. The customers responded with an anecdote about someone who they worked with in their sales business world who started a teacher training course in History but couldn't do it. They ended this little conversation with, 'We'll be back in soon to see how long you lasted'. They have a point: nearly a quarter of new teachers leave within three years (DfE, 2021) and a reason for job dissatisfaction given by 83% of teachers is government and policy (DfE, 2024b).

You will also have to deal with the mediated and cultural definitions of your age group, whether you are seen as being 'too old' or 'too young'. We have both known a mentor to ask us, referring to an older trainee teacher: 'Why does she want to go into teaching at her age?' If you are in your 20s, or even possibly 30s, you will no doubt be aware of the derogatory term 'snowflake' which can be bestowed on younger generations (often by smug and self-deceiving members of older ones). There is a stereotype of Generation Z (those born from 1997 to 2012) as a generation which is not resilient, and this idea sometimes gets repeated to us by mentors. It is nonsense, of course. We are individuals who belong to, but are not defined by, our generation. Age group is just another social discourse which comes with expectations and permissions, including the extent to which we can share feelings and express individuality; Generation Z was given greater permission in the way that our generation (X) was not. When examples of 'snowflake-ness' come up, it is easy for mentors to jump to the stereotype – and stereotypes can act as weapons. On the other hand, this 'snowflake' stereotype gets reinforced on occasions, such as when one of our trainee teachers said to her mentor, on being given a timetable: 'You can't do this because it will damage my mental health'. Another trainee, who had not followed instructions properly, said to one of us: 'You have exceeded my cognitive load and therefore it is your fault that I do not know it'. Impressed as we were by the way that they could articulate one of the central messages in their training programme that pupils must not be given more information than they could handle, such comments do not bode well for anyone starting a profession where the learning comes thick and fast. All we can suggest is having awareness of the stereotype and realising that some of the comments you may hear (whether you are Generation Z or not) are probably not really directed to 'you' but cultural expectations and stereotypes. We also agree with Bruce Daisley (n.d.) who famously pointed out that just telling someone to be more resilient would never work:

> Never in the history of resilience, has someone become more resilient by being told to be more resilient.

Resilience comes from looking after yourself, so that you can protect and sustain yourself.

Well-being

One irony of teaching is that over-worked trainee teachers often have to teach pupils about well-being. You are the children's guide for how to balance life and make sense of their place in the universe. How can you help children to cope with their lives when you do not always feel able to cope with your own? You have to be a champion of Social, Emotional and Mental Health (SEMH) needs and teach Relationship and Sex Education (RSE). Even if your life feels like a Country and Western song in which your partner and dog have just packed their bags and run off to live with the man who came to repossess your house, and when you finally manage to walk many miles to one of the few remaining public payphones (as they took your mobile and drove off in your car) even your mum isn't answering. The balance of 'being real' about yourself and your life while performing the role of a teacher who safeguards children can be a difficult act – but it is an act. You have to play your part in the theatre of a school and no matter what else may be happening in your life, you must not bring it into the building because you have a priority of safeguarding and teaching children there.

If you are to survive a placement – and we have been on the other end of so many tearful conversations with trainees that we know it is not easy – you should try to ensure your own well-being. Some well-being advice can give you more tasks to do: do some yoga, try mindfulness, manage your time better, try colouring in a picture of a bunny. In our current jobs, we are given a 'well-being day'. But what we would really like is to more time to get on with our jobs so we can have a day off on Sunday. Each time, the well-being advice is to act as an individual, rather than to join in a collective pressure group to work together to improve work conditions. If you are stressed, it is because you have not done enough of whatever you were told to do to alleviate it (and so your fault). Meanwhile, an overload of tasks may be what is really 'stressing you out'. Furthermore, this way of thinking makes the issue your problem which is why it may be popular with policymakers: it means they do not have to address the all too often untenable conditions of work. We recommend the following, based on our experience of seeing how trainee teachers cope with the year:

- Give yourself time to reflect on your practice. Think and self-talk. Treat this as a necessary part of your development. This can be done whenever and wherever – on the bus, walking the dog, etc.

- Outside school, become a person again with hobbies, friends and a family. It is easy to get lost in the workload and, in teaching, this workload will never disappear. It is also all too easy to start being a teacher at home and that will not go down well with parents, partners and housemates.
- Care for yourself. There is no reason in the world not to be kind to yourself. Praise yourself and have treats and rewards. Why not? Speak to yourself in the way you would speak to a friend and in this way you will find yourself giving kinder responses. Do this out loud if you like (although perhaps best not to do so while in school).
- Parkinson's Law states: 'Work expands to fill the time available'. This means that whatever task you have to do, given an hour or given three hours that is how long it will take. Learn to focus for a short time and concentrate on the task in hand and you will be more effective.
- Find private space to work in school and try to do as much as you can while you are there. Trainee teachers who remove themselves from communal areas may be seen as being anti-social and not wanting to be part of the team, but try to find a balance between being a team player and being in a quiet place where you can focus on your work. (This balance was not found by the trainee teacher who was caught playing computer games with the IT technician in what he thought was his 'spare' time; he had an 'uphill struggle' for the rest of the placement.)
- Remember that you are in the learning business and are supposed to make mistakes, so give yourself permission to. Even the game-playing trainee made it through in the end.

Conclusion

One of us was recently talking to an ex-teacher who said he wondered where the years had gone after 34 years in the classroom. There was not one ounce of regret about his years in school nor did he recall a bad moment. Instead, he reminisced with pleasure about the school trips and being an integral part of the community of the school; making a different in people's lives, were what he was missing. It reminded us of the advice of the poet W.H. Auden, who was a teacher in Malvern for three years (The Downs, n.d.) – watch the eyes of those who are dedicated to their professions to see their drive and fire. If you could have seen that ex-teacher's eyes, it would have reminded you of the joys and privileges of teaching and being part of young people's lives. You are the lucky ones, being at the start of your chosen career. You do, nevertheless, need to go into the teaching profession with your eyes open to the way it is controlled and find your own freedoms of activity and expression. This agency comes when you have demonstrated to teachers, mentors and those running your Training Provider that you can be trusted to safeguard and teach children – so work on this first. Earlier in this chapter, we mentioned the denigrating comment from George Bernard Shaw's play about those who cannot do ending up as teachers and will end with a much older saying from ancient Greece: 'Those that know, do. Those that understand, teach' (Aristotle, c.384–322 B.C.).

··· **REFLECTIONS**

What do you think of when you say, 'I am training to be a teacher'? How do you feel about yourself? How do others respond to this statement? What are your own thoughts about being labelled as a 'teacher'? Do you think that they give a true picture of who you are and want to be? The idea that your thoughts are not 'you' is a big realisation which can have the effect of freeing you up from your current state of mind and actions. You will need to talk back to your thoughts in order to give counterpoints. This is why written reflections are so important: they create spaces to not only write about how you are thinking and feeling but to present other possible interpretations.

Remember times when life has been tough and you have persevered. What did you rely on? If you struggled and had to give up, what did you learn from this experience? It may be that you learnt to be more forgiving and understanding of yourself.

···

··· **ACTIONS**

Your curriculum will be written by your Training Provider but it will be partly based on the ITTECF. It is worth accessing this document, which is available from:

https://assets.publishing.service.gov.uk/media/661d24ac08c3be25cfbd3e61/
Initial_Teacher_Training_and_Early_Career_Framework.pdf

Find the links to key research literature and note the guidance about best practice.

Try tracking your emotions on a chart. It may seem unnecessary when you feel good but it might reveal patterns when you do not. On a Tuesday night, for example when you have the Year 9 class you dread teaching in the morning. It will also be a useful reminder that things tend to get easier on a placement as you settle into it.

···

Case Study 1

Dan Bevan took a Drama and English degree and then an English PGCE in 2018–2019. He had two placements and despite the rather awkward second school trying to 'poach' him, had already accepted a job at the first, where he has been ever since. Dan reflects on his time in teaching and considers what it means to be resilient.

I think resilience is about accepting the fact that you don't know everything and that you never will know everything because if you're the type of person that has to get things right first time and can't take any feedback, can't take any criticism, then it's very difficult to be resilient in that situation because in education you find yourself always needing to improve. It's an ever-evolving profession so you need to be an ever-evolving person. What makes you resilient is 'riding the waves' and accepting that what you've done one day might not work tomorrow, and that's difficult. The school changes suddenly sometimes, as it did when our head teacher passed away, then we had a new head teacher, then we had a pandemic, and mixed in with this we've had **Ofsted**.

The school I am in is very family-orientated with everybody looking after everybody and the head teacher was very much in charge with very clear leadership, and clear direction, and micromanaged us a lot, and this filtered down to the point where you knew what you're doing every point of the day. When she was ill, suddenly the school was run by a Senior Leadership Team (SLT) and there was a kind of a vacuum at the top. I learned that the head teacher is very important in terms of school as they set the tone of the SLT and that is then filtered down. I also learned that the hierarchical structure of school worked right down to me. When they changed above, I had to change.

Before I started teaching, I would question everything but you realise that in a school you have to be wise and 'toe the line.' There is a culture of compliance in school so I find myself having to verbally agree with people and statements that I don't agree with, really. I find myself saying, "That's a good idea. Why don't we try this as well?" in the vain hope that they just forget about their bit and keep mine. I also find myself working out what the head teacher's strategy is as I know this will be expected of me.

When you are a trainee and in your first year as an Early Career Teacher, there is a 'sweet spot', when management leaves you alone and you are allowed just to do the job of teaching. After two years, you are expected to progress and keep yourself relevant. If you don't take on responsibility, you can become ignored and seen negatively as school 'dead wood'. I got a promotion in my third year as head of house role, which is a pastoral role. I got another for a curriculum role with Looked After students. I teach them **literacy** for an hour a week and mostly, I use it for emotional support or whatever they need. When something is not done well in the department, I will work at this part and improve it. I replanned the mark schemes for next year and redesigned the entire standardisation process so I put myself at the forefront of the assessment process.

You have to learn to patch up the gaps. With experience, I can see the issues and the pitfalls arising and rather than having to deal with the fallout of them later. I find a little section where I can 'dig in' and make a little difference. Sometimes, there is a sort of storm brewing, that you don't know how to navigate and you don't know what to do. It is as if your house is being rained on by torrential rain and every single window and every single door is open, and the roof is leaking so you find a window or door you can shut; just find one thing you can do to make it better.

This is a job of decision-making. I am constantly making decisions which will have an impact on somebody else. I am self-driven and self-motivated and usually I won't be beaten by anything but on one particular occasion I got upset by the politics of an interview situation and having not been given a promotion and ended up the same day sitting in a head teacher's office of another school and being offered a job and a £7000 pay-rise. I stalled on a decision and it was raised to £9000 and then I stopped and something wasn't right so turned it down. I think that you need this kind of judgement as if I had accepted, I may have walked into a nightmare. It is difficult working in just one school as I am never wholly sure what is out there and have to imagine what it would be like in another school. I take inspiration from a colleague who has worked at the school for 18 years. She has good relationships with all, and she's content. Like me, she loves the school and the demographic of pupils, because they are children from challenging backgrounds, challenging home lives, and I make a difference in their lives. I have a sense of purpose that I don't think I would find in a more privileged area.

I don't think that we ever finish our jobs as teachers. If you work in retail, you finish when that shop shuts as you can't sell anything but when I get home I'm still thinking about lessons and pupils and considering what I'm doing next. The quicker that, as a trainee teacher, you learn that you will never finish and change your mindset about work it is easier to understand the profession and fit into it. At university you have assignments and deadlines and there is an end in sight and there is a grade coming and now I've realised that summer isn't even the end because I'm having conversations about designing for next year. I will often go home and think, "I'm tired...yeah good" and I'm interested in that good tired feeling, that point when you are tired in teaching but there's a sense of satisfaction behind that tiredness. When those children smile, when they come and tell me about their day, good or bad, that makes me feel fulfilled. No matter how terrible the thing they're disclosing is, I think, "They trusted me with that," and you don't get real trust just 'plucked out of the air'.

I have kept my hobbies out of school. I am a photographer specialising in wrestling and I love music. Even this is not separated from school because with some pupils who love wrestling, that is my link with them. I go to the gym so instead of sitting there all night thinking of standardisation, or whatever, I sit there thinking about how many reps I did. I listen to music in my free periods and check my gym performance in the day and so my hobbies come into the school building. Some teachers leave their lives at the door and they're like robots but I'll use my outside life as a benefit. I know there are groups of pupils who love wrestling and some of them won't engage with school, but they will engage with me when I talk about wrestling. School does not like my tattoos and I have to keep them covered but if a pupil is hard to reach and struggling and I find they are interested in tattoos, I'll roll up my sleeves and they get a little bit of me and it gives them something to cling on to. I'm like a magician, something for every pupil, but I would have nothing in school if I hadn't got my home life because I bring it in. What else would I show them? A bar graph to show their progress over the past three terms?

I am one of the lucky ones. I enjoy teaching so much. I'm happy in education. It was always my plan to be a teacher. I never swayed. I never even looked at anything else since being in Year 10 in my English lesson with Mr Neville I wrote a war story during a lesson on a *Romeo and Juliet* module because I was fed up of the play, and I showed it him, and rather than admonish me for not concentrating on Shakespeare, he loved it, and a couple of lessons later I found myself annotating my own work that he'd given out as an example and I just thought, "This is phenomenal. What a man! I'm gonna be a teacher," and that's what I've done, and I've no regrets doing it. I never sit there and think I wish I trained for something else because it's the perfect place for me. What else would I do?

............................WHAT TOOLS ARE IN YOUR TOOLBOX NOW?

- Understanding that there is a curriculum your Training Provider has to teach.
- Permission to question the structures you find yourself in and to find agency within it as you form your own views on what works for you.
- Ways of supporting yourself through what might be a challenging year.

Places to Get More Tools for Your Toolkit

Bethune, A. and Kell, E. (2020) *A Little Guide for Teachers: Teacher Wellbeing and Self-care*. London: SAGE.
'Look after yourself' is the message of this practical self-help book.

Gomes, B. (2020) Teacher Workload: How to Master it and Get Your Life Back. Independently Published.
Written by a UK-based teacher about teaching with an independent publisher and mindset.

References

Adams, D. (2002) *The Salmon of Doubt: Hitchhiking the Galaxy One Last Time*. London: Random House.

Daisley, B. (n.d.) *Resilience and Inner Strength: How to Build It – Bruce Daisley, Author, Fortitude*. Available from: https://changemakers.works/podcasts/bruce-daisley-fortitude/

DfE (2019a) *ITT Core Content Framework*. Available from: https://assets.publishing.service.govuk/government/uploads/system/uploads/attachment_data/file/974307/ITT_core_content_framework_.pdf

DfE (2019b) *Early Career Framework*. Available from: https://www.gov.uk/government/publications/early-career-framework

DfE (2021) *School Workforce in England*. Available from: https://explore-education-statistics.service.gov.uk/find-statistics/school-workforce-in-england/2021

DfE (2024a) *Initial Teacher Trainee and Career Framework*. Available from: https://www.gov.uk/government/publications/initial-teacher-trainee-and-early-career-framework

DfE (2024b) *Working Lives of Teachers and Leaders: Wave 2 Summary Report*. Available from: https://www.gov.uk/government/publications/working-lives-of-teachers-and-leaders-wave-2/working-lives-of-teachers-and-leaders-wave-2-summary-report

The Downs (n.d.) *About the Downs: History of the School*. Available from: www.thedownsmalvern.org.uk/about-the-downs/history-of-the-school.html

2
How Schools Work

What this chapter will cover

- School life
- Types of schools
- School management systems
- Expecting unexpected events
- Training Providers

Introduction

This chapter explains and explores the way schools operate to give you a greater understanding of the world you have chosen to enter. There is no single type of school because there are many options for children's education including home schooling, Pupil Referral Units (PRU), Social, Emotional Mental Health (SEMH) schools, independent schools, faith schools, grammar school, academies, free schools and so on. This chapter explains the natures of some of these different schools and the hierarchy of school management structures within them. We also explore the move from a state comprehensive system to a market-driven one to give you a sense of some of the financial pressures schools operate under. There is guidance about some typical key roles in schools and advice on who you can learn from and gain support from on aspects of teaching. Emergencies and everyday disruptions to routines are also covered here to prepare you (as much as it is possible) for atypical events which may punctuate the school day. This chapter concludes with a section on how a school and a Training Provider (which runs your course) might work together and the differing roles they play in working towards the same end.

School Life

One of the mentors we were working with, when explaining why she was so tired, said: 'I have to make three decisions per minute'. That is a fair calculation, we think. It means that in the eight hours you are likely to be in the school building from 8 a.m. to 4 p.m. (and you will be lucky if you have as short a working day as this) you could make 1,440 decisions. One of them could be where to park your car. If you arrive at 8 a.m. you may not find a space in the car park, and will have to park on a street and annoy one of the school's neighbours. You will now be later than you wanted to be and the choice of which drink you will make yourself and question of how on earth to find a clean mug to do it in will have been overtaken by the need to attend briefing, which happens at 8.15 a.m. You will have not been able to check your emails or the Virtual Learning Environment (VLE), and if you get caught doing this in briefing you will be frowned on from a great height. Printing out resources for the first lesson is a priority but by this time someone has probably broken the machine. The next printer is in another block, and when you get there someone will have decided to teach *War and Peace* and mistakenly put the whole book on to copy 30 times. Standing a little closer to the person copying does not tend to speed matters up, but in such desperate situations you might as well give it a try. Eventually, you will have the resources for the first lesson, but not the chance to check the technology in the room. You will notice in this hypothetical situation that you have been excused from form time and assembly. In comes another colleague to ask about a pupil in your lesson, and another five minutes goes by. Your class has arrived outside while this is happening (and your increasingly annoyed mentor, who is outside of the classroom monitoring them). None of this narrative is very edifying and perhaps speaks more about our practice in school than yours, but it gives a picture of a school day that is busy from start to finish and which requires you to be constantly making decisions large and small. In this narrative, we have not yet reached even 9 a.m.

Decision-making can be tiring. Should you upbraid a pupil for wearing earrings? Should you talk to the pupil who is working but making too much noise at the same time? If we rely on making all these decisions in-the-moment, it would be overwhelming – especially as some decisions can have a critical impact on someone's future; for instance, did you just see a pupil talk in an exam? You are not sure, but if you decide 'yes' it could mean the end of that pupil's examinations with consequences for their future, a 'sliding doors' moment (a phrase from a popular film in which a character catches a train and then the scene is replayed as if the train had been missed) because the difference this one act could make in their lives could be played out in two simultaneous narratives – in one, they passed the exams and went on to university.

In order to survive this constant decision-making, prepare as much as you can in advance. Most Training Providers and mentors will expect all of the resources for lessons to be shared two days in advance of the lesson. This means two working days – so Monday's 11 a.m. lesson has to be shared by the previous Thursday at 11 a.m., at the latest. Expectations will vary: you may get given the lesson plans, or you may have a mentor who does not mind about seeing plans in advance and relaxes the rules.

For each of these lessons you are going to teach, you will need to know:

- the pupils' prior learning, and how secure it is;
- what knowledge, skills and understanding are to be taught;
- what pupils are expected to know and be able to do;
- what the barriers to learning of pupils in the class will be; and
- how you will respond to these barriers.

Added to this, we think, you should anticipate what you will do when likely events happen. Of course someone will tap a pencil, of course someone will call out the answer to a question and so on. Eventually, your response will become automatic but for now, plan. Planning (presentation, resources, rehearsal of instructions, questions and possible responses) is critical for new teachers and you should know what you are going to say and do, and in what circumstances.

Beyond lessons, the day can seem like a series of endless happenings... because it is. As former UK Prime Minister, Harold Macmillan, described the most difficult part of his job: 'Events, dear boy, events' (QI, 2020). Few of these events are vital in themselves, but each one is a part of what makes the teacher's day – for instance:

- a conversation with a form tutor about a pupil,
- contact with the Safeguarding Officer,
- arrangement for a school trip, and
- a phone call to a parent/**carer** to praise a pupil.

Each punctuates what you are there to do – to safeguard and teach hundreds of children each day. Every moment is an opportunity to work on a problem or celebrate a success, and it can be very tiring. The sheer amount of different activities – and we list some, in no particular order, below – makes it so. These can also be exhilarating and motivating; adrenaline is always a teacher's friend (until you want to sleep, that is).

Activities at School Directly Involving Pupils

- Chat to pupils around the school.
- Attend school trips.
- Teach lessons.
- Undertake bus and playground duty.
- Monitor school corridors and implement school behaviour policy.
- Check that diaries have been signed and communication with parents/carers is being carried out.
- Be a teacher of Relationship and Sex Education (RSE).
- Be a subject tutor.
- Be a teacher of literacy and **numeracy**.
- Be a teacher of Personal, Social, Health Education (PSHE).
- Be a model of well-being.
- Take registers.
- Be a form tutor.
- Check uniforms and school equipment.
- Anything we have missed.

Activities in School Not Directly Involving Pupils

- Attend briefings.
- Prepare for and attend parents' evenings.
- Contact parents/carers.
- Attend and take part in meetings.
- Mark pupils' work.
- Plan schemes of work.
- Plan and participate in school trips.
- Liaise with Teaching and Learning Assistants.
- Plan lessons.
- Create resources for lessons.
- Check emails and VLE.
- Respond to absences in registers.
- Prepare rooms before a lesson.
- Tidy up rooms after a lesson.
- Attend Continuous Professional Development (CPD) meetings.
- Write reports for all pupils.
- Keep up to date with subject knowledge.
- Keep up to date with curriculum changes.
- Liaise with Safeguarding Officer.
- Liaise with form tutors.
- Anything we have missed.

Types of School

Among the many types of school there are:

- academies: state-funded schools which operate as independent financial organisations.
- character schools: schools which concentrate on attitude and well-being.
- city technology colleges: state-funded schools which focus on science and technology.
- faith schools: run by religious organisations.
- pupil referral units: state-funded schools which teach those who have been excluded from mainstream education.
- private/independent schools: largely funded by parents/carers.
- state boarding schools: state-funded education but boarding is paid for by parents/carers.
- special schools: state-funded schools for children who need an education which focuses on these needs: cognitive, emotional, mental health, sensory, physical and communication.

There are subdivisions for each. For example, schools may be called 'university technical colleges' or 'studio schools'.

In the United Kingdom there is a primary sector and a secondary sector; some local authorities have a straddling middle school system. Take Worcestershire as an example. There are 112 schools, 30 of which are secondary, 19 are middle schools (typically for 11–14-year olds) (Worcestershire County Council, 2024). The county's major city, Worcester, has five mainstream secondary schools including an 11–19 language specialist school, Christopher Whitehead. There are also seven independent schools including the prestigious The King's School and Royal Grammar School, both of which charge around £18,000 per year (KSW, 2024; RGS, 2024) with scholarships and bursaries for anyone academically very advanced. There are faith-based state secondary schools in the city such as Blessed Edward Oldcorne Catholic College, Bishop Perowne Church of England College and the independent The River School which: 'Wholeheartedly honours God with every fibre of our being' (The River School, 2024). Any child permanently excluded from mainstream education might end up at Worcester's Newbridge School (2024) which reminds parents/carers on their website of Section 7 of the **Education Act** (2011): 'The parent/carer of every child of compulsory school age shall cause him/her to receive efficient full time education...Either by regular attendance at school or otherwise'. When not 'otherwise', Newbridge School provides specialist education to around 70 pupils who are excluded from mainstream schools so acts as a PRU. Children with a Statement of Special Educational Need (SEND) and an Education Health and Care Plan might go to Riverside School, up to a maximum of 68 pupils, as this is their capacity (Riverside, 2024). Any child with particularly complex needs could go to nearby Bromsgrove's Chadsgrove School and those with less complex needs to Regency High School (Chadsgrove, 2024; Regency, 2024). As we write, the Multi Academy Trust (MAT), Oasis, is behind a new school build in Worcester (Worcester News, 2022) that will initially cater for 600 pupils which may not sound like much, but this will be Year 7 only and this new school will grow to at least five times this figure in the next five years. This is only some of the provision of secondary education in one area. Worcestershire does not have a state grammar school system, which affects the nearby city of Birmingham, where the most academically advanced are 'creamed off' into eight grammar schools, all run by the King Edward VI Foundation (KES, 2024).

This variety of provision is a world away from the 1940s–1970s dream some politicians had of a system where all children get the same experience – a comprehensive education. A comprehensive system, as it was first envisaged, aimed to give all children an equal education regardless of their background. In 1970, Basil Bernstein, an expert on education and social class, concluded that this was a dream rather than a reality; the title of one of his journal articles stated: *'Education Cannot Compensate for Society'*. In other words, the children of wealthy parents/carers were doing better from state system education than those from economically poorer ones. Forty years later, education philosopher Richard Pring (2011) examined the idea that if all schools taught in exactly the same way and focused on the 'science of teaching' and empirically tested methods that all pupils regardless of background would succeed the same, but Pring came to the same conclusions as Bernstein:

> Those 'delivering what works' (the teachers) and those 'in receipt of the delivery' (the young people) dwell in a world of ideas through which they interpret the social worlds they inhabit. The students bring with them to the school understanding and interests which are rooted in the cultural lives of their families and social groups. It is not surprising that the targets set for them seem totally irrelevant – indeed inimical to their conception of what is worthwhile and in their interest. Similarly with the teachers. They too come to school with understandings of what is educationally worthwhile and rooted in a professional culture as teachers of literature or history or whatever. The school is where these different cultures interact, and the good teacher is engaged in a dialogue between these different cultural worlds. A straightforward account of causality (where a particular intervention can be predicted to have a desired effect) is hardly applicable in human affairs...In that sense, 'education cannot compensate for society' – and so much educational policy and intervention, based on that assumption, is grossly mistaken. (Pring, 2011: 157–8)

Despite misgivings from Bernstein – and later on Pring – there was a political will for a comprehensive system in the 20th century until the 1980s, when a Conservative government was 'hell-bent' on moving everything it could to a 'free market', including (as much as it would be possible to do so) schools. The changes this government put in place moved the United Kingdom to a neoliberal system, one which favours private enterprise above state-funded institutions. By handing the job of education over to market-driven schools which could act as independent businesses, the various governments since the 1980s side-stepped the need to make sure all children get an equal chance with education. Instead, they order schools 'to provide a level playing field' to those who come from a more economically disadvantaged background by giving extra targeted support to a group of pupils more likely to underachieve.

In order to explain the changes to schools since the 1980s, we will choose a single case, Northampton School for Boys (NSB) – the first teaching school for one of us. With a foundation going back to 1541 (NSB, 2024), this school owned land it could gain income from or sell in order to fund its expansion and facilities, and it did so when it was allowed to become a Grant Maintained School (GMS) in the 1990s. This meant that the school could become independent of the local authority, get funding directly from central government and supplement this with any funds it could create itself. Further freedoms for NSB to act as a private company were given with 'academy' status. The first round of academisation was in the 2000s when the New Labour government legislated that any school which failed an Ofsted inspection must be taken out of local government funding control and apply for sponsorship from business, churches or voluntary bodies (West and Wolfe, 2018). The next round of academisation – the Academies Act (2010) – allowed NSB to become, effectively, an independent school (Lexis Nexis, 2017) albeit one which got most funding from the state (and therefore the taxpayer). With its 'independent' wealth and strong alumni system (former students are known as Old Northamptonians and there is a thriving rugby and social club under this name) they refurbished the theatre, added a swimming pool and dance facility. National titles were won in rugby, basketball, football and rowing (NSB, 2024), many actors and dancers went on to work on the nation's stages, and NSB was voted Educational Establishment of the Year in 2017 (NSB, 2024). This does not mean that NSB is a comprehensive school – even while one of us was there, they seemed to be polishing up the old grammar school sign above their door. The freedoms of being an academy allowed the school to specialise and select students from beyond the geographical catchment area. It may be a more selective school but at the same time, provides top education and facilities for pupils in the area and its present high-flying reality can be contrasted to the comprehensive school days one of us was told about, where there were plenty of fights (although at least the teachers seemed to win most of them). NSB expanded from its single site to become a Trust to run the Northampton School (2024), a new school, and if legislation allows, no doubt will continue to expand. New schools can be called free schools (Gov.uk, n.d.), but they still operate as academies. One headteacher of a free school in Birmingham took this a bit too far when he paid himself a double salary (TES, 2020) – perhaps, to be fair to him, misinterpreting the word 'free'.

Within the fee-paying sector there are many types of provision, including that offered by Montessori and Steiner schools which focus on pupil autonomy, expression and creativity. Parents/carers can join up in community schools, and this increasingly happens. In Birmingham, for example, there are 168 secondary schools (Birmingham City Council, 2024); it might be a big place, but if all of them took 2000 pupils, we would have to question what was 'in the water', as they say, 11–16 years ago. With the liberalisation of school control, there has been a growth of small, mainly faith-based schools in the last few years. A.S. Neil's Summerhill School stands as a famous (and sometimes when the media coverage gets negative, infamous) example of a school that allows the pupils freedom to learn or not to learn. The choice of school is out there but the reality is constrained by funds, geography, transport and catchment areas (parents/carers cannot choose any school but have to apply and may not get their first choice). For all of the complexity of the secondary school landscape, 80 per cent of schools are academies/free schools and they teach 79 per cent of all secondary school pupils (Gov.UK, 2022); these as mainstream schools might still be recognised as the 'local comp'.

Training Providers

Teacher training in a formal sense has been with us since before the 1870 **Forster Act**, the creation of a **Board of Education** in 1899 and the 1902 Education Act, which established a national system of schooling alongside training for teachers paid for by taxation and administered by regional governments. Before this, there were places such as The Battersea Normal School in 1841 (If you think your mentors are strict, they are nothing compared to what you would have had then). There were notable similarities with today's teacher training, including two school placements. A century later (things moved much more slowly then) the **McNair Report** (1944) established teacher training centres, many of which went on to become today's universities. An example is Coventry Ladies' Teacher Training College, established in 1948 (Warwick, 2024) and still on the same site today as the Centre for Teacher Education, University of Warwick. The **Education Reform Act** (1988) launched a **National Curriculum** and an organisation that would enforce government requirements onto schools, training providers and teachers: Ofsted. By the time New Labour came to power, in 1997, much of the 'spadework' had been done to transform teacher education, especially the Education Act (1994) which established a governing body - the **Teacher Training Agency** - to oversee and fund training providers. The New Labour government (1997–2010) claimed,

> Our top priority was, is and always will be education, education, education.
> (Blair, 2001)

which signalled the 'end of an era' (Furlong, 2005: 120) for the universities and teacher training colleges that had dominated the sector in the latter half of the 20th century. New Labour's policies revisioned the whole idea of a teacher and teacher trainer as professional - from someone who is deemed worthy of holding a position of respect and authority with an inner **core** of moral and behavioural standards into someone who is 'managed' (Furlong, 2005: 120).

Increasingly, Training Providers are managed and told what to teach and how to assess but this instruction is framed around the language of 'free choice' and **neoliberalism**. There has been an opening up of the market to schools and private businesses such as Ambition (2024). You might be on a school-led programme. New Labour launched the first of these with the Graduate Teacher Programme (GTP, 1998) in 1998. It was aimed at mature learners who wanted to try out teaching as paid, **unqualified teachers**, and learn 'on the job' (TNA, n.d.). Teach First was also launched during the New Labour years, alongside the promotion of School Centred Initial Teacher Training institution (SCITTs) where schools could bypass universities and train their teachers in-house. The Conservative-Liberal Coalition government of 2010–2015 made no secret of its desire to continue the process of private companies and schools running teacher training, and initiated the School Direct programme. The government of the time seemed to be more comfortable with trainee teachers being taught by schools than university academics who the then **Secretary of State for Education** called 'The Blob, in thrall to Sixties ideologies' (Gove, 2013). The government aimed for half of trainee teachers to be allocated directly to schools and this was largely realised by 2018, with 47 per cent at university-based training and the remaining 53 per cent divided between school-led (35 per cent), SCITT (14 per cent), Teach First (9 per cent) and PGTA (4 per cent) (DfE, 2018).

Regardless of who your Training Provider is, the Post Graduate Certificate of Education (PGCE) course (as it is often termed) is normally a one-year course and the undergraduate route is normally three years although both can be taken part-time, in which case the time typically doubles. For the academic aspect of the qualifications, you will probably be in the hands of a Higher Education provider who might let you exit the course with a Level 6 qualification which may be called a Professional Certificate in Education or Professional Graduate Certificate in Education. Most trainees get a **Level 7** PGCE. Level 7 PGCEs bring 60 **credits** (a third of a **Master's degree**) or 90 credits (half of a Master's degree). At 120 credits, the award becomes a Post Graduate Diploma in Education (PGDE) and this is essential to teach in Scotland (Teach in Scotland, 2022). Anyone with a PGDE requires only 60 more credits to achieve the full 180 credits and to be awarded a full Master's degree in education; these credits are usually gained through a dissertation. The PGCE academic qualification is not necessary to teach in England – and some Training Providers do not offer it or will allow you to gain Qualified Teacher Status (QTS) without it – but schools may be wary of employing a teacher without it.

There are 210 accredited Training Providers; 142 of them are schools or MATs (GOV.uk, 2023). Training Providers offer QTS and if they are not universities, often work with such Degree Awarding Bodies (DAB) who award an academic qualification such as a PGCE. One of us worked for a DAB which taught the PGCE for the Training Provider Teach First. At the time, Teach First wanted 'top' students from 'top' universities and by the very nature of the connection between family income and academic success, they were often from the upper echelons of society and then placed in schools in the most deprived areas of the country. One of our Teach First English trainee teachers recalled a creative writing lesson in which they told the class: 'Let's imagine ourselves in a beautiful desert island where the sand is clean, and the sea is clear. Look away from those dismal, grey flats out of the window and. . .' A pupil, understandably indignant, interrupted with, 'That's my home!' Although there was sometimes a 'culture clash', Teach First's intentions were and are good – to put 'top' graduates into school, give them an up to 80 per cent timetable and solve the problem of recruitment in the most difficult schools. Teach First (2024) followed the pattern of Teach for America (Allen and Allnutt, 2017), including bringing in Brett Wigdortz from that organisation with his evangelical zeal to reform schools. Teach First is usually a two-year QTS course, with the idea that you teach first and go onto do something else – with over

40% of its trainee teachers doing just this after two years (Allen and Allnutt, 2017). Training Providers such as Teach First are allowed to train teachers and recommend QTS to the **Department for Education** (who are the only ones who can approve the status but there is no record of them ever refusing a Training Provider's recommendation).

The relationship between your Training Provider and a DAB may be a strained one, or not fully 'joined up'. Training Providers often 'shop around' for a DAB who is easy to work with, or cheap, or both. Some DABs are in different parts of the country and there can be little actual contact with trainee teachers. Into this gap, the trainee teacher has to enter. You need to keep positive relations with your Training Provider and with the DAB (they may be the same thing) but the main place you need to focus on is your placement school. We have often been in discussions with colleagues about trainee teachers whose performance on the university side is less than desired but, 'they are good in school' or 'they are good teachers' and this seems to resolve the issue. Nonetheless, you have a lot of relationships and connections to consider. Teacher training is ever-changing. In 2025, Teacher Degree Apprenticeships will add another layer of complexity and a four year partly on-the job route. We have not even mentioned Troops to Teaching or NowTeach because life is too short... as was the funding for these initiatives.

School Management Systems

School systems are stubbornly hierarchical and vertical. Power is held at every level but each has to look up to the other which may, to steal the punchline from an old comedy sketch, be a 'pain in the neck'. As there are many types of school, this structure may not be how all operate, but the vast majority do. Management and management structures are a bit like rabbits, we find, as they keep reproducing themselves. Here are some of the titles you may encounter:

- Chief Executive Officer: ultimately in control of the schools.
- Trustees: voluntary members who oversee all of the Trust's actions.
- Governors: voluntary members who are responsible for governance of individual schools.
- Executive Head: person who runs several schools.
- Senior Leadership Team for Trust: oversees the leadership teams in schools.
- Associate Head Teacher: runs a single school in a MAT.
- Head Teacher: runs a single school that is not in a MAT.
- Senior Leadership Team – supports the head teacher.

Below this upper management system comes teachers with responsibilities in schools. These are sometimes called Teaching and Learning Responsibility (TLR) role or a +1 or +3, as taking on responsibility increases a teacher's salary by stages. Usually, a teacher has to work one year in order to go up one level on the teacher's pay 'spine' (+1) but if responsibility is accepted, progress is speeded up. Here are some responsibility roles in a school which are likely to be in place.

- Head of Subject – responsible for the coordination of the teaching of a subject and will probably be accompanied by a deputy (or two).
- Head of Year (or Head of House) – coordinates the education of a year-group.
- Literacy Lead – devises school policy, checks and supports the teaching of English in all its forms.
- Numeracy Lead – devises school policy, checks and supports the teaching of maths in all its forms and skills.
- Personal Social Health and Economic (PSHE) lead – organises the whole-school teaching of wider life skills.
- Special Education Needs Coordinator (SENCo) – looks after the policies and processes of education and care for children who need extra support in school; sometimes called Special Education Needs and Disabilities Coordinator (SENDCo).
- Safeguarding lead – responsible for the policies which guard children.
- Lead Practitioner – teachers who models excellent practice and contributes to school improvement.

Expecting Unexpected Events

We both observe lessons regularly. One of us raised both eyebrows when the trainee teacher we were observing chose to use a countdown timer which ended in a bomb explosion sound, in a school which had had three emergency evacuations caused by a hoax-bomber in the previous week. As well as evacuating, schools may 'lock down' if there is a threat from outside or inside. Lockdowns are a desperately regrettable feature of modern life, but surely preferable to the lack of awareness or process which commonly existed before tragedies such as the 1996 Dunblane massacre in Scotland. Events such as these, which remain unthinkable even after they have taken place, have resulted in schools preparing themselves for emergencies. You must know what the school emergency policy is, how it is enacted and what it means for you and the pupils.

Fires and floods may also happen. It is hard to set fire to a school (you would have to really try!), but it happens. Fires tend to affect schools out of school time and while in England there were only 87 secondary school fires between 2015 and 2020 (Zurich, 2021), fires in both primary and secondary schools affected 389,830 hours of teaching time in this period. In 2007, when the water table was at its height in this country, in Hull alone 95 out of 98 schools were damaged by floods (Floodflash, 2021). As a teacher, you must be reflexive to the situation and respond in-the-moment; your primary concern must be for the welfare of the children. Alongside Fire and Flood, we even face a future where another Horseman of the Apocalypse, Famine, might not stay as far away as we would hope. Schools have had to adapt to the challenges of what has been termed a 'cost-of-living crisis' that sees children arrive either under-fed or under-nourished. Ironically, this has come at the same time as being tasked with addressing a rise in childhood obesity created by ultra-processed foods. Teachers and schools also got the burden of responsibility when yet another horseman turned up and Pestilence affected schools with the Covid-19 pandemic.

Conclusion

It is not that you have no choice about complying with school policy - you have all the choice in the world, but you will not survive your school placement unless you know, understand and conform to it. It would be an incredibly arrogant act to go in, as a trainee teacher, and try to change it. It is difficult to predict what your school will be like, but you can be sure that it is going to be a busy place. As a teacher, you are at the bottom of a chain of control and you should expect to be strongly directed in terms of your actions. You will be expected to respond to management in a positive manner and to protect the pupils if the worst happens. All of this, and the amount of roles and decisions that teachers have to take and make, can - unsurprisingly - lead to tiredness. You probably will feel tired, but we hope that it will be the 'good tiredness' which comes from doing a job you love and making a difference in the lives of others.

·····REFLECTION

You are likely to have four institutions to keep happy:

- Two placement schools,
- Training Provider, and
- Degree Awarding Body.

Are you aware of who these institutions are? Do you have a main contact for each one with whom you can discuss progress? Many Training Providers will not allow you to exit a course with just QTS; you have to get the academic award, such as a PGCE, as well. You are training to be a professional, so reflect on how you can be proactive and take control of the process.

·····ACTIONS

Locate the main people who you can contact about:

- School – you should have contact with the person who is the head of Initial Teacher Training (ITT) and a subject mentor.
- Training Provider – you should have contact with the head of secondary ITT.
- Degree Awarding Body – if you are on a PGCE, you should know who the key contacts are and should also know the requirements to pass.

Case Study 2

Lewis Hyde was as ready-made for a teacher training course as students come. He had experience tutoring pupils for the 11+ examination, a passion for his subject and the confidence and presence to engage a class. Nevertheless, during his second placement, he got to a point where he could not go in to the school. Here he recounts his experiences and reflects on how his placement schools differed, in order to give you a sense that your first school may well give you a different experience to your second. The names of the schools and mentors have been altered. Having successfully gained a PGCE and QTS, Lewis was accepted onto a PhD course at the University of London and is also teaching on a part-time basis.

I had two great mentors at my first school, St Andrew's – Gerald and Dave. I remember Gerald saying that one of the things he loved about teaching was that he loved his subject and you could see that in his enthusiasm for his lesson and I tried to replicate this. I feel like Dave and I were quite similar and when I was not teaching and even though it was not on my timetable, I would go in to his bottom set class. There were only 8 or 10 of them in the class. Despite there being two of us, they were still rowdy, but we spent the lesson laughing, talking and 'bouncing off' the pupils' responses and doing what we had to do to create a positive learning atmosphere and take care of the children in the room. I learned the importance of relationships from Dave. The school had a positive way of forming relations rather than putting them against a 'brick wall' of disciplinary procedure. Much as I enjoyed St Andrew's, the third school, The Grove Academy, was closer to what I was looking for. The best way I can put it is that its approach to supporting pupils 'spoke to me'. It was a standard old-fashioned comprehensive school. While there was a mindless management culture the building suited me as it was open and light, and the atmosphere among the staff was similar. The teachers would have a cathartic rant amongst themselves but they were totally engaged in the life of the school and it felt like they enjoyed being there. For example, my mentor, Safina, knew people across the department very well and was very friendly with the pupils and had been there for years so knew their parents/carers. She was a mother at home and brought some that maternal care with her; obviously you can mother your class too much but it was an example of how you can form individual relations with pupils. I found that the teachers there were protective about their pupils.

The third school, Ball Park Academy, was the one I had problems with. Physically, I felt like I was in a prison library. It was a 1960s building with thin corridors and not much light. The welcome for me and other trainees was not great – but then it hadn't been at St Andrew's either. Ball Park Academy, though, had not even got chairs for us in the staffroom and we were told to stand when it was busy, such as at briefing. When I stepped into the building, I could tell that this was a place that was struggling with its discipline. Unlike at the first placement, the pupils did not seem to want to be there and it was as if the pupils were against the system. There were rules in the school which did not suit me either. The pupils could leave a lesson at any time for a toilet break but they locked all toilets except one in another annex of the school, far from the teaching buildings. The pupils knew that at any time they could leave a lesson and join the fun of the queue for the toilet. There was a member of staff monitoring it (not much of a fun job, I always thought) but it gave any pupil a break from the lesson at any time and they would arrange to meet with friends on the way they just go wandering. There had been a disconnect between the frontline teaching staff in the management at both the third and second school, but at Ball Park Academy, it felt like that disconnect was significantly wider. At Ball Park I was given these very black and white presentations to deliver and I had little say about the content, which did not suit me either.

Ask any trainee about the school they go to and this list of issues may be repeated. I knew that doing a PGCE was hard – everyone had told me this. My tutor even told me that I would find my own way in which it would be hard but I still did not expect to get to a point when I could not physically go into a school building. I was eight weeks away from QTS and a PGCE but there was nothing I could do to go in. If I reflect on why that may have been the case, firstly, although I can teach perfectly well, I am not much of a communicator and so the constant need to interact with teachers and mentors was a strain. Secondly, as much as I loved my subject in university, I did not enjoy teaching it in the way I had to. I wanted to be able to teach more creatively, fluidly and teach things that I enjoyed. My lack of enthusiasm must have shown as I was slowly having my confidence eroded. I felt that the teacher feedback on my lessons was becoming more and more negative, and with good reason. Perhaps my character and natural reticence meant that my desire to get involved was not coming over. The department was all female except one male who did not mix with the others so perhaps this was a factor as well. I struggled to get involved with the conversations in the subject department room. The 'crunch' point came when the Head of English told me in a public space that I was being lazy and slacking. In one lesson, I had perched on a table to talk with the pupils and she complained to my mentor about this as well and it upset me that firstly this was a problem and secondly that she did not come to me directly. I was told by my mentor, who was lovely, to be on my best behaviour around this head of subject. On one day I had three lessons and all of them went badly. I felt humiliated by the criticism and awareness that this had happened and I also felt shame. I felt like an idiot and I could have lived with this feeling if it was not for my additional feeling that I did not enjoy the content I was teaching and felt that I was stuck in a machine and, all in all, I could not walk through the school doors again.

Since then, of course, I have found the place I want to be – some teaching, some studying. I look back on my experiences during the PGCE with pride because I persevered. As a result, I do not regret a moment, even the hard parts as they were the ones which taught me most about myself and the kind of trajectory I wanted my life to follow.

······················**WHAT TOOLS ARE IN YOUR TOOLBOX NOW?**

- Understanding about what is expected of a trainee teacher.
- Understanding of the way schools work as systems.
- Understanding about the way the PGCE works.
- Knowledge of some of the types of school.
- Knowledge of some of the roles in school.

···

Place to Get More Tools for Your Toolkit

NASUWT (n.d.) School Lockdown Procedures. Available from: https://www.nasuwt.org.uk/advice/health-safety/school-lockdown-procedures.html
This site provides teachers and schools advice about lockdown and safety procedures.

Capel, S., Leask, M. and Younie, S. (2019) Learning to Teach in the Secondary School (8th edn). London: Routledge.
Favourite book of trainee teachers through its many editions.

Governors for Schools (2024). Available from: https://governorsforschools.org.uk/
See the section titled 'Types of School Governor and Governing Boards' to learn more about how schools are run and consider becoming a school governor in the future.

References

Academies Act. (2010) London: The Stationery Office. Available from: www.legislation.gov.uk/ukpga/2010/32/contents

Allen, R. and Allnutt, J. (2017) The impact of Teach First on pupil attainment at age 16. *British Educational Research Journal* 43(4): 627–646.

Ambition (2024) *Teacher Training.* Available from: www.ambition.org.uk/programmes/teacher-training/

Bernstein, B. (1970) Education cannot compensate for society. *New Society* 38: 344–347.

Birmingham (2024) *Birmingham Schools and Admissions Data.* Available from: www.admissionsday.co.uk/area/birmingham-:~:text=BirminghamCityCouncilhas339,while298settheirown

Blair, T. (2001) Speech by Rt Hon Tony Blair *the Prime Minister Launching Labour's Education Manifesto at the University of Southampton.* Available from: www.theguardian.com/politics/2001/may/23/labour.tonyblair

Chadsgrove School (2024) Available from: www.chadsgroveschool.org.uk/web/

DfE (2018) *Initial Teacher Training (ITT) Census for the Academic Year 2018 to 2019, England.* Available from: https://assets.publishing.service.gov.uk/government/uploads/system/uploads/attachment_data/file/759716/ITT_Census_2018_to_2019_main_text.pdf

Education Act (2011) London: Stationery Office. Available from: https://www.legislation.gov.uk/ukpga/2011/21/contents

Education Reform Act (1988) London: Stationery Office. Available from: https://www.legislation.gov.uk/ukpga/1988/40/contents

Education Act (1994) London: Stationery Office. Available from: https://www.legislation.gov.uk/ukpga/1994/30/contents

Floodflash (2021) *Flood Risk in England.* Available from: www.floodflash.co/england-flood-risk-which-areas-have-it-worst/

Furlong, J. (2005) New Labour and teacher education: The end of an era, *Oxford Review of Education* 31(1): 119–134.

Gov.UK (2022) *Schools, Pupils and Their Characteristics.* Available from www.exploreeducation-statistics.service.gov.uk/find-statistics/school-pupils-and-their-characteristics

Gov.UK (n.d.) *Types of School.* Available from: www.gov.uk/types-of-school/free-schools

Gov.uk (2023) *Initial Teacher Training Census.* Available from: www.explore-education-statistics.service.gov.uk/find-statistics/initial-teacher-training-census/2023-24

Gove, M. (2013) I refuse to surrender to Marxist teachers hell bent on destroying our schools. Available from: www.dailymail.co.uk/debate/article-2298146/I-refuse-surrender-Marxistteachers-hell-bent-destroying-schools-Education-Secretary-berates-new-enemies-promiseopposing-plans.html

GTP (1998) *Graduate Teacher Programme.* Available from: www.tda.gov.uk/Recruit/thetrainingprocess/typesofcourse/gtp.aspx

KES (2024) *Raising Aspirations.* Available from: www.kingedwardvifoundation.co.uk/

KSW (2024) *Shape Your Future.* Available from: www.ksw.org.uk/

Lexis Nexis (2017) *Are Academies Legally Obliged to Comply with Department of Education Statutory Guidance?* Available from: www.lexisnexis.co.uk/legal/guidance/are-academies-legally-obliged-to-comply-with-department-of-education-statutory-guidance-if-so-what-is

McNair Report (1944) *London: His Majesty's Stationery Office.* Available from: www.educationengland.org.uk/documents/mcnair/mcnair1944.html

Newbridge School (2024) *Headteacher's Welcome.* Available from: www.newbridgeschool.org/about-us/headteachers-welcome/

Northampton School (2024) *The School.* Available from: www.northamptonschool.co.uk/page/?title=The+School&pid=7

NSB (2024) *NSB.* Available from: www.nsb.northants.sch.uk/

Pring, R. (2011) Can education compensate for society? *Forum* 53(1): 153–162.

QI (2020) *Events, My Dear Boy, Events.* Available from: www.quoteinvestigator.com/2020/08/31/events/

River School (2024) *The River School.* Available from: www.riverschool.co.uk/

Riverside School (2024) *Riverside School.* Available from: www.riversidesschool.co.uk/information/admissions/

Regency (2024) *Our Community Succeeds Together.* Available from: www.regency.worcs.sch.uk/

RGS (2024) *RGS Worcester.* Available from: www.rgsw.org.uk/

Teach First (2024) *Our Mission.* Available from: www.teachfirst.org.uk/our-mission

Teach in Scotland (2022) *Routes in Teaching.* Available from: www.teachinscotland.scot/become-a-teacher/routes-into-teaching/

TES (2020) *Barred from Running Academies.* Available from: www.tes.com/magazine/archive/liam-nolan-barred-running-academies

TNA (n.d.) *Teacher Training.* Available from: www.nationalarchives.gov.uk/help-with-yourresearch/research-guides/teacher-training/

Warwick (2024) *How Did CTE Begin 75 Years Ago?* Available from: www.warwick.ac.uk/fac/soc/cte/about/news-and-events/newsfeed/cte75/#:~:text=How%20did%20CTE%20begin%2075,address%20the%20need%20for%20teachers

West and Wolfe (2018) *Academies Vision Report.* Available from: www.lse.ac.uk/social-policy/Assets/Documents/PDF/Research-reports/Academies-Vision-Report.pdf

Worcester News (2022) *Oasis Community Learning Confirmed for New Worcester School.* Available from: www.worcesternews.co.uk/news/23097110.oasis-community-learning-confirmed-new-worcester-school/

Worcestershire County Council (2024) *School Statistics and Data Collection.* Available from: www.worcestershire.gov.uk/council-services/childrens-services/schools-education-and-learning/school-statistics-and-data-collection

Zurich (2021) *More than 1,100 Classrooms Gutted by School Blazes.* Available from: www.zurich.co.uk/media-centre/more-than-1100-classrooms-gutted-by-school-blazes

3

Working With Your Mentor

What this chapter will cover

- **Coaching** and mentoring
- Working with your mentor
- Mentoring your mentor

Introduction

The very first mentor entered literature over 26 centuries ago in Homer's *The Odyssey*. Mentor was supposed to look after Telemachus's personal development – a process interrupted when he was replaced by the goddess Athena who took his form. It is fitting that even right at the beginning of the concept of mentoring, it was never simple to understand, easy to do or without conflicts. Jean Rhodes (2018) even suggests that: 'Mentor presided over utter havoc...bullied Telemachus and harassed his mother'. We do hope that your mentor does not harass your mother. *The Odyssey* has been described as: 'a quest for self, in the company of another, the mentor...a metaphorical journey of courage, challenge, creativity and ultimate self-discovery' (Bennetts, 1998: 1). Training to be a teacher does not quite involve the death-defying acts Telemachus went through in search of his father Odysseus (who was disguised as a beggar...it's complicated!) but *The Odyssey* gave us the word 'mentor' and we like the idea that the training year is also a 'quest for self' – to find out who you are, and who you are as a teacher, guided by a knowledgeable, experienced, and (we hope) kindly person. Those assessing teacher training believe such mentoring is 'vital' (Ofsted, 2020), those who helped design the current teacher training curriculum stated it is 'critically important' (DfE, 2015: 40), those who run it agree that it is 'very important' (DfE, 2023: 25) and teacher trainees agree that it is a 'key aspect' (Hobson, 2002: 5) of their training. We agree with this agreement: the mentor plays a crucial role in your course. This chapter aims to enlighten you about the nature of mentoring and the type of mentor you may end up with, and emphasises a key message from us – take control of the process, and mentor your mentor.

Coaching and Mentoring

The Education Endowment Foundation report *What Makes Great Teaching?* (Coe et al., 2014) steered school mentoring to follow a coaching mode. Coaching is a form of mentoring which: 'relies on job-related tasks or skills and is accomplished through instruction, demonstration, and high-impact feedback' (Hopkins-Thompson, 2000: 30). While the focus may be on practical direction, there is still a need for this coaching to be done 'in an environment of trust and support' (Coe et al., 2014: 44). A coaching model encourages clear goal setting, modelling, monitoring and feedback (EEF, 2021). It has been widely adopted in many countries including Australia, where mentors are known as 'Supervising Teachers' (AITSL, 2020: 13) who are guided by a 'Mentoring Capability Framework' which instructs that the process should be 'explicit coaching' (Department of Education and Training, 2019) of 'Provisionally Registered Teachers' (PRTs). Titles help to define roles, and calling trainee teachers PRTs and mentors Supervising Teachers implies that Australia's system facilitates a 'fast track' of learning teaching skills (Ambrosetti, 2014). Some UK Training Providers ask for this style of mentoring by basing it on Jim Knight's (2023) Instructional Coaching Model (ICM), a seven-stage model of improvement based on, 'impact...data...system' (ICM, 2024) These words should reveal that this mentoring scheme is not going to be a touchy-feely, 'have a good cry on my shoulder' set-up. Rachel Lofthouse (2022) has worked to Anglicise the American ICM approach, modifying it away from being too 'formulaic or scripted'.

The need for a mentor to be flexible, responsive and, let's face it, human, is not always expressed in the Initial Teacher Training and Early Career Framework (ITTECF) which describes a coaching model:

> Receiving clear, consistent and effective mentoring, through structured feedback from expert colleagues on a particular approach – using the best available evidence – to provide a structured process for improving practice. (DfE, 2024: 7)

As part of this structured feedback, you have entitlement to 1.5 hours with your mentor per week which includes an observation of your teaching (DfE, 2022) – so time is not made available for an immersive deep experience.

Despite the coaching model being widely adopted, the term 'mentor' is often used in schools and in the ITTECF; the term can be confusing as 'mentoring' typically implies a more holistic purpose and approach, although, in fact, definitions of 'mentoring' vary. Fletcher (2000: 1) considers mentoring in education to be an amalgamation of: 'coaching, counselling and assessment' which potentially means that you can be told that you are failing by the same person who offers you the couch and wants to know how you feel about it. Kram (1983) found that mentoring can provide functions that are psychosocial – delving into your mind and supporting your ability to interact with others. For some, mentoring is giving 'general advice and motivation regarding one's career and life' (Yost and Plunkett, 2009: 110). For others, mentoring is the rather scary-sounding: 'intense interpersonal exchange' (Russell and Adams, 1997: 2). It is not that there are no definitions of what a mentor should be, it is just that 'definitions are not definitive enough' (Cox et al., 2018: xxxi).

We have worked with hundreds of mentors and see at least as great a variation in their practice as there are definitions. This is, in a sense, a relief; some of our trainee teachers, at the start of their first placement, cannot even find their school, and are mystified as to why anyone would expect them to wake up before 8 a.m. – such trainees need a more nuanced approach with compassion and understanding of human nature. Mentoring always involves a 'mentor' and 'mentee', and the former helps the latter develop professionally. It is, like so many aspects of teaching, an interactive relationship. Hobson and Malderez (2013: 90) gave a useful definition of the role of a school mentor:

> a one-to-one relationship between a relatively inexperienced teacher (the mentee) and a relatively experienced one (the mentor) which aims to support the mentee's learning and development as a teacher, and their integration into and acceptance by the cultures of the school and the profession.

Working With Your Mentor

The mentoring role has traditionally been unpaid and often not directly part of anyone's job description. So, perhaps unsurprisingly, mentoring has been, overall: 'Not as good as it should be' (DfE, 2015: 15). Mentoring can be seen as a Cinderella role (Murtagh and Dawes, 2021) – a low priority for schools, and lacking recognition and reward. A mentor's negative behaviour, as Buckingham and Goodall (2019) identified, can trigger the mentee to reject the information they have been given. Being mentored is not always positive and having a negative experience with your mentor can be more damaging than if you had none at all (Eby et al., 2010). The experienced teacher trainer Trevor Wright noted: 'there are mentors who still regard the teaching placement as a sort of work experience' (2009: 1). This may mean placing the trainee teacher into the classroom unsupported and seeing if they 'sink or swim', with a critical eye on the process as to whether they are 'up to it' or not. If considered not up to it, the trainee may be ignored or targeted with criticism until they leave. Having given little or no support, the mentor has their expectations confirmed if the trainee 'sinks'; the mentor cannot 'lose' with this way of thinking. On your teaching placement, you may notice such mentors. They tend to see themselves as assessors. Mentors like this will look at what you do and inform you – through body language, tone of voice/email, what they say to you, what they do not say to you or what you hear they have said through others – whether they think you are, or are not, fit to be a teacher. We have been told by mentors, many times, that a trainee teacher will never be a good teacher, only for the trainee to become just that. While the vast, vast majority of mentors are (if you make them cups of tea) excellent, these other types also exist:

- Judge-mentor – ready to give their instant assessment that a trainee is or is not suited for teaching.
- Tor-mentor – 'I had to do it the hard way, and so should you'. Just like the Victorian schoolmaster with his cane ready, discipline is the way forward according to this type of mentor and they are likely to set a series of impossible tasks, designed to – in their view – toughen you up and squash you into place.
- Don't-want-to-be-a-mentor – in our first year of university lecturing, one of us was assigned a mentor who immediately turned to a colleague, complained at length about her job, then ended up with, 'And now I have been given him to mentor!' – thus severing the relationship immediately.

The vast majority of mentors are good, well-meaning, busy, tired teachers, who enjoy the company of trainee teachers and want to help in any way they can. Most mentors have experience, are hard-working (and hard-worn) teachers who model good practice, understand the nature of teacher training, and are kind. It is kindness, above all, that we look for in a mentor, because even if the placement is not going well, we can rely on them to act with openness, honesty and fairness. Should the trainee teacher not be passing the placement we can rely on them to put in place realistic steps to improve while being open and clear about the possibility of failure, and mindful of the trainee teacher's well-being.

Mentors are very much in demand in school, because Early Career Teachers also need a mentor for two years; this requirement is 'stretching' schools' capacities, and means more people are becoming mentors, some unwillingly, rather than schools 'cherry-picking' those most suited to the role. It can be difficult to attract teachers to the role (Ofsted, 2020) so the school may have to pick the person who did not say 'no' quickly enough. There have been great changes in mentoring since the 2019 reforms. One change is that mentors now have to be provided with mentor training sessions: One change is that mentors now have to be provided with mentor training sessions, and they may not want to do this training, and they may not want to do this training, may resent it - and even resent you, the trainee, for causing it. In an ideal world, though, schools and Training Providers are in a joint culture with the same purpose to build the next generation of teachers, and it is always hoped that this mutually beneficial aim will underpin the collaboration.

Mentoring Your Mentor

No matter how understanding your mentor is (or is not), one point that you must be aware of is that the mentor–mentee relationship involves a balance of power that is neither equal nor in your favour: 'the supervisor has authority over the protégé' (Ambrosetti and Dekkers, 2010: 44). Mentors are heavily involved in the assessment of trainees and this is a factor which can hurt the relationship. Power could be described as: 'the ability to get someone to do something that they do not particularly want to do' (Jackson and Carter, 2006: 94). All professional learning environments contain relationships that are affected by power; the mentor–mentee relationship is, in this sense, nothing new. Trust may be an important factor of the mentor–mentee relationship but we have found that when our trainee teachers confide in their mentors about how hard the course is, and how over-demanding the placement timetable, we get phone calls from mentors who are not sure the mentee is 'up to it'. How much should you trust your mentor? We recommend caution: after all, the mentor is one of your assessors, not your 'mate'. There are plenty of people, we hope, who can listen to your troubles and share your burdens - but your mentor has power, so proceed with caution. You might be lucky and end up developing a relationship of trust, or perhaps not so lucky and be guided into the 'correct mindset' (Kay, 1990) by a mentor, or even unluckier and fall into the 'deficit model' of mentoring where all that is focused on is what you are doing wrong. You may well become a mentor in the future. If you do, you will understand more how you are expected to deal with a new individual who comes packaged with different problems, strengths and weaknesses to the ones that you had. It always amazes us, when we have former trainees who have become mentors, how they can somehow miraculously forget their former struggles, and risk treating their mentees with the same disregard and criticism they were in our offices crying about five years earlier.

To mentor a mentor, we advise the following:

- Understand they will be very busy as the position does not come with many (if any) hours of remission from teaching.
- Understand that your mentor is just a person trying their best, regardless of how effective they may seem as a teacher or a mentor. They have their view of teaching and may try to impose this on you, in which case you have to be guided by it, but the more you can show them that you have your own style that works, the more they will relax.

- Understand that a mentor wants nothing more than for you to be successful. Apart from the altruistic desire for the good of others, and apart from the fact you are now teaching some of their lessons, it looks good on them if they have a successful trainee teacher. This is something you can work on: aim to be someone they will be proud of.
- Understand that the relationship is hierarchical and the school will always support the mentor - a permanent member of the teaching staff - over you. At times, you may have to leave your pride at the school door and accept your position. If you take any other approach - combative, resistant or negative - there will probably only be one outcome and it will not be in your favour. A school is unlikely to upset a permanent member of staff for the sake of a very expendable trainee teacher.

Mentors can be impatient, irascible and difficult (as all people can be). But you have to learn how to work with colleagues and, potentially, line managers who can be like this. Schools are intense, emotional places and dealing with the everyday, constant stress factors of school can exacerbate characteristics. We advise you to be proactive in setting your agenda and find ways to control the situation as much as you can. Set your own targets, while accommodating the ones your mentor chooses. If it seems as if all you are getting is criticism, it can lower your morale. Why not see mentor meetings as a chance to collect data on your 'current reality' to help you understand what you need to develop? See comments on how you can improve positively, even if they may have been framed negatively by your mentor - if your mentor tells you that you are not moving around the room enough, make a note that you need to move around the room more. One piece of advice we can pass on is to focus on the content of the mentor feedback, not the expression. Write down the actual words. Take the hurt you might feel - along with the sense that someone is belittling you, or the fact that they do not seem to like you - out of the equation. Find out what needs to be done, and try to do it. As you write it down, repeat it back to the mentor to check if you have understood it correctly. The chances are that when you do this, the mentor will be able to see how negative it sounds and may well temper their judgement. On a placement, you are in the survival business. If you have got through another day and you are still in school no matter what the feedback, you are still in there fighting, so take control, and try to guide the situation in a positive direction. We will pass onto you the advice of Kegan (1994: 303):

- Be a self-directed learner (take initiative and set your own goals and standards).
- Use experts, institutions and other resources to pursue your goals.
- Read about teaching actively (rather than only receptively) with purpose in mind.
- Write to yourself and, if you can, bring your mentors into this self-reflection. Ask them and write down their response.

Trainees sometimes fail themselves by deciding that they can no longer work in their school or with their mentor. Before you 'press the button' which destroys your placement, try taking control of your learning and do not become the 'victim' of a mentor. If your mentor suits you, then great. If your mentor does not suit you, then no matter. You will probably never see them again after this placement has ended (unless you have a masochistic streak in you). This person is not the only source of learning; you have books, friends, colleagues, your experience, other teachers and a personal tutor with your Training Provider. If you really want that one person to rely on in school, find a person who does inspire you and try to observe them as much as possible. Mentoring is important in all fields of work and the person you choose to be your mentor may not be the person who is assigned to you. Terry Wogan was a seasoned professional radio broadcaster, for 22 years the 'morning voice' on BBC Radio 2. A fellow presenter, Jeremy Vine, once met him in the lift and said: 'Good grief, Terry. It's 28 minutes past seven. You're on air in two minutes'. He replied, 'Yes, I'm early this morning' (Vine, 2016). Jeremy Vine spoke of Terry Wogan as a true mentor, someone with experience who made the job seem effortless and enjoyable (on being asked by Queen Elizabeth how long he had worked at the BBC he replied that he had never worked a day there in his life) and someone who had the time and patience to help others. We hope that you find someone like this in your school, whether it is your assigned mentor, or someone else. But remember that if a placement ends, it is probably not the end of your attempt to be a teacher. Nor is it the end of the world. If you fail a placement, you can usually try again.

Conclusion

Not everyone is fond of mentoring as it is usually practised in schools, with one person in a hierarchical power relation telling the other person what to do and even how to think. For some, it is the 'Godfather' (Ragins and Verbos, 2007) approach, with the implication that you will be given plenty of offers you cannot refuse. For Carl Rogers, a one-way system where the 'mentor who does not see the process as an opportunity for learning but as a way of passing on his/her expertise or is patronizing' (Rogers, 2004: 24). You may well be patronised (or matronised) and perhaps by someone younger than you. So when you step into the role of mentee, realise that here you are a learner rather than a teacher, and be ready, open and conscious about the process of change. We find that much of what happens in mentoring is just instructions, such as, 'I want a lesson plan by tomorrow morning' or, 'your Do Now Activity needs to be trimmed down from 30 minutes to 10', or, 'do it, or else'. Some mentoring we encounter seems more like 'dog training' to us: do this and I will pat you (metaphorically) on the head. As the relationship changes, the dynamic alters, particularly when trust is in place, and there develops a shared sense of how to progress. As teacher trainers, we can see that mentors can affect trainee teachers much as coaches affect their sports teams. The football manager Brian Clough, for example took Nottingham Forest, which had in the previous century only ever won the FA Cup, to the top of what is now the Premier League; they were crowned as European Champions - twice. Sarina Wiegman took England's national team to the World Cup final as European Champions. Put simply, the difference between a failing and winning side can be an individual who not only knows strategy and training regimes but can bring out the best in those they are training. Just as with school mentors, there is no one single way of being a great sports coach - Wiegman, we are sure, would not employ Clough's bring-you-down-to-earth tactic of asking Stan Bowles (one of the most famous and skilled players of his time) what his name was at their first training session. David Clutterbuck (n.d.) is a wise communicator of mentoring experience and he sums up some values which we hope to see in mentors:

> Firstly, a deep reflection on one's own experiences – the basis of wisdom. . .Secondly, the skills of using personal experience to stimulate and support the client's thinking. Thirdly, understanding of a range of psychological and behavioural issues rarely emphasised in coach training – for example, the conscious and unconscious exercise of power, and the skills of being an effective role model. Fourthly, an appreciation and acquisition of relevant knowledge and expertise in specific applications of mentoring, such as ethical mentoring (requiring an understanding of the psychology of ethicality) or diversity.

And here we take a deep mental breath and envision all those thoughtful, wise, kindly, skilled people we have known who have acted as mentors in the past and fulfilled this amazing brief.

REFLECTION

A narrative will build around you, and will do so quickly. If the narrative is positive – that this is a hard-working trainee who is 'born to teach', for example – the likelihood is that your errors will be deemed learning opportunities to be embraced. Think about the kind of impression you have given to your mentor and imagine what kind of a character you are presenting. Imagine yourself through your mentor's eyes, and think about how you might try to counter any negative impressions you have given to stop a negative narrative from 'snowballing'.

ACTIONS

The ITT Early Career Framework has 'Learn How To. . .' elements which can provide useful starting points for steering discussion with your mentor. Try using the language of the framework to ask for 'expert input', 'opportunities for practice' and for 'feedback' on stated aspects of teaching. It may take some time in your training to gain the confidence and understanding of your skills to be able to sustain an effective coaching dialogue, but once you and your mentor are able to develop this approach, it can be empowering and give you a sense of agency in your own development.

Jim Knight (2023), a leading proponent of Instructional Coaching in the United States, offers mentors guidance which we have 'flipped' to make the following suggestions for the trainee teacher:

- Try to do most of the talking.
- Try to focus on one aspect of practice at a time.
- Ask for clarification when you are not certain what is being said.
- Prepare yourself for coaching opportunities through reflection on your developing practice.
- Be open to being coached.

Borrowing from Jean Piaget's (1936) original theory of learning stages, consider how you will learn the following:

- Categorisation: where things go. Learn how your school, the department and classroom work. Learn where the books go, and where the pens are kept.
- Perceptions: how to view things. Learn about your school's purpose and ethos and how the nature of education is interpreted by all you encounter.
- Ideas: what is out there. You will be bombarded by new words, acronyms and initialisms. Learn what they mean and how to respond to them.
- Objects: things and what they mean. The world of your school is partly conceptual and partly physical. Learn which rooms you go to, how long can you stay in a place, and whose seat in the staff room you had better not sit in.
- Actions: what to do and how to do it. Learn what is acceptable behaviour, vocabulary and body language in school.

Case Study 3

Elizabeth Lawson is as experienced a mentor as they come. She mentored since her second year of teaching in 2002 as a classroom teacher of English, as Head of English, Lead Practitioner, Assistant Headteacher, Teaching School Director, Induction Tutor, Vice Principal and the (rather strangely termed) Appropriate Body Lead across 12 schools. Here, she recounts what she loves about the role of mentor. You will see that her interpretation is 'hands-on', 'full-on,' and far more intensive than a coach who only has 1.5 hours to spare.

I would say that mentoring is one of my most enjoyable and rewarding aspects of teaching and I continue to welcome every opportunity to mentor. For me, mentoring is a gift: a true joy of teaching and a real privilege to play a part in a teacher's career. It involves a positive mindset and a desire to champion the student. The mentor becomes the advocate for the student within the department and school setting, liaising with staff for/ with/on their behalf and encouraging the student to embed within the setting and have the confidence to speak to staff independently and with confidence. Students thrive when they have the opportunity to learn within a whole school community and it certainly 'takes a village' to 'raise' a student effectively. The role of the mentor is the support the student to navigate this new and often 'alien' context and guide them through the process, until able to increasingly separate from the 'home' support given. The mentor needs to become slowly and increasingly 'surplus' in the classroom in order for the student to gain confidence. This can be a strange dynamic as often students hope the teacher will step in. It can also challenge your sense of ego as a mentor, as you step aside. Especially on the final placement, I feel that the teacher needs to move to the background and enable the student to flourish and take full ownership of the class. The class should react to the student allowing the mentor to slowly move from their usual lead position and enable the student to move to the spotlight and have a realistic experience of leading a class 'front and centre'.

Fundamentally, as a mentor I see my role to nurture each student's talents and it is my role to learn about their uniqueness and react to this in order to judge how to effectiveness nurture and support. This could be by exposing and guiding the student to different teaching styles, spotlighting/highlighting good practice and creating opportunities to direct the student to grow with new learning moments. Articulating these experiences, overtly, either from talking through their findings or teaching side-by-side. Pointing out something of good practice, really can enhance a students' experience and learning. This could be something as seemingly obvious as walking through the school together and stopping to notice something – 'do you notice how …?'; 'what do you think about…?'; 'did you see that teacher/ leader talking there and how they…?' – to evaluating the latest lesson observation within a formal mentor meeting. Through these small, perhaps seemingly insignificant points of interest the mentor can start to 'plant the seed' of deeper learning about culture, and teacher behaviours and mindsets, we want to nurture in the profession. Mentoring is a process of interpreting and building understanding, at an appropriate pace for the trainees, in order to support the trainees to navigate their placement in a safe and supportive environment.

Every trainee is unique and it is my aim to quickly and conscientiously learn about who they are, what has led them to want to become a teacher, and how I might work with the student in order to get the best out of them. It is not my aim to make 'carbon copies' of me, or indeed of any other teacher, it is for me to observe and watch what skills and qualities the student has to start with and then match this with experiences, encounters, and opportunities in school, which will help to develop the student to be their authentic self and able to react to new learning and new challenges with resilience and confidence. This is the magic of the journey of mentoring, because, at the start we have no idea what that 'excellence' may look like for them (although we have the Teachers' Standards to be reached) or indeed, if it will happen on the placement. If I can see that a trainee presents as sensitive and quieter in their initial presentation in front of a class I may suggest a form tutor who displays similar qualities but who is respected through their consistent but gentle form of class control, so that the trainee can see examples from teachers who have similar qualities. I direct the trainee to watch, and 'magpie' different qualities and tools they see to 'hook' their interest and affirm their place in education and build their own unique and special teacher identity. This can also work with the opposite approach: encouraging a 'louder' trainee to see a quieter style and allow the student to reflect on what they notice, and how the teacher contrasts to the style they typically adopt. Encouraging a thoughtful process and displaying best practice in terms of style of delivery leads to useful conversations about how teachers adhere to their growing philosophy of what it means to be a teacher and/or challenge their original thinking/considerations whilst on practice.

An effective mentor has a vested interest in each trainee as a person/human being - asking (internal) questions such as: 'who are you?'; 'What makes you tick?'; 'What educational journey have you been on?'; 'What inspires you to teach?'. Teaching holds the mirror up to you as a teacher and any insecurities as scrutinised by others, especially teenagers. Building self-esteem and stamina is about knowing what makes you 'tick,' and altruistic career choice can easily break the strongest of people. The role of the mentor is to build from this intuitive connection a genuine desire to nurture and support, with honesty and integrity, the person on their journey, and help to build the necessary stamina, intelligence, adaptability, and resilience.

Some of my proudest moments have been mentoring students over years and then watching them take on leadership roles, knowing that their strong foundational years in teaching enabled them to 'fly'. Through mentoring, I can guide trainees to see the 'unknown unknowns' – something in them that they had not recognised consciously – ambition, perhaps, or potential in a new area of the school. I would suggest that any trainee documents such moments of realisation where the 'windows of understanding' open up; try to make it a place of (tired) wonder.

.... WHAT TOOLS ARE IN YOUR TOOLKIT NOW?

- A greater understanding of what school mentoring is.
- A greater sense of your mentor as an individual doing their best.
- Tips to deal with difficult mentoring situations.
- Encouragement to take control of the mentoring relationship.

Places to Get More Tools for Your Toolkit

Kegan, R. (1994) *The Evolving Self: Problem and Process in Human Development.* Massachusetts: Harvard University Press.

There are many books on how to be a successful mentor – far more than how to be a successful mentee. We mentioned Robert Kegan in this chapter; while his is a 'heavy tome' to digest, especially on a teacher training year, it has a suitable level of depth and understanding about how humans create meaning to be career-transforming.

Early Career Hub (2024) *An Introduction to Instructional Coaching.* Available from: https://my.chartered.college/early-career-hub/an-introduction-to-instructional-coaching/

The Chartered College gives a clear outline of instructional coaching approaches and gives useful links for those entering teaching.

References

AITSL (2020) *Guidelines for the Accreditation of Initial Teacher Education Programs in Australia*. Available from: www.aitsl.edu.au/docs/default-source/default-document-library/accreditation

Ambrosetti, A. (2014) Are you ready to be a mentor? Preparing teachers for mentoring pre-service teachers, *Australian Journal of Teacher Education* 39(6): 30–42.

Ambrosetti, A. and Dekkers, J. (2010) The interconnectedness of the roles of mentors and mentees in pre-service teacher education mentoring relationships. *Australian Journal of Teacher Education*, 35(6): 42–55.

Bennetts, C. (1998) *Traditional Mentor Relationships in the Lives of Creative People*. Available from: https://core.ac.uk/download/pdf/42604393.pdf

Buckingham, M. and Goodall, A. (2019) *Nine Lies about Work*. Massachusetts: Harvard University Press.

Clutterbuck, D. (n.d.) *From Coach to Professional Mentor*. Available from: www.davidclutterbuckpartnership.com/from-coach-to-professional-mentor/

Coe, R., Aloisi, C., Higgins, S. and Elliot Major, L. (2014) *What Makes Great Teaching? Review of the Underpinning Research*. Available from: www.suttontrust.com/wp-content/uploads/2014/10/What-Makes-Great-Teaching-REPORT.pdf

Cox, E., Bachkirova, T. and Clutterbuck, D. (2018) *The Complete Handbook of Coaching*. London: SAGE.

DfE (2015) *Carter Review of Initial Teacher Training*. Available from: government/government/publications/carter-review-of-initial-teacher-training

DfE (2023) *Induction for Early Career Teachers (England)*. Available from: www.gov.uk/government/publications/induction-for-early-career-teachers-england

DfE (2022) *ITT Reform*. Available from: www.assets.publishing.service.gov.uk/government/uploads/system/uploads/attachment_data/file/1079080/ITT_Reform_Accompanying_Document.pdf

DfE (2024) *ITT Criteria and Supporting Advice*. Available from: https://assets.publishing.service.gov.uk/media/65ccac0ec96cf300126a3718/2024-25_ITT_criteria_and_supporting_advice.pdf

Department of Education and Training (2019) *Mentoring Capability Framework*. Available from: www.vic.gov.au/effective-mentoring-program

Eby, L., Butts, M., Durley, J. and Ragins, B. (2010) Are bad experiences stronger than good ones in mentoring relationships? *Journal of Vocational Behavior* 77(1): 81–92.

EEF (2021) *Effective Professional Development*. Available from: www.educationendowmentfoundation.org.uk/education-evidence/guidance-reports/effective-professional-development

Fletcher, S. (2000). *Mentoring in Schools: A Handbook of Good Practice*. London: Routledge.

Hobson, A. (2002) Student teachers' perceptions of school-based mentoring in Initial Teacher Training (ITT), *Mentoring and Tutoring: Partnership in Learning* 10(1): 5–20.

Hobson, A. and Malderez, A. (2013). Judgementoring and other threats to realizing the potential of school-based mentoring in teacher education, *International Journal of Mentoring and Coaching in Education* 2(2): 89–108.

Hopkins-Thompson, P. (2000). Colleagues helping colleagues: Mentoring and coaching. *NASSP Bulletin* 84(617).

ICM (2024). *Instructional Coaching*. Available from: www.instructionalcoaching.com/

Jackson, N. and Carter, P. (2006) *Rethinking Organisational Behaviour: A Post-structuralist Framework*. Essex: Prentice Hall.

Kay, R. (1990). Mentoring: Definition, principles and applications. In T. Bey & C. Holmes (Eds.), *Mentoring* (pp. 25–38). Reston, VA: Association of Teacher Educators.

Kegan, R. (1994) *The Evolving Self: Problem and Process in Human Development*. Massachusetts: Harvard University Press.

Knight, J. (2023) *The Definitive Guide to Instructional Coaching: Seven Factors for Success*. Melton: John Catt.

Kram, K. (1983) Phases of the mentor relationship. *Academy of Management Journal* 26(4): 608–625.

Lofthouse, R. (2022) *Here be Dragons: Mythbusting Instructional Coaching for Teaching*. Available from: https://www.leedsbeckett.ac.uk/blogs/carnegie-education/2022/01/here-be-dragons—myth-busting-instructional-coaching-for-teachers/

Murtagh, L. and Dawes, L. (2021) National standards for school-based mentors: The potential to recognise the "Cinderella" role of mentoring? *International Journal of Mentoring and Coaching in Education* 10(1): 31–45.

Ofsted (2020) *Consultation Proposals for the Framework to Inspect the Quality of Teacher Education*. Available from: https://www.gov.uk/government/consultations/initial-teacher-education-inspection-framework-and-handbook-2020-inspecting-the-quality-of-teacher-edu cation/consultation-proposals-for-the-framework-to-inspect-the-quality-of-teacher-education-from-september-2020

Piaget, J. (1936) *Origins of Intelligence in the Child*. London: Routledge & Kegan Paul.

Ragins, B. and Verbos, A. (2007) Positive relationships in action. In Dutton, J. & Ragins, B. R. (Eds.), *Exploring Positive Relationships at Work* (pp. 91–116). New Jersey: Lawrence Erlbaum and Associates.

Rhodes, J. (2018). *Evidence-based Mentoring*. Available from: www.evidencebasedmentoring.org/who-was-mentor-a-stunning-revelation-with-important-lessons/

Rogers, C. (2004) *On Becoming a Person*. London: Constable and Robinson.

Russell, J. and Adams, D. (1997). The changing nature of mentoring in organizations. *Journal of Vocational Behavior* 51: 1–14.

Vine, J. (2016) *The Day Sir Terry Put Me in My Place – And Proved His Genius*. Available from: www.dailymail.co.uk/news/article-3425821/The-day-Sir-Terry-place-proved-genius-JEREMY-VINE-beloved-broadcaster-broke-listener-records-mind-spoke-one.html

Wright, T. (2009) *How to Be a Brilliant Teacher*. Abingdon: Routledge.

Yost, P. and Plunkett, M. (2009) *Real-Time Leadership Development*. Chichester: Wiley.

4

Subject Knowledge: Being the Expert in the Room

What this chapter will cover

- The importance of subject knowledge
- Knowing and modelling subject excellence
- The bodies which inform what the subject is
- Communities of Practice
- Teaching beyond your subject

Introduction

Subject knowledge is like a seam running through the rock of teaching in a secondary school. It underpins, it overarches, and we could go on with the metaphors, but essentially they all mean the same: subject knowledge is crucially important. This chapter will consider practical steps that can be taken to ensure your subject knowledge is (at the very least) acceptable. The National Curriculum, **Assessment Objectives**, subject bodies and the role of support organisations will be explored. The chapter also considers how subject expertise needs to become the province of the pupils: moving your love, knowledge, and skills of the subject over to them.

The Importance of Subject Knowledge

The easy part of subject knowledge is substantive knowledge: the facts. The birthdate of a major figure, such as Shakespeare (relatively easy in this case, as no-one is sure of the exact date) and how many major religions there are (six, although some claim 20, and what does 'major' mean anyway?). 'Disciplinary' knowledge makes sense of, gives purpose, and uses substantive knowledge in a particular way. This depends on what the subject is for (developing reasoning skills, calculation, expression, for example) and why it makes sense to learn it. We suggest that you download an exam syllabus and read its 'fluffy preamble' as this will tell you about the disciplinary principles of the curriculum. Alongside these two types of knowledge, skills are vital in every subject. Art is an obvious example where the ability to communicate an idea in a 2D or 3D form is highly valued; drama demands speech skills; science skills include how to turn on the gas tap without blowing up the room.

Beyond these two types of knowledge and skills, there is what we are going to call 'mist'. The National Curriculum gives teachers a moral, cultural, social and spiritual development role. This mistiness is found, for example, in the National Curriculum in English: the English teacher has to ensure the pupils have a 'love of literature' (DfE, 2013: 2). How do you teach love? How do you quantify the amount of love they have achieved? Do they love it enough? What is love anyway? Can you write a report that includes the words: 'progress in love needs to improve'? The word love is in the Greek word 'philosophy' which means love (philo) of knowledge (sophos): all subjects have this at their heart. Like love, 'learning' is a misty abstract noun; you cannot feel it, but you can experience its effects like an energy. Learning is a kind of energy for humans. And so the love of learning is a twice abstracted concept. You can probably see why we call it mist – it just seems easier. Sometimes, teaching is about facts (substantive), sometimes it is about what to do with these facts (disciplinary) and sometimes it is about how to perform an act well (skills). But you will also have to teach mist, such as how to generate a positive attitude towards a subject, the motivation to learn it, or the creativity to take it further.

In history, the substantive knowledge is present in, for instance, the dates of the First World War, the major battle places and the treaties signed between nations. Being able to use these facts to form opinions on the war involves disciplinary knowledge. These opinions need to be 'weighed up' by drawing conclusions about which facts should be believed, and why.

The ability to reflect, rethink, and to create something new from knowledge are skills to be developed. These cognitive skills can enable a pupil to question the subject: how do you feel about war? Why? Should nations exist? What about if. . .? The mistiness comes in ensuring engagement about a topic that happened over a hundred years ago about countries which may not mean too much to the pupil who has, perhaps, emigrated only last week from Indonesia. The very nature of getting the pupils to care enough to gain the knowledge and develop the skills is part of the teacher's job – in respect of all pupils, and regardless of background.

Like mistiness, learning has a 'fuzzy edge' because people are not machines or computers but heuristic by nature; we have the ability to distil what we know into a feeling which allows us to think and act quickly. The human brain is attached to the body, which affects what the brain does (although the education thinker Ken Robinson (2006) had a very fair point that academics seem to think the body is there to take the head to meetings). Mistiness is also in such issues as 'cultural capital' which is generated when the topics taught are likely to allow the pupils to gather more respect in the wider society. The ability to casually quote Ovid in Latin, for example can give an individual a greater sense of self-worth and a chance of impressing others. After all, no-one wants to end up like the Roman poet and have to declare: 'barbarus hic ego sum' (Ovid, Tristia 5 – 'here it is that I am a barbarian').

Knowing and Modelling Subject Excellence

It is not the job of your Training Provider to teach you subject knowledge, nor your school mentor. It is, instead, their job to give you the Pedagogical Content Knowledge (commonly referred to as PCK, a term given us by Shulman in 1987): ways of teaching the knowledge (substantive and disciplinary) /skills/mist that you already have. An expert, in the form of your subject specialist mentor, will be provided for this purpose, and you will be given access to subject specialist sessions. Training Providers may go over some problematic subjects or go to the areas where there are so-called 'misconceptions', and there are Subject Knowledge Enhancement courses which pre-service trainees might take if their degrees were not in the subject. Otherwise, you have to make sure you know your subject well enough to teach it. The Training Provider audits you to check your subject knowledge and help you to isolate the areas of weakness but, frankly, if you have not got enough subject knowledge to teach 11–18-year olds you ought to make the decision to take yourself out the classroom and learn it first. Subject knowledge is assessed by the Training Provider on entry and if they were not satisfied that you had it, you would (or should) not be on the course. Usually, a trainee teacher has studied the subject up to undergraduate degree level, but one of us taught Biology having studied a degree in Chemistry and had to rapidly revise a subject not learnt since A Level. The unspoken rule of education is that you should be qualified in a subject one step above what you are teaching – so having passed Biology A Level was considered sufficient to teach it, but only because we also had a degree in a related subject. Here, we are writing 'should be' and 'ought to' because there is no strict ruling on what level of qualification is required. We all have new topics to learn, we all need to refresh knowledge and may resort to using breaks in the lesson to have a quick look over our notes – for example to check, as one of always had to every time it was taught, what the atrioventricular node actually does.

The subject knowledge you need can be found in the following places:

- The National Curriculum (or a locally agreed subject curriculum) – the minimum content requirement for the subject.
- Assessment Objectives (AOs) – the subject criteria to be assessed in examinations.
- Examination board specifications – based on the National (or local) curriculum and the AOs.
- School schemes of work (SoW) – based on the National or local curriculum, AOs, examination boards and little bits of magic dust (i.e. whatever was on a previous scheme of work that the creator liked, or didn't want to remove because they had prepared all of the materials for it).

Your knowledge of your subject is internal, but what is taught is externally defined. What you teach will not be exactly the subject that you have previously learnt; ultimately, what you teach will be determined by the government which has been advised by experts. An independent school (including an academy) may choose its own curriculum but it has to be justified to external agencies such as Ofsted. If it is not the same as the National (or local) curriculum, there has to be very good reasoning behind the choices made and so most schools defer to established sources of subject knowledge. The government has prescribed the AOs for examination boards, so there is not much room for manoeuvre anyway. One example of local curriculum relates to Religious Education. Since the 1988 Education Reform Act, every local authority has to have a SACRE – Standing Advisory Council for Religious Education (we imagine they are allowed to sit for meetings) which decides on a curriculum for religious study, and on the nature of religious worship, in the area's schools.

School 'subject leads' will be responsible for creating long-term, medium-term and short-term plans for their subject. Schools vary as to how much teaching material is offered to teachers, with some not offering it at all and others putting resources on the intranet somewhere you cannot find. Our trainee teachers sometimes respond with bemusement when we mention SoWs and long-term plans. In these cases, the training teacher has to go back to the National Curriculum (or locally agreed subject content) and AOs to create their own plans. There is nothing really wrong with this because it develops their subject knowledge and independence. It is increasingly the case, though, that schools give the teachers (including trainees) comprehensive lesson content, resources and presentations, and ask merely for adaptation and delivery. You are likely to be expected to:

- Enter a lesson with sufficient knowledge of the content of the lesson.
- Give a fluent explanation or exposition presentation of information.
- Answer questions that are related to that content level of the curriculum.
- Be able to model a top-grade answer and do so live in front of the class.

You are not expected to:

- Have a grasp of the whole curriculum and the connections between its parts.

Communities of Practice

Much like nostalgia, teaching is not what it was. We have to keep stopping ourselves from referring regretfully to 'how it was better in the old days'; for instance, with regard to the way we used to link up with other teachers of our subject across local schools. That was before schools were put in a competitive marketplace when there was a greater role for Local Education Authorities to train and link up professionals. One of us went to the English and Media Centre in Northampton, for example, to get training and meet fellow professionals. Such days are no longer with us, but schools are, increasingly, in Multi Academy Trusts (MATs) and so there is an opportunity there to meet colleagues and share subject knowledge and enthusiasm about your subject. There are also online ways of meeting, which is a great improvement on the days when, after work, we would have to drive our (t)rusty old Ford Fiestas to a nondescript building in a town centre.

The phrase 'Community of Practice' (COP) was coined by Jean Lave and Etienne Wenger and referred to: 'a duality of participation and reification' (Wenger, 1998: 63). This means, in plainer English, that you get together with colleagues to make sense of what the subject means today. The 'reification' part refers to the signs and symbols and unspoken truths of your subject. These are a code which you have internalised, but which outside of your 'subject bubble' may well make little sense. COPs are usually comforting because you are with your subject tribe, as it were, and the ways you make sense of the world in relation to your subject can be shared. As we are now feeling all warmly linked up to fellow professionals, we will borrow a little of the Department for Education (DfE)-funded Practice Supervisor Development Programme's (2020) advice about forming or belonging to COPs:

- Evolution – allow COPs to change according to need in terms of regularity and form.
- Internal and external dialogue – get other voices to come in as well as share knowledge and passions.
- Participation at various levels – do not get 'hung up' on who attends or who does the bulk of the arranging.
- Focus on the domain – keep to the subject of teaching the subject.
- A rhythm – try to keep a regularity of contact time.

You are unlikely to need to create this community from scratch: there are plenty out there already meeting. The best way of discovering them is through national associations such as the National Association of Teachers of Religious Education (NATRE, 2024) and the National Association for the Teaching of English (NATE, 2024). If you put the words 'national association of teachers of' and then your subject in a search engine, you will begin to connect.

Teaching Beyond Your Subject

As a teacher you have to do more than just teach your subject. You are not only a teacher of your subject but of Maths, English, digital literacy, social skills, emotional skills, mental health skills, relationship skills, sexuality, spirituality, morality, cultural skills and more.

There are also many 'literacies' that teachers need to attend to, including digital, health, financial, and visual. The legal framework around teaching insists that you include specific teaching of English and Maths in your lessons. The Teachers' Standards, against which you will be judged at the end of your training, state that: 'Teaching includes clear development of pupils' literacy and numeracy skills within the subject' (DfE, 2011). Part Two of the Professional Standards for teachers includes the need to: 'Address the mathematics and English needs of learners and work creatively to overcome individual barriers to learning' (DfE, 2011). As for the third of what are traditionally known as key skills, **Information Technology** (sometimes called ICT or Information Communication Technology) – as Lord Sutherland observes: 'The DfE policy on ICT is there is no policy on ICT' (SecEd, 2013). Despite this, you will still have to teach the pupils how to use IT safely, and to optimise their learning. The two key subjects that you will not only have to teach, but also prove your abilities in, are English and Maths. Training Providers are required to 'assure' that you 'demonstrate competence' in these areas: speaking, listening and communicating and writing; using data and graphs to interpret information and solve mathematical problems (DfE, 2024).

There is a moral imperative to teach children the skills to explore their worlds, which was beautifully summed up by former Secretary-General of the United Nations, Kofi Annan.

> Literacy is a bridge from misery to hope. It is a tool for daily life in modern society. It is a bulwark against poverty, and a building block of development, an essential complement to investments in roads, dams, clinics and factories. Literacy is a platform for democratization, and a vehicle for the promotion of cultural and national identity . . .. Literacy is, finally, the road to human progress and the means through which every man, woman and child can realise his or her full potential. (Annan, 1997)

Inadequate literacy levels of pupils who leave school are a perennial problem. By 2015, the DfE was reporting that around 42 per cent of employers needed to organise additional training for young people joining them from school or college. It is as if the message is a stuck record which goes something like this: pupils' literacy standards are not good enough and here are our rather unclear plans for what we are going to do about it. For example, in 2016, the then Education Secretary Justine Greening (2016–2018), suggested that we: 'Don't let young people hit a brick wall in English and Maths' (TES, 2016). This painful fate was to be remedied, once again, by government plans but such plans have a history of not solving the problem. When government plans fail, of course, it is the schools' fault that literacy levels are not good enough and, by extension, the teachers' fault: 'Too few schools currently develop reading skills effectively' (Ofsted, 2012, p. 30). In order to 'move English forward' as Ofsted (2012) once so ineloquently put it, all teachers need to embed, among the many other skills of literacy, the following skills into their lessons: skimming, scanning, reading for detail, using an index, using a glossary, paragraphing, appropriate language use, punctuation and vocabulary.

For Maths, all teachers (including trainee teachers) need to teach pupils how to use data, create tables, charts and graphs. You need to support pupils with understanding of how to complete mathematical calculations: add up, take away, multiply, estimate and round up and down. You also need to teach pupils to solve mathematical problems including: time (the nature and calculation of it); money (how to calculate its use); ratios; measurement of distance and area; conversion between currencies; fractions; decimals; averages; range and estimation.

Look for opportunities in your subject teaching to reinforce pupils' literacy and numeracy skills. Pupils need to be able to transfer skills between subjects, and English and Maths are ideal for interdisciplinary ways of thinking. One further point: there should not be a perverse pride in not being good at Maths, so do not communicate this to pupils (especially if you are their Maths teacher).

Conclusion

We all have to 'fake it until we make it'. Read around topics. As you do, have a few 'choice cuts' of additional knowledge that you can casually scatter among those pupils who are hungry for more. You may also have to teach qualifications outside of the mainstream GCSEs, such as the International Baccalaureate or the American Curriculum and Post-16 (T-Levels included) which makes deep subject knowledge even more important. We are advocates of 'point of need' teaching, which means that you should not try to cram knowledge into your heads before the course, or during it, but find out the essential material which you need to learn in order to teach it in your next lesson. Be direct about what your pupils need to know. If possible, try to read beyond the essential curriculum material in the lesson, so that you can extend pupils' knowledge and respond to pupils' questions to inform you about what else you will need to know in the future. You can also be brave enough to learn from the pupils. One interviewee wisely told us: 'Although they are young people, they are still people'. This is a good point. The pupils are not objects, or vessels, to be filled but living, breathing, thinking human beings who may well know more than you about the subject being taught in th lesson, so the humility – or common goodness – to acknowledge this and learn from children is a positive teacher trait and one which the pupils will value. We also think that pupils will give you some room to be human, and admit that you do not know the answer (praise the pupil's question while you admit this). As well as learning from the pupils in an open and honest way, you can use the following strategies to deal with questions you do not know the answer to:

- 'Come back to me at lunch time and I will tell you' (do not worry, they probably will not).
- 'That's a great question and I'm going to set this for homework' (may not be too popular, but hey ho!).

Secondary trainee teachers usually come into teaching because they love their subject. If that is the case for you, then you are one of the fortunate ones: you can share this passion in the classroom. If not, you will have a more objective understanding of what needs to be taught. There can be some benefits in this. Regardless of your reason for teaching, you not only need to know the facts but also the reasons why your subject includes them. You need to develop the disciplinary skills and then teach *mist*. It is not easy, but surely you would not have come into this profession if you wanted something easy. When it works, the phrases 'lightbulb moment' and 'lighting of fires' are often used, because there is something magical about the moment a child learns something new.

....**REFLECTION**

Imagine that the subject you teach was a person – what type of person would it be? What characteristics would it have? PE, for example (and please do disagree with us) might be a positive, competitive, people-person. History might be a storyteller, deeply engaged and passionate about knowing more. Having written these characteristics, consider each against your own. To what extent did you choose your subject or it choose you? Philip Larkin (1983), who was prone to depressive thoughts, once wrote that he did not choose poetry but it chose him, and so did his subject matter: 'deprivation is for me what daffodils were to Wordsworth'.

....

....**ACTION**

Read through the National Curriculum (or local curriculum) and create a checklist of key subject knowledge. Consider your confidence and familiarity with each aspect. Your Training Provider will probably have given you a subject knowledge audit which you can use. Start with the easy substantive knowledge, then go through the disciplinary. Think about what skills are needed then consider what else you will need to do to make sure the children love the subject as much as you do. Then think about your subject's mist – what else is needed, beyond knowledge and skills, to bring the pupils to love your subject as much as (we hope) you do?

....

Case Study 4

Karen Teasdale completed a Post Graduate Certificate of Education (PGCE) at Birmingham University in the 1990s and has worked in three secondary schools and two universities. She trained as a Geography teacher but ended up teaching Drama because that was what her school needed. Here, Karen relates aspects of her life in teaching and discusses the communities of education she encountered between her first teaching job and her third school in the 2010s. Based on her many years of experience, she provides advice about schools, professionalism and how you should approach a school.

I came from a very monocultural world of the Cotswolds and with my first school I was suddenly in the very multicultural Handsworth in Birmingham but was blessed that, at that point, we had people like Section 11 teachers – specialists in school who you were able to help teachers make the curriculum accessible to all, including those who had **English as an additional language**. I am indebted to the pupils and the staff that I worked with because it was such a wonderful 'voyage of discovery' and there was a sense that schools and teachers were working together for the good of all. As part of the school's **Continuing Professional Development** (CPD) teachers would get together – a proper opportunity to form a community. I would meet with all the Drama practitioners and get a sense of the context that they were working in and discuss shared difficulties and challenges. I also had a wonderful staffroom where teachers could rant, cry, and celebrate, and it was a safe space for teachers to be together. I was given a scheme of work and themes to teach, but I created my own lessons and prepared my own resources. I was respected as a professional and able to choose, to an extent, what I did. On Friday lunchtimes most of the staff went to the pub for lunch – it sounds odd today but it was something you did, and it built a sense of community. When I started, each department had a visit from Her Majesty's Inspector of Schools (Ofsted's more friendly forerunner) and it was one professional talking to another professional. No-one questioned my professional values because I was a teacher.

In my first year, I have a vivid memory of having the worst English classroom right at the end of the corridor with a Year 11 bottom set and I had chosen to have a conversation with one of these naughtier pupils who had been disruptive in the corridor. I could feel the presence of the Deputy Head Teacher beside me, and she just said, "Is everything okay?" I really felt in that moment that she was saying, "Do you need me? I am here if you do," but also, "I don't want to tread on your toes or undermine what you are doing." In that moment, she empowered me; it was like her saying, "I've got your back." Perhaps all teachers feel this but for me, my first experience of school was a golden time for education when schools worked as teams with a shared sense of professionalism. The school funded my Master's degree in education and my development seemed to matter to them.

When I returned to teaching in schools after 10 years working at Birmingham City University, I realised that the form of professional was different from when I started but I think that people's reasons for going into the profession are still the same – at the heart is the belief that you're going to make a difference. If you look at school websites, there is the same message – we treat the pupil as a person, look at them holistically and look after their mental health and wellbeing. The problem comes with such pressures as the e-baccalaureate and Progress 8 where schools are rated and ranked by examination results. I think that there are too many external pressures on schools about results. I also found that there was more of a focus on compliance when I returned to schools. For me, professional does not necessarily mean always doing what you're told. It's about being able to question and say, "Actually, I disagree with that and here's why." Equally though, professionalism has always meant that I am part of a team and that I need to consistently implement the school ethos and if I really dislike this then I need to be working somewhere else.

I was very lucky because even in my latest school when I did not agree with the new management regime I was largely left alone because I was a one-person Drama department and partly because of the professional respect that had developed for me from the Senior Leadership Team who had been in the school for years. It was still difficult because things that we were all told to like Do Now Activities, behaviour pink slips, Exit Tickets, and taking pupils to a central place of detention did not match with my **pedagogy** or personal philosophy. It is not only teaching that had changed. When I returned to school, I did so as a parent and I couldn't watch a school production without bursting into tears of pride. I came back more maternal and my identity had changed, as in addition to everything else I was, I was a mother.

One thing I learnt to do is to own mistakes and that one of the most powerful tools you have is an apology. Often there is total silence and bemusement as those young people, possibly for the first time, hear a genuine apology and an adult admits that they are wrong. I say to the pupil, "You might not be prepared to forgive me straightaway but I would like us to keep building on this relationship," which may sound corny but it also vocalises that we are in a pupil-teacher relationship, and we both need to work on this together. In doing this, I also give a message that I expect pupils to make mistakes and I tell them that this is one of the ways that you learn. When I see trainee teachers, they seem to want to get it perfect on that first day and you cannot possibly do this. You are probably never going to get perfect in a whole career but instead you have to keep learning: learning from the pupils, learning from your colleagues, learning from the latest manifesto or publication, and so on. Teachers model everything for the pupils including being a lifelong learner and so I make sure I show them that I am. I focus on communication and make sure everybody in the room has a 'voice' because talk is a key to learning. I would remind trainees that you are a guest in school so be on your best behaviour! I would advise you to go into a classroom with open eyes and be willing to learn. You should realise that when you go into a classroom, you may think that the behaviour is good but you have not witnessed the battles and 'coastal erosion' that went on to get them in this position. You have not done this yet with a class, so they will be different with you. Good trainee teachers are developing their professional identity and being reflective, questioning; they have a passion for their subjects, and an enthusiasm, and high value for the role of education and belief in themselves, their new colleagues, and the children.

.... **WHAT TOOLS ARE IN YOUR TOOLKIT NOW?**

- Greater understanding that knowledge is more than knowledge – that it includes what to do with the knowledge in your discipline, skills, and the promotion of wider human qualities.
- Greater understanding about where subject content comes from.
- Advice about what subject knowledge expectations your Training Provider and schools may have.
- Understanding of your responsibility in developing pupils' English and Maths.

....

Places to Get More Tools for Your Toolkit

We are very fortunate, in the United Kingdom, to have a public service broadcaster whose remit is to educate as well as inform and entertain. If you want to know more about your subject, use the resources available for pupils at: https://www.bbc.co.uk/bitesize

During the Covid-19 pandemic Oak National was a temporary solution to the need to education pupils online. They are still with us, with lessons resources and invaluable information about how to teach a subject: https://www.thenational.academy/#teachers

References

Annan, K. (1997) *Secretary-General Stresses Need for Political Will and Resources to Meet Challenge of Fight against Illiteracy.* Available from: http://www.press.un.org/en/1997/19970904.sgsm6316.html

DfE (2011) *The Teachers' Standards.* Available from: www.assets.publishing.service.gov.uk/media/61b73d6c8fa8f50384489c9a/Teachers__Standards_Dec_2021.pdf

DfE (2013) *English Programmes of Study.* Available from: www.assets.publishing.service.gov.uk/media/5a7b8761ed915d4147620f6b/SECONDARY_national_curriculum_-_English2.pdf

DfE (2024) *Initial Teacher Training (ITT): Criteria and Supporting Advice.* Available from: https://www.gov.uk/government/publications/initial-teacher-training-and-early-career-framework

Larkin (1983) *Required Writing: Miscellaneous Pieces.* London: Faber and Faber.

NATRE (2024) *National Association of Teachers of Religious Education.* Available from: www.natre.org.uk/

NATE (2024) *National Association for the Teaching of English.* Available from: www.nate.org.uk/

Ofsted (2012) *Moving English Forward.* Available from: www.assets.publishing.service.gov.uk/media/5a7b44bc40f0b66a2fc0648b/110118.pdf

PSDP (2020) *Practice Supervisor Development Programme.* Available from: www.practice-supervisors.rip.org.uk/wp-content/uploads/2021/01/StS_PT_Developing_a_community_of_practice_in_your_org_Final.pdf

Robinson, K. (2006) *Do Schools Kill Creativity.* Available from: www.ted.com/talks/sir_ken_robinson_do_schools_kill_creativity/transcript

SecEd (2013) *The DfE Policy on ICT Is There Is No Policy on ICT.* Available from: www.sec-ed.co.uk/content/news/the-dfe-policy-on-ict-is-there-is-no-policy-on-ict

Shulman, L. (1987) Knowledge and teaching: Foundations of the new reforms. *Harvard Educational Review* 57(1): 1–22.

TES (2016) *Justine Greening: 'Don't Let Young People "hit a Brick Wall" in English and Maths'*. Available from: www.tes.com/magazine/archive/justine-greening-dont-let-young-people-hit-brick-wall-english-and-maths

Wenger, E. (1998) *Communities of Practice: Learning, Meaning, and Identity*. Cambridge: Cambridge University Press.

5

What You Need to Know About the Law, Policy and Regulation

What this chapter will cover

- Legal and **regulatory** framework of teacher training
- Laws which protect the training teacher
- The Teachers' Standards
- Fundamental **British Values**
- **Keeping Children Safe in Education**

Introduction

In the Wild West, if the movies are to be believed, there were laws, with sheriffs in every town to uphold them who tended to end up getting shot in the process. We have, in the past, been in plenty of schools which resembled this world, but they are few and far between today because, in general (and not necessarily in your placement school) there are more regulations and more sheriffs (known as Senior Leadership Teams) to implement them. In this chapter, we examine the national laws which lie behind school regulation. The legal status of trainee teachers in school will be explored, alongside an introduction to organisations and the specific regulation and legislation which support trainee teachers. The Teachers' Standards will be outlined and we will explain how and why these Standards are integrated into Training Provider curricula. The differences between law, policy and regulatory advice will be discussed, with distinctions between the 'musts' which have to be obeyed and the 'shoulds' which direct practice. A school has a duty not only to comply with the law and fulfil regulation, but also to make sure its staff (and, temporarily, its staff will include you) know and obey them. In all of this, there is no more important factor in schools than what is known as 'safeguarding', and the importance of this will be stressed. You have to expect when taking on the teacher's role of a guardian of children, that your behaviour – inside and outside of school – will be regulated. *As ignorantia juris non excusat* (or in English, ignorance of the law is no excuse) it is a very good idea to keep close to the laws outlined in this chapter and to make sure you know and follow school policy with regard to law and regulation.

Legal and Regulatory Framework of Teacher Training

The word 'reasonably' underscores many legal requirements and this word comes down to interpretation – what the police, judge or jury may decide, based on evidence and prior examples. You cannot reasonably be expected to read, comprehend and alter your actions to every clause of every law, any more than you can reasonably be expected to be responsible for every child in the school at the same time. It is the school's job to make sure you know what to do, and as long as you work as others do in the school you will be acting within the law unless (and there are always caveats, or exceptions, in law) you do something stupid. There are relatively few prosecutions of schools, and jail terms for teachers for offences (other than sexual ones) are rarer. The United Kingdom is a devolved country and so each country has its own laws, although a centralised UK parliament means there are many similarities between them, particularly on the important issues of education and child safety.

If you break the law, you can be arrested, charged and – if found guilty by a judge or jury – punished by the state's authorities by fines, community service or imprisonment. Regulations, on the other hand, are the rules about what you *should* do. If you do not follow them, you can be punished by the governing powers put in place by the Department for Education (DfE). Regulatory bodies such as the **Teacher Regulation**

Agency (TRA) and Ofsted who are given power by the government to act in ways that fine schools, or close them, or remove individuals from the teaching register and so prevent them from teaching.

Neither regulations nor laws are easy to understand in their raw form. You might think that they would be, considering their serious consequences, but each law requires interpretation. The reason for this is that there may be circumstances leading to why something happened; perhaps it was somehow justifiable not to do what the law states or not to do what the law states you should. Legally you cannot, for example, steal a cauliflower, but if you only did so to throw it at a person who was about to be hit by a bus, to alert them to the danger, we are fairly sure there would be some leniency in court. There are many 'shoulds' in both regulation and the law – far more than 'musts'. 'Shoulds' are what schools and individuals 'ought to do'; 'Musts' on the other hand, if not must-ed, can lead to prosecution. Some of these 'musts' come well-qualified in legislation documents by an 'unless' or 'if reasonable', which often makes the decision of whether the law has been broken complex. The main laws which affect trainee teachers are examined below: the Education Act, the **Equality Act**, Children and Young Persons Act, Children and Families Act, the Children Act, Common Law Duty of Care, Knives Act, Offensive Weapons Act, Sexual Offences Act, Online Safety Act and Copyright Law.

The Education Act

Education policy in the United Kingdom is like a ping-pong ball to political parties as it keeps going one way when Labour get in, then back again when the Conservatives are in power. Such policy is a relatively low cost, high impact way of imposing an ideology on a country, in a place which will do much to define the next generation. It can feel, by those who have to keep changing their practice in schools, like not so much ping-pong but pong-pong, with political parties taking education policy and ponging it against a wall.

The first Education Act of 1870 (known as the Forster Act) made education compulsory for children from five to 13 years old (British Library, n.d.). The 2008 Act updated the age at which compulsory education or training ends to 18 years old (Education and Skills Act, 2008). The 2011 Act abolished a lot of the laws the previous government had put into place and put a legal foundation in place for the radical curriculum reform which, at the time of writing this book, still informs what schools do. The last four significant updates to the Education Act were in 1996, 2002, 2011 and 2018. Sometimes, the changes are seen as being so significant that they produce a completely new Act of Parliament, such as the Education Reform Act (1988) and the Education and Inspections Act (2006). The Education Reform Act (1988) brought the education system of England and Wales under central government control, away from the control of Local Education Authorities (LEAs), and introduced a National Curriculum. Since 1988, the Secretary of State for Education of the day can act in a political manner to affect what happens in all schools: 'the design of education was moved away from the intellectuals, the educationists, and firmly placed in the hands of politicians' (Goodson, 1999: 294). This political will is clearly seen in the Education and Inspections Act

(2006) which speeded up a process of marketisation of schools – creating a competitive environment for central government funds – that had been in place since the 1980s. The Act gave the legal basis for Trusts to be formed which meant that schools could then run as private businesses; this 'right' has been encouraged and supported ever since, for example, with the creation of Multi-Academy Trusts (MATs) which are allowed to act like businesses, taking over other schools, cutting costs through expansion and so on.

The Education Act not only defines the legal framework on school curricula and ownership, it also informs teachers and schools about the limits of what can be done in a classroom when a child is unruly. The Education Act (1996 sections 550ZA and 550ZB) allows a Head Teacher to search a pupil or to delegate this role to staff. The search must be by someone of the same sex and in the presence of another member of staff (unless – here is the caveat – it is 'urgent'). The Head Teacher (or delegated member of staff) must not remove clothes (but – caveat – can remove a hat and coat). In 2013, this law was updated to make clear that physical contact with a pupil must be: 'proper and necessary'. This includes the use of restraint. What if, for example, you are female and suspect a male pupil has a knife, and have heard that they are about to use it? Could you search the pupil in this instance? Without being the same sex and having the permission of the Head Teacher, the answer is 'no'. There is a caveat to this because 'reasonable force' is allowed, regardless of sex and permission, and then there is Duty of Care law which states that if you do not do something to prevent injury, you are liable to be prosecuted. You can see that when Charles Dickens (2001) called the law an 'ass' he may have been unfair to the animal. With such complexity, it is best to rely on the school's instructions and your school mentor, and always err on the side of caution.

To give you a further 'flavour' of the laws a school must operate within, we have isolated one section from the Education and Inspections Act (2006) Section 90, which gives legal power to discipline a child. First, it defines the issue of 'disciplinary penalty' as something which is:

> imposed on a pupil, by any school at which education is provided for him, where his conduct falls below the standard which could reasonably be expected of him (whether because he fails to follow a rule in force at any such school or an instruction given to him by a member of its staff or for any other reason).

So, it is the 'standard which could be reasonably expected of him' (we imagine that it applies to 'her' or 'them' too) that can allow discipline – but whose expectation would the pupil be up against and what if the standards were unfair? What if the pupil had been falsely accused? The Act then defines the right of the school to enforce this discipline:

> The imposition of the disciplinary penalty is lawful if…reasonable in all the circumstances … made…by any paid member of the staff of the school…or…by any other member of the staff of the school, in circumstances where the head teacher has authorised the member of the staff to impose the penalty on the pupil.

If you examine this, you will see that a ***non-salaried*** trainee teacher (i.e. the vast majority of trainee teachers) needs authorisation from the Head Teacher to sanction a pupil. But even so, how would you know what would be 'reasonable in all the circumstances?' The law can be a slippery snake. Schools tend to rely on 'custom and practice' (repeating what they have always done themselves and what other similar schools have done) and government advice from non-statutory guidance such as the *Use of Reasonable Force in Schools* (DfE, 2013).

The Equality Act

The Equality Act (2010) safeguards everyone (including you) against discrimination because of 'protected characteristics'. By specifying age, disability, gender reassignment, marriage and civil partnership, pregnancy and maternity, race, religion or belief, sex and sexual orientation, the Equality Act works as a legal protector, ensuring that who you are, or choose to be, will not result in prejudicial action against you. If a school discriminates against you because of your faith, for example, then you have recourse to this law to prosecute the school. The existence of the law means that, probably, the school will not be discriminatory. In terms of how you yourself treat others, we hope you would comply with the Equality Act out of common decency and humanity. If not, you could be prosecuted, and the Act makes it clear that it relates to teachers:

> Thus, if a teacher belittles a pupil and holds her up to ridicule in class because of a disability she has, this could lead to a court case alleging unlawful harassment. The same unacceptable treatment directed at a lesbian pupil, or based on a pupil's religion, could lead to a case claiming direct discrimination. The practical consequences for the school, and the penalties, would be no different. (The Equality Act, 2010)

Children and Young Persons Act/Children and Families Act

The Children and Young Persons Act (2008) is concerned with **looked-after children (LAC)** and gives details to the school about provision and the need to give a Designated Teacher responsibility. This was updated in the Children and Families Act (2014) where a 'virtual school head' was included as someone to monitor the provision. LAC is the term for those in local authority care which may mean living in a residential home, with foster carers or even with parents and relatives. Those pupils who are assessed as needing this extra support can access funds and a system of support.

Common Law Duty of Care

The Common Law Duty of Care is legislation which can act on anyone who has neglected to do what is 'reasonably expected' to safeguard another person. Someone can be prosecuted for doing nothing in a situation where action could have restored safety. Every adult is liable to this law, in and out of school. For the safety of all children, the teacher (including the trainee teacher) must monitor the classroom, be aware of health and safety risks, and do all possible to prevent the pupils from engaging in dangerous behaviour. Leaving a group of 14-year olds with a box of matches unattended in a science laboratory, for example, would constitute neglect.

The Children Act

The Children Act (1989, 2004) focuses on vulnerable children and gives recommendations about who should care for them. This Act formalised the key term 'safeguarding', which covers the welfare of children with these words: 'reasonable in all circumstances for the purpose of safeguarding or promoting the welfare of the child' (Children Act, 1989). The term 'safeguarding' was taken up by Ofsted and schools, and was further emphasised in guidance documents such as *Working Together to Safeguard Children* (DfE, 2018a) which, importantly, gave the clear requirement that teachers should know who to report cases to, but not investigate them themselves. So, find out who the Safeguarding Officer is in school and do not act independently when there are concerns about child safety.

Knives Act/Offencive Weapons Act

The Knives Act (1997) states that it is an offence to carry any sharp or bladed instrument in a public place if the blade is longer than 3 inches (or 7.62 cm). As this criminalises any freelance chef, there is the caveat that a longer blade can be carried if there is 'good reason'. This is not an easy law to enforce – anyone stopped with a vicious machete might claim to be taking it to their mother's house to carve a tough melon. The law was created out of the government's response to media attention to crimes involving knives by young people – what they often call 'getting tough on knife crime'. The Knives Act (1997) prevents children from buying knives and allows the police to search people for them, but tends to be used, sadly, to prosecute only after a knife attack has occurred. In school, there is no good reason to carry a knife – unless, perhaps, it is a scalpel in biology, or a paint knife in art, or a knife in food technology, or a Sikh kirpan and so on. A child baptised into the Sikh religion may carry a kirpan (knife) because the Offensive Weapons Act (2019) was amended in 2019 to specifically allow them to carry one, and the Equality Act (2010) protects their religious rights. So, despite the Knives Act (1997) and the Offensive Weapons Act (2019), which also focuses on blades but extends legislation to corrosive substances, guns and anything else you would hope to never see used as weapons in school, knives can be very much part of school life. Their use needs to be monitored and regulated by the Common Law Duty of Care, as any person or organisation can prosecute another because they neglected to do what is 'reasonably expected' to safeguard another. The nature of care towards others (regardless of whether they are pupils or not) is an everyday, every moment concern for everyone.

Sexual Offences Act

Anyone over the age of 18 who touches a child (legally, under the age of 16) in a sexual manner is committing a legal offence which is punishable by imprisonment. Those who are in a 'position of trust' – and the Sexual Offences Act (2003) specifically states that this includes teachers – are liable to be prosecuted if the child is under the age of 18. Thirty-five per cent of all cases of teachers being banned from the profession involve male teachers committing sexual offences and 70 per cent of those banned from teaching are male (BBC, 2018). One of the 30 per cent, Rebecca Joynes, was arrested for having sex with a 15-year-old pupil, and while on bail had sex with a 16-year-old pupil with whom she had a baby (BBC, 2024a). The baby was taken from Joynes 24 hours after birth and she was sentenced to six-and-a-half years in jail, with the words of the Greater Manchester Police following her: 'Women can still be paedophiles; this term is not reserved only for men. Men and boys can still be victims of sexual abuse' (BBC, 2024b). These are relatively rare events (although depressingly, there seems to be a new one reported at least once a year). They bring much salacious news coverage and negative publicity with three outcomes: legal (may result in jail), regulatory (struck off the teacher register by the TRA) and social (being placed on the sex offender's register and branded as a paedophile brings potential social danger). The same is true of what the law calls 'pseudo-photographs' (the law was written in the relatively early days of the internet) to outlaw sexualised imagery of children under the age of 18. The trainee teacher who, on being shown a sexualised picture of a child by a pupil, recorded it on their phone to show the Safeguarding Officer (a bang-our-heads-against-a-wall moment for us teacher trainers) did so in breach of the law and was quickly dismissed from their placement. There must be no sexualised contact between a trainee teacher and a pupil; that is a 'must' with absolutely no caveat.

The Online Safety Act

This Act was passed through Parliament in 2024 and specifically criminalises online harm (Gov.uk, 2024) including:

- Encouraging or assisting serious self-harm.
- Cyberflashing (sending sexually explicit images without receiver's consent).
- Sending false information intended to cause harm.
- Threatening communications.
- Intimate image abuse (taking, sharing or threatening to share explicit images without subject's consent).
- Epilepsy trolling (sending content intended to trigger a seizure).

Trainee teachers need to know what to do if they encounter cases of pupils who might be sharing explicit and/or endangering images of themselves or others. The Teachers' Standards Part Two already regulates your behaviour, so if you were found to have acted in any of the above ways, you would be put before a disciplinary committee and, if found guilty, more than likely removed from the TRA's register of teachers. Based on this law, the legal process would then begin.

Copyright Law

The Educational Recording Agency and the Copyright Licensing Agency are used to allow schools to reproduce the work of others and so prevent prosecution under Copyright Law.

The phrase 'fair dealing' sums up the permissions granted. There are rules about what can be copied and shown, including:

- The material reproduced must be used purposefully for education.
- The material reproduced must not be for commercial purposes – so beware if you are charging for an event.
- The material reproduced must have the source acknowledged.

Some works are not permitted with this licence and musical texts are not allowed to be reproduced – here comes the caveat again – except small extracts. Schools pay subscriptions to companies that grant some freedom: the Copyright, Designs and Patents Act (1988) allows images to be reproduced; the Educational Recording Agency (ERA, 2022) and the Copyright Licensing Agency (CLA, 2022) allows 'fair dealing' (IPO, 2014) so that teachers can use pictures, text, sounds and moving images from published sources. Your school should guide you about copyright law, but in general, you should reproduce copyrighted work as little as possible, and ensure that it is always acknowledged and used purposefully.

Laws and Regulation Which Protect a Trainee Teacher

The laws are not all out to get and constrain you. Some laws protect you from the Training Provider and school. You also have a regulatory framework, which outlines expectations and gives you the right of appeal and complaint. Here is some legislation and guidance you may need during your placement and course: Competitions and Markets Authority, Office for Students, Office of the Independent Adjudicator, Trade Unions, the Education Act, the Employment Rights Act, Health and Safety at Work Act, and Initial Teacher Training regulation.

Competitions and Markets Authority

The 77-page *UK Higher Education Providers – Advice on Consumer Law Protection* (Gov.uk, 2023) makes very clear by referring to students as consumers 182 times. You have the Competitions and Markets Authority (CMA) Practical Law (CMA, 2022) to protect you if your course did not provide what it advertised or if it demanded money for something which was not pre-warned. You could address this in court, but the threat of legal action alone would usually be enough for you to get satisfaction from the Training Provider. Whatever your Training Provider offers should be in writing (and it is worth trying to get confirmation of any promises made about the course in this form) but even what you are told verbally has legal standing – though it can sometimes become 'one person's word against another'. Any promise you have been given, written or verbal, is a form of contract between you and the Training Provider, and if it is not fulfilled you have a legal ground for complaint.

Office for Students

While you are studying to be a teacher, you are a student and so may call on the advice, protection and support of the Office for Students (2024). This does not include school-based training. The Office for Students regulates the Higher Education sector and you can appeal to them directly if you feel that you have been unfairly treated. Usually, the threat of doing so will work to alert your Training Provider to take your complaint seriously and it is advisable to go to them first.

Office of the Independent Adjudicator

Before appealing to the Office of the Independent Adjudicators (OIA, 2024) you will need to have exhausted the Training Provider's complaints system first and proved that you have tried to find a resolution through them, preferably gaining a Letter of Completion. The OIA then acts as an external judge and jury to see if the organisation which took you on as a student has dealt with your complaint fairly. The OIA is clear that the term 'student' includes trainee teachers and includes those based at schools and Trusts. Likewise, someone on the **apprenticeship** route can use the OIA's services, as it has regulatory power over any organisation which takes on students.

Unions

You have a legal right to join a union (Gov.uk, n.d.) and no employer can stop you though we have (ironically) known some 'free schools' try to. The National Education Union (NEU, 2024a) is the largest, with around 500,000 members (TUC, 2024); National Association of School-masters and Union of Women Teachers (**NASUWT**) is close behind with 300,000+ members (NASUWT, 2024). As a trainee teacher, you are allowed full union rights. The union provides you with courses, training, advice and support. It also gives you access to legal teams which act on your behalf in disputes. We suggest you join a union as soon as you start your training.

The Education Act

As part of the Education Act's role to ensure a legal basis to what teachers and schools must do, it governs teacher pay and conditions – which are also outlined in the guidance document *School Teachers' Pay and Conditions* (DfE, 2021). Apart from those on the Salaried route, trainee teachers are not legally employed by their schools and so cannot benefit from the legal rights given to teachers. Salaried trainee teachers, however, are entitled to a 'reasonable break' (whatever that might mean; unions in the past have defined it as 40 minutes). The working year is restricted to 190 teaching days and five training days, leaving 170 days free from either. Salaried trainee teachers have a right to a written contract within two months of starting training, which includes a job title and the work that would be expected of you. Full-time teachers get 10 per cent of their timetable as Planning Preparation and Assessment (PPA) time (NEU, 2024b) so you are entitled to at least this – although teacher training comes with its own stipulation about how much you should be teaching anyway. PPA time is to be used for covering absent teachers 'only rarely, and only in circumstances that are not foreseeable' (DfE, 2021: 51).

The Employment Rights Act and the Health and Safety at Work Act

For Salaried trainee teachers, the Employment Rights Act (1996) gives details of contracts, breaks and the information you should expect from your employer. The Health and Safety at Work Act (Gov.uk, 1974) gives legal power to the need to safeguard you, regardless of your salaried status, from physical and mental harm while in the workplace. In a world of constantly changing laws, that these two laws are firmly based in the late 20th century and have not been updated since implies that perhaps they are not exactly government priorities, but in the event of any injury or abuse by an employer they are the acts to refer to - with guidance from a legal representative or union.

The Teachers' Standards

Your Training Provider will have integrated the Teachers' Standards (DfE, 2011) into their own assessment criteria which will determine whether you get Qualified Teacher Status (QTS) or not. At the end of the course, by meeting the Training Provider's assessment criteria, you will have also fulfilled the Teachers' Standards. The idea of an externally based set of criteria which needed to be fulfilled was not put in place until 1997 (DfEE, 1997). Before this, the judgement about awarding QTS was down to the experience and instinct of professionals: fellow teachers, Head Teachers and teacher trainers. To an extent, this is still the case: these people will decide whether you are fit to be a teacher and give the final judgement on you. They will, though, have to base their decisions on criteria which you need to see, understand, internalise and, eventually, prove that you have fulfilled. Imagine that you are in a court of law and someone is pointing at you and accusing you of not being a teacher - you have to go to the Training Provider's criteria to give evidence that you are. The Standards, on which the Training Provider's criteria are based, are in two parts: Part One concentrates on your professional development in teaching, with eight Standards focused on delivery of your subject through effective lesson planning, delivery, assessment and behaviour management; Part Two concentrates on your personal and professional conduct. In one lesson, you can fulfil many requirements of Part One of the Standards, but to gain QTS you must have done so consistently through the year. Here, we present each Standard with an explanation of what it means and how it can be fulfilled.

Standard 1: Set High Expectations Which Inspire, Motivate and Challenge Pupils

Standard 1 requires you to do the following:

- Establish a safe and stimulating environment for pupils, rooted in mutual respect.
- Set goals that **stretch and challenge** pupils of all backgrounds, abilities and dispositions.
- Demonstrate consistently the positive attitudes, values and behaviour which are expected of pupils.

There are three separate strands here: the classroom environment you create for pupils; the goals your lesson sets; and the way you are in the classroom. You need to make sure that:

- You expect pupils to want to learn and be engaged in learning.
- The aims of the lesson are pitched correctly in terms of what the curriculum demands at a particular age level and what will ensure the pupils to progress with their learning.
- You are on time, with resources planned, enthusiastic about the lesson and respectful of all.

The key phrase for this Standard is 'high expectations'. What if the class does not want to learn, or one particular pupil does not? Your expectation is that they will, and you will take action to do all you can to ensure that they can and are engaged. This is about you and your actions, rather than what the class does.

Standard 2: Promote Good Progress and Outcomes by Pupils

Standard 2 requires you to do the following:

- Be accountable for pupils' attainment, progress and outcomes.
- Be aware of pupils' capabilities and their prior knowledge, and plan teaching to build on these.
- Guide pupils to reflect on the progress they have made and their emerging needs.
- Demonstrate knowledge and understanding of how pupils learn and how this impacts on teaching.
- Encourage pupils to take a responsible and conscientious attitude to their own work and study.

The key word for this Standard is 'progress'. You must ensure that pupils learn what they need to, and that this is evidenced. There is an interesting comment in the Core Content Framework (CCF) about 'misleading factors, such as how busy pupils appear' (DfE, 2019: 23). This Standard ensures that you cannot go into a lesson and, effectively, babysit a group; you must have a reason for teaching each and every lesson. To fulfil this Standard, you will need to:

- Have a record of prior achievement in the subject for each individual.
- Be able to use data to inform how your lesson will aim the subject at each individual.
- Ensure that each pupil understands their level of learning of the subject and has a mechanism to take action to modify knowledge or practice.
- Work on the attitudes of the pupils so they want to learn.

Standard 3: Demonstrate Good Subject and Curriculum Knowledge

Standard 3 requires the following:

- Have a secure knowledge of the relevant subject(s) and curriculum areas, foster and maintain pupils' interest in the subject, and address misunderstandings.

- Demonstrate a critical understanding of developments in the subject and curriculum areas, and promote the value of scholarship.
- Demonstrate an understanding of and take responsibility for promoting high standards of literacy, articulacy and the correct use of Standard English.

To fulfil this Standard, you will need to:

- Know the subject you are teaching.
- Understand the National (or local) curriculum of the subject.
- Keep up to date with the way the subject is to be taught in school.
- Be a teacher of literacy as well as your subject.

Standard 4: Plan and Teach Well-Structured Lessons

Standard 4 requires you to do the following:

- Impart knowledge and develop understanding through effective use of lesson time.
- Promote a love of learning and children's intellectual curiosity.
- Set homework and plan other out-of-class activities to consolidate and extend the knowledge and understanding pupils have acquired.
- Reflect systematically on the effectiveness of lessons and approaches to teaching.
- Contribute to the design and provision of an engaging curriculum within the relevant subject area(s).

This Standard deals with the smooth running of the lesson. You will need to:

- Plan each lesson thoughtfully so that the timing is decided in advance, and adapted as the lesson requires.
- Make good use of directed study time – give purposeful homework and tasks to do outside the lesson.

Having 'chunked' your lesson into manageable learning stages in advance, changed the pace according to pupil responses, and made sure there is extension work for all, you need to focus on yourself to fulfil the rest of this Standard:

- Ensure that pupils know about how much you care about your teaching subject and the content of the lesson.
- Be able to self-assess each lesson and satisfactorily be able to know strengths and weaknesses.
- Be part of the subject department by helping to develop resources and teaching schedules.

Whenever the Standards turn to you as a trainee teacher and how you behave, they become easier to fulfil as you are independent of the school, the pupils or other outside factors. You can fulfil these by being, acting and communicating that you are 'living and breathing' the subject as it is taught in the school.

Standard 5: Adapt Teaching to Respond to the Strengths and Needs of all Pupils

Standard 5 requires you to do the following:

- Know when and how to adapt your teaching? appropriately, using approaches which enable pupils to be taught effectively.
- Have a secure understanding of how a range of factors can inhibit pupils' ability to learn, and how best to overcome these.
- Demonstrate an awareness of the physical, social and intellectual development of children, and know how to adapt teaching to support pupils' education at different stages of development.
- Have a clear understanding of the needs of all pupils, including those with special educational needs; those of high ability; those with English as an additional language; those with disabilities; and be able to use and evaluate distinctive teaching approaches to engage and support them.

The key word here is 'adapt'. You need to:

- Give a different lesson to each pupil as needed.
- Know strategies to support those with specific learning needs.
- Understand the stages of child development and the expectations of learning at different ages.
- Target those whose learning is more advanced, those for whom English is not their first language and those who have learning and/or physical disabilities.

Standard 6: Make Accurate and Productive Use of Assessment

Standard 6 requires you to do the following:

- Know and understand how to assess the relevant subject and curriculum areas, including **statutory** assessment requirements.
- Make use of formative and **summative assessment** to secure pupils' progress.
- Use relevant data to monitor progress, set targets and plan subsequent lessons.
- Give pupils regular feedback, both orally and through accurate marking.
- Encourage pupils to respond to the feedback.

Successful assessment – diagnostic (before a lesson), formative (during a lesson) and summative (after a lesson) – are the keys to fulfilling this Standard. This starts with knowledge gained from reading about teaching, the advice from your mentors and other professionals and training courses, applied with **reflexivity** and sensitivity, in the classroom. To fulfil this Standard you will need to:

- Understand both the school's and the government's ways of assessing pupils in a summative manner.

- Successfully use in-class checks on learning and examinations.
- Be clear about the purpose of any assessment and ensure that judgements about learning are founded on valid assessments.
- Use pupil data to plan lessons to cater for each individual pupil in the room.
- Correctly and supportively give feedback to pupils.

Standard 7: Manage Behaviour Effectively to Ensure a Good and Safe Learning Environment

Standard 7 requires you to do the following:

- Have clear rules and routines for behaviour in classrooms, and take responsibility for promoting good and courteous behaviour both in classrooms and around the school, in accordance with the school's behaviour policy.
- Have high expectations of behaviour, and establish a framework for discipline with a range of strategies, using praise, sanctions and rewards consistently and fairly.
- Manage classes effectively, using approaches which are appropriate to pupils' needs in order to involve and motivate them.
- Maintain good relationships with pupils, exercise appropriate authority and act decisively when necessary.

This Standard is about what you do and is centred on the word 'manage'. To fulfil this Standard, you will need to:

- Establish the school's rules in your lesson, and exercise sanctions and praise to ensure they are adhered to.
- Be able to motivate pupils to learn.
- Be a figure of control who the pupils can relate to.

You are not 'the law' in a school, but the upholder and enforcer of it. Each school has its own policy for behaviour management, and it is your job to know it and make sure that any breaches of it, if needs be, are sanctioned.

Standard 8: Fulfil Wider Professional Responsibilities

Standard 8 requires you to do the following:

- Make a positive contribution to the wider life and ethos of the school.
- Develop effective professional relationships with colleagues, knowing how and when to draw on advice and specialist support.
- Deploy support staff effectively.
- Take responsibility for improving teaching through appropriate professional.
- Development, responding to advice and feedback from colleagues.
- Communicate effectively with parents with regard to pupils' achievements and well-being.

In order to fulfil this Standard, you will need to:

- Help the school and pupils beyond what you do in the classroom.
- Understand and consult other professionals in the school, including those with specialist responsibilities.
- Be able to purposefully direct anyone who is supporting your lesson.
- Act on professional advice in a positive and constructive manner.
- Be in regular contact with parents.

You are to become part of the life of the school and are not allowed to hide in a cupboard until lesson time (we have had trainees who resorted to hiding in the toilets, which was hardly fair on the rest of the staff).

Teachers' Standards: Part Two

Part Two of the Standards governs the minimum expected behaviour of a teacher inside and outside school, including the following:

- Treating pupils with dignity, building relationships rooted in mutual respect and at all times observing proper boundaries appropriate to a teacher's professional position.
- Having regard for the need to safeguard pupils' well-being, in accordance with statutory provisions.
- Showing tolerance of and respect for the rights of others.
- Not undermining fundamental British values, including democracy, the rule of law, individual liberty and mutual respect and tolerance of those with different faiths and beliefs.
- Ensuring that personal beliefs are not expressed in ways that exploit pupils' vulnerability or might lead them to break the law.
- Teachers must have proper and professional regard for the ethos, policies and practices of the school in which they teach, and maintain high standards in their own attendance and punctuality.
- Teachers must have an understanding of, and always act within, the statutory frameworks that set out their professional duties and responsibilities.

The Teachers' Standards have legal power (although there is the usual caveat, 'unless there is a good reason not to'). The 'must' on the Teachers' Standards allows schools to break a contract if any Standards are proven to be transgressed. If, for example, you were to express intolerance of a faith on social media, you would have broken the code (and would expect to be dismissed from the placement and training programme) and you may have also broken the law (the Equality Act) against which you could be judged separately on criminal grounds. As with many other professions which come with additional legal requirements (such as the armed forces or the emergency services) there is an internal process of investigation and punishment. The TRA intervenes when there is concern over a teacher's behaviour. The TRA is controlled by the DfE which, in turn, is controlled by the Secretary of State for Education. Before the case gets to the person in this role, there is a lengthy process of review by an independent panel which has a legal adviser who will determine whether: 'the behaviour of the person concerned has been fundamentally incompatible with being a teacher' (Gov.uk, 2021). If this is the case, the person is 'prohibited' from teaching in schools, sixth form colleges and any youth institution.

Fundamental British Values

In 2007, the Chancellor of the Exchequer Gordon Brown said:

> when people are. . .asked what they admire about Britain, more usually say it is our values: British tolerance, the British belief in liberty and the British sense of fair play. (Guardian, 2007)

We may well be relatively 'good eggs' on the worldwide stage these days but as a nation there is a counterargument that 'British' and 'Values' are ones we should not be too proud of, as the representatives from 12 Commonwealth countries calling on King Charles to acknowledge and apologise for the impacts, and ongoing legacy, from British 'genocide and colonisation' (Independent, 2023) would tell you. Marika Sherwood expresses this view:

> When children were taken from the workhouses and marched up to the Lancashire factories in the mid-19th century, was that 'liberty'? Or when children on the streets were picked up and shipped out to the colonies as cheap labour? Or when political activists in Britain were exiled and those in the colonies jailed? . . . just how many millions of enslaved Africans did Britain transport across the Atlantic and Indian Oceans?

Many schools re-badge Fundamental British Values as the school's values, or human values. Regardless, as a teacher you must never 'undermine' - that is, oppose - these qualities; you must promote them:

- democracy,
- the rule of law,
- individual liberty,
- mutual respect, and
- tolerance of those with different faiths and beliefs (DfE, 2014b)

Keeping Children Safe in Education

Try this one, if you like: ask a Head Teacher what the main task of a school is, and they will not reply 'learning' but 'safeguarding'. Of all the roles you have in school, safeguarding children is the priority and parents will, primarily, be concerned that you keep their child safe. The judge, Lord Esher, agreed, in a case where a headmaster had been found guilty of neglect by leaving phosphorus accessible to pupils: 'The schoolmaster was bound to take such care of his boys as a careful father would' (Williams v. Eady, 1893). Initially, such responsibility was very much seen as a male thing but in 1962, a judge finally redressed the gender balance by summing up a case where the LEA, Middlesex County Council, was prosecuted for not acting as 'a prudent parent' (Lyes v. Middlesex County Council, 1962) would, when it fitted a pane of glass that could shatter in a school. The phrase 'prudent parent' is still the one used in the DfE-produced document on health and safety in schools (DfE, 2014a). Note that you are identified as being 'in loco parentis' (in the place of the parents). In order to fulfil this role, you will need to be knowledgeable about *Keeping Children Safe in Education* (*KCSiE*) (DfE, 2024 – this guidance has been updated annually for some time and you should refer to the most up-to-date version) which explains the legislative framework for schools regarding safeguarding. *KCSiE* runs to 178 pages and usefully sums up the laws protecting children for schools, including the Sexual Offences Act, the Children Act and so on. It has 744 'shoulds' and 118 'musts'. The 'shoulds' will be monitored when Ofsted comes calling and the 'musts' may result in prosecution if any of them are breached. School leaders have a responsibility to ensure that staff (including all trainee teachers) have read and are familiar with at least Part One of the statutory guidance document which, thankfully, is only the first 23 pages.

We can sum up some of the *KCSiE* document for you here:

- You need to be trained by the Training Provider and schools on how to spot signs of abuse.
- You must not investigate anything yourself.
- You must also never promise a child confidentiality.
- You need to be vigilant for any signs of emotional, sexual and physical abuse, including neglect.
- Suspicions of criminal exploitation, female genital mutilation and bullying (peer-on-peer) all need to be reported to the Safeguarding Lead.

If neglect or abuse is confirmed, it should be reported by means of a multi-agency system, which includes the local authority. If there are safeguarding concerns about another member of staff, these concerns should be reported to the Head Teacher. If there are safeguarding concerns about the Head Teacher, then these concerns go to the governors. *KCSiE* is an invaluable guide, and it includes whistleblowing procedures. It states that three processes must be in place in a school:

- pupil behaviour policy,
- staff behaviour policy (code of conduct), and
- safeguarding arrangements.

Staff training for these processes is compulsory at **induction**, which must be updated through the year.

Conclusion

You cannot possibly internalise all of the laws and regulations during your first year in school so focus on the priorities. The first priority is to safeguard the children so absorb what you need to know from *KCSiE*. You also need to know how your Training Provider will assess you so make sure you know how they have re-visioned the Teachers' Standards. From thereon, follow your placement school's policies and codes, and learn from your mentor. Your own study of law and regulation should be an ongoing focus, so that you are up-to-date, knowledgeable, and aware of your professional rights and responsibilities.

·· **REFLECTIONS**

Is it reasonable to do the following and if so, when?

- Remove disruptive children from a classroom when they have refused to follow instruction.
- Prevent a pupil leaving the classroom.
- Prevent a pupil attacking staff or student.
- Restrain a pupil from self-harming.
- Confiscate inappropriate items.
- Detain pupils at the end of school.

You will need to know the answers, as these are common acts in school. To find the legal answers, you could negotiate the 'shoulds' and 'musts' and then the 'unless' and 'reasonable' clauses, but it is probably best to ask an experienced member of staff and to learn from observation and experience.
··

·· **ACTIONS**

There are legal experts in school who oversee policy, so your main action is to read, revise and internalise school policy on all matters. Keep within this guidance and you have fulfilled your duties. Also, read Part One of *KCSiE* and revise it. As a trainee teacher, your actions will be mediated by a mentor but you still have a human responsibility to look after children and work to eliminate the awful, immoral abuse of those who cannot yet protect themselves.
··

Case Study 5

Melisa Watkins qualified in 2024 and gained a position in her second placement school as an English teacher. This extract of an essay she wrote while on her Post Graduate Certificate of Education (PGCE) course shows that the topics you choose to study for your assignments can be both original and important to you, as Paganism was to her. In this essay extract,

Melisa reminds us that, teachers need to be aware, sensitive and open to the beliefs of all pupils.

Paganism is still one of the most misunderstood, and for some, feared religions. These fears and misconceptions mean that many Pagans face judgement, despite new legislation that explicitly prohibits discrimination against religion or belief. The Equality Act (2010) was a great step forward for making sure those that needed it had protection by drawing together nine separate anti-discrimination laws and legislation and further strengthening them to protect an identified number of characteristics including belief. This is relevant to me as a Pagan and a teacher. I taught a child in my placement school who identified as a Pagan and we are not alone as according to the 2021 Census (ONS, 2021) 74,000 people in the UK identified their religion as Paganism.

Paganism stands on its own as a religion but also serves to function as an umbrella term for a variety of nature-based polytheistic religions, such as: Wiccan, Witchcraft, Druid, Heathenry, Hellenism, Neopagans, etc. (The Pagan Federation, n.d.). Paganism is an ancient religious outlook that is identifiable by its focus on three specific areas: nature, polytheism incorporating gods and goddesses. As the religion is not dogmatic, many variations of Paganism have surfaced in recent times, but all implicitly believe in tolerance, kindness, and the importance of nature. Paganism is a 'nature religion that stresses the immanence of the divine rather than transcendence, which in turn leads to a strong emphasis on responsibility, rather than rules' (Jarvis, 2008: 44). Despite propaganda stating the reverse, Pagans do not class themselves as Satanists, anti-Christian, and do not even believe in the Devil. Instead, they see themselves as 'keepers of the 'Old Religion', whose ancestors had practised Paganism for centuries, often secretly and 'underground' since its suppression by the Christian Church' (Crowley, 2019: 171).

Evidence of ancient Paganism can still be found in all areas of our lives today where Christianity adopted rather than erased traditions. The very days of the week and months of the year are named for Pagan Gods and Goddesses: Wednesday – Odin's day, Thursday – Thor's day (Rosen, 2004). Many popular British festivals follow the ancient Pagan festivals, the cycle of the seasons or eight Sabbats, and these have been merged with the Christian calendar. Easter replaced Ostara with its traditions of painted eggs to symbolise the new life of spring; Christmas replaced Yule where greenery was traditionally brought into the home to keep it safe until the Horned God made his rebirth into the world. Although these holidays are celebrated widely as Christian holidays the one Sabbat that is still commonly associated with Pagans is Samhain, popularly called Halloween, which is the Pagan New Year festival. The UK school curriculum is often focused on the British calendar year with celebrations around: Christmas, Diwali, and Eid; however, the autumn festival of Halloween is usually avoided and considered by a vast number of teachers to be inappropriate to study or celebrate in schools (Plater, 2013). If all religions are protected by law, then why is the Pagan New Year festival deemed inappropriate?

Although they are technically separate, the relationship between the church and the government has had a pivotal role in the development of the education system (King, 2010). Whilst standard secondary schools in the UK may claim to be independent of religion, Niens et al. (2013: 910) argue that religion, and more specifically Christianity, is in fact still incorporated into the school life through assemblies, events, religious studies and the hidden curriculum. The 'hidden curriculum' refers to the unwritten, unofficial, and often unintended lessons, values, and perspectives that students learn in school (Sabbott, 2013).

The 'hidden curriculum' is potentially problematic for Pagans with the lack of representation in Religious Education lessons and the lack of festival celebrations, but it can even be a problem upon a closer inspection of the National Curriculum texts within English. Shakespeare, for example, is openly discriminatory to Pagans and his work makes up a portion of the English curriculum. In 1604, under King James I's rule, witchcraft was made a capital offence, and historical witch hunts took place in the UK. Shakespeare's *Macbeth* was heavily influenced by the witch hunt phenomenon, and I have observed it being taught in the English classroom on both placements as a GCSE text. A key theme in Macbeth is the supernatural. Witches as a trope, then and now, have often been seen as a threat to the Christian patriarchy. They often appear in literature to reflect the growing anxieties when the image of woman changes, and although the killing has stopped, the witch is still an icon of evil (Baker, 2019). Shakespeare explicitly refers to Hecate, a main goddess in Paganism. Hecate was worshipped in Ancient Greece as a goddess who would bestow luck, health, or wisdom and today Pagans worship her as the goddess of witchcraft, a source of positive energy. In *Macbeth*, she is presented as a negative force (Chakrabarti and Sarkar, 2021: 8). During my placements I observed teachers exploring how the characters of the witches and Hecate are inherently evil, and how reference is made to the good characters who followed the 'light' of Christianity. The teachers did not seem to be aware that Hecate is still relevant and worshipped to this day.

Pagan pupils and staff may feel the need to assimilate their religious identity into the majority religious culture in their desire to avoid prejudice and discrimination and fit in with their peers and the social norms of the school (Niens et al., 2013: 910). I observed something like this on placement A. Whilst having a discussion with an openly Pagan member of staff, she explained to me that when she was a pupil at school, she did not have the confidence to be public about her religion. She was a pupil in a local Catholic school and was fearful of the reaction she would receive from the teachers, her peers and even her own parents. She told me that this led her to 'act out' as a teenager until she found a group of friends outside of the school who shared the same beliefs. It is important to highlight that this is not just relevant to pupils. According to King (2010: 287) 'staff in faith-based schools are generally expected to be of the same faith as the school or supportive of the values and practices of that faith'. Sandberg (2014) agrees with this and adds that in some cases the religious opinions of staff can be taken into account when considering hiring, promotion etc. and that whilst they may not be openly discriminated against, a staff member of the same faith is more likely to be promoted. This can be further evidenced when we consider the dress code. The 2010 Equality Act protects a person's right to wear religious clothing or symbols without harassment or discrimination. Faith schools are able to work around this law by adding a dress policy to the contract of employment. Once a member of staff signs this document with that **inclusion**, they cannot then claim that their religious freedom has been infringed upon (Sandberg, 2014: 15). This, of course, would be unlikely to be an issue if they were wearing religious symbols of the faith school's religion.

..............................WHAT TOOLS ARE IN YOUR TOOLKIT NOW?

- Knowledge of education law and how it defines what can be done in school.
- Understanding of the importance of safeguarding.
- Awareness of laws that are applicable in schools.
- The ability to refer to supporting bodies including unions, the CMA and the OIA if your Training Provider and Degree Awarding body are not acting fairly and within the regulations.

Places to Get More Tools for Your Toolkit

DfE (2024, updated regularly) *Keeping Children Safe in Education.* London: HMSO. Part One gives a detailed guide to safeguarding responsibilities for staff and the best practice to support the children in your care.

Blatchford, R. (2020) *The Teachers' Standards in the Classroom.* London: Learning Matters. This book gives good, honest advice on what the Teachers' Standards are and how to best fulfil them.

Newlance, A. (2021) *Becoming a Teacher: The Legal, Ethical and Moral Implications of Entering Society's Most Fundamental Profession.* Camarthen: Crown House Publishing. Chapter 3 is on law and subtitled as 'The teacher you must be'. It gives clear, no-compromise instruction about staying on the right side of the law.

References

Baker, K. (2019) *Representations of Witches and Witchcraft in Children's Literature.* https://scholarworks.calstate.edu/downloads/1g05fh019

BBC (2018) *Teacher Bans: Sexually Motivated Conduct Is Most Common Cause.* Available from: www.bbc.co.uk/news/uk-england-44643267

BBC (2024a) *Rebecca Joynes: Teacher Guilty of Sex with Two Boys.* Available from: www.bbc.co.uk/news/uk-england-manchester-69026069

BBC (2024b) *Teacher Who Sexually Abused Two Schoolboys Jailed.* Available from: www.bbc.co.uk/news/articles/cn08y6785xqo

British Library (n.d.) *Synopsis of the Forster Education Act 1870.* Available from: www.bl.uk/collection-items/synopsis-of-the-forster-education-act-1870

Chakrabarti, R. and Sarkar, S. (2021) The weird 'others'. *Rupkatha Journal on Interdisciplinary Studies in Humanities* 13(1): 1–12.

Children Act (1989) London: The Stationery Office. Available from: www.legislation.gov.uk/ukpga/1989/41/contents

Children Act (2004) London: The Stationery Office. Available from: www.legislation.gov.uk/ukpga/2004/31/contents

Children and Families Act (2014) London: The Stationery Office. Available from: www.legislation.gov.uk/ukpga/2014/6/contents

Children and Young Persons Act (2008) London: The Stationery Office. Available from: www.legislation.gov.uk/ukpga/2008/23/contents

CLA (2022) *Copyright Licensing Agency.* Available from: www.cla.co.uk

CMA (2022) *Competitions and Market Authority.* Available from: www.gov.uk/government/organisations/competition-and-markets-authority

Copyright, Designs and Patents Act (1988) London: The Stationery Office. Available from: www.legislation.gov.uk/ukpga/1988/48/contents

Crowley, V. (2019) *Nature Religion Today.* Edinburgh: Edinburgh University Press.

DfE (2011) *The Teachers' Standards.* Available from: www.assets.publishing.service.gov.uk/media/61b73d6c8fa8f50384489c9a/Teachers__Standards_Dec_2021.pdf

DfE (2013) *Use of Reasonable Force in Schools.* Available from: www.gov.uk/government/publications/use-of-reasonable-force-in-schools

DfE (2014a) *Health and Safety: Advice on Legal Duties and Powers for Local Authorities, School Leaders, School Staff and Governing Bodies.* Available from: www.assets.publishing.service.gov.uk/government/uploads/system/uploads/attachment_data/file/279429/DfE_Health_and_Safety_Advice_06_02_14.pdf

DfE (2014b). *Promoting Fundamental British Values as Part of SMSC in Schools.* Available from: www.gov.uk/government/uploads/system/uploads/attachment_data/file/380595/SMSC_Guidance_Maintained_Schools.pdf

DfE (2018) *Working Together to Safeguard Children.* Available from: www.gov.uk/government/publications/working-together-to-safeguard-children-2

DfE (2019) *Core Content Framework.* Available from: www.gov.uk/government/publications/initial-teacher-training-itt-core-content-framework

DfE (2021) *School Teachers' Pay and Conditions.* Available from: www.gov.uk/government/publications/school-teachers-pay-and-conditions

DFE (2024) *Keeping Children Safe in Education.* Available from: www.assets.publishing.service.gov.uk/media/6650a1967b792ffff71a83e8/Keeping_children_safe_in_education_2024.pdf

DfEE (1997) *Circular Number 10/97*. Available from: www.educationengland.org.uk/documents/dfee/circular10-97.html

Dickens, C. (2001) *Bleak House*. London: Wordsworth Classics.

Education Act (1996) London: The Stationery Office. Available from: www.legislation.gov.uk/ukpga/1996/56/section/550ZA

Education and Inspections Act (2006) London: The Stationery Office. Available from: www.legislation.gov.uk/ukpga/2006/40/contents

Education and Skills Act (2008) London: The Stationery Office. Available from: www.legislation.gov.uk/ukpga/2008/25/section/1

Education Reform Act (1988). London: The Stationery Office. Available from: www.legislation.gov.uk/ukpga/1988/40/contents

Employment Rights Act (1996) London: The Stationery Office. Available from: www.legislation.gov.uk/ukpga/1996/18/contents

Equality Act (2010) London: The Stationery Office. Available from: www.legislation.gov.uk/ukpga/2010/15/contents

ERA (2022) *Educational Recording Agency*. Available from: https://era.org.uk

Goodson, I. (1999) The educational researcher as a public intellectual, *British Educational Research Journal* 25(3): 277-297.

Gov.uk (n.d.) *Joining a Trade Union*. Available from: https://www.gov.uk/join-trade-union/trade-union-membership-your-employment-rights#:~:text=You%20have%20the%20right%20to,on%20pay%2C%20terms%20and%20conditi

Gov.uk (1974) *Health and Safety at Work Act*. Available from: https://www.hse.gov.uk/legislation/hswa.htm

Gov.uk (2021) *Teaching Regulation Agency Corporate Plan: 2021 to 2024*. Available from: www.gov.uk/government/publications/teaching-regulation-agency-corporate-plan/teaching-regulation-agency-corporate-plan-2021-to-2024-:~:text=investigating serious misconduct,where a,to have committed serious misconduct

Gov.uk (2023) *UK Higher Education Providers – Advice on Consumer Protection Law* Available from: www.assets.publishing.service.gov.uk/media/64771faeb32b9e0012a95f30/Consumer_law_advice_for_higher_education_providers_.pdf

Gov.uk (2024) *Online Safety Act: Explainer*. Available from: www.gov.uk/government/publications/online-safety-act-explainer/online-safety-act-explainer-new-offences-introduced-by-the-act

Guardian (2007) *Gordon Brown Speech*. Available from: www.theguardian.com/politics/2007/feb/27/immigrationpolicy.race

Health and Safety at Work Act (1974) London: The Stationery Office. Available from: www.legislation.gov.uk/ukpga/1974/37/contents

Independent (2023) *Commonwealth Representatives Ask for Reparations and Apology Ahead of Coronation*. Available from: www.independent.co.uk/news/uk/british-charles-iii-commonwealth-new-zealand-australia-b2332113.html

IPO (2014) *Intellectual Property Office: Exceptions to Copyright*. Available from: www.gov.uk/guidance/exceptions-to-copyright

Jarvis, C. (2008) Becoming a woman through Wicca: Witches and Wiccans in contemporary teen fiction, *Children's Literature in Education* 39(1): 43-52.

King, C. (2010) Faith schools in Pluralistic Britain: Debate, discussion, and considerations, *Journal of Contemporary Religion* 25(2): 281-299.

Knives Act (1997) London: The Stationery Office. Available from: www.legislation.gov.uk/ukpga/1997/21/contents

Lyes v. Middlesex County Council (1962) 61 LGR 443.

NASUWT (2024) *About Us*. Available from: www.nasuwt.org.uk/about-nasuwt.html

NEU (2024a) *About the NEU*. Available from: https://neu.org.uk/about-neu

NEU (2024b) https://neu.org.uk/advice/your-rights-work/workload-and-working-hours/planning-preparation-and-assessment-ppa-time-tips-for-reps#:~:text=Make%20sure%20PPA%20time%20is,at%20least%2030%20minutes'%20duration

Niens, U., Mawhinney, A., Richardson, N. and Chiba, Y. (2013) Acculturation and Religion in Schools: The views of young people from minority belief backgrounds, *British Educational Research Journal* 39(5): 907–924.

Offensive Weapons Act (2019) London: The Stationery Office. Available from: www.legislation.gov.uk/ukpga/2019/17/contents/enacted

Office for Students (2024) *Welcome to the Office for Students*. Available from: www.officeforstudents.org.uk

OIA (2024) *Office of the Independent Adjudicator*. Available from: www.oiahe.org.uk/about-us/our-scheme/our-rules/guidance-on-the-rules/rule-2/

ONS (2021) *Religion, England and Wales - Office for National Statistics*. Available from: https://www.ons.gov.uk/peoplepopulationandcommunity/culturalidentity/religion/bulletins/religionenglandandwales/census2021

Plater, M. (2013) Children, Schools and Hallowe'en, *British Journal of Religious Education* 35(2): 201-217.

Rosen, R. (2004) *Time and Temporality in the Ancient World*. Pennsylvania: University of Pennsylvania Museum of Archaeology and Anthropology.

Sabbott (2013) *Hidden Curriculum Definition*. Available from: https://www.edglossary.org/hidden-curriculum

Sandberg, R. (2014) *Religion, Law and Society*. Cambridge: Cambridge University Press.

Sexual Offences Act (2003) London: The Stationery Office. Available from: www.legislation.gov.uk/ukpga/2003/42/contents

The Pagan Federation (n.d.) *Introduction to Paganism*. Available from: https://www.paganfed.org/paganism

TUC (2024) *NEU*. Available from: https://www.tuc.org.uk/unions/neu#:~:text=Together%20for%20education.,for%20teachers%20and%20education%20professionals

Williams v. Eady (1893) 10 TLR 41 CA.

6
Cognitive Science

Introduction

Back in the deep, dark mists of time, one of us was walking to a school training session titled 'Improving Learning' when an 'old hand' teacher muttered: 'When I came into teaching, nobody ever said anything about learning'. Teaching is not learning, that much is true; they are two different acts, and you should never presume that what you teach is what pupils learn. A teacher can turn up for an hour, conduct a lesson, ask questions, and yet at the end of the lesson none of the required learning has been achieved, by one or possibly many more of the pupils. Those pupils who are not attending to the lesson are nevertheless still learning – by thinking, talking to others and using all their senses to create something new – but not necessarily learning what the teacher wants them to learn. Not only is your lesson just one of many sources of learning in the room, it may well be the least attractive. We offer, in this chapter, a recipe for success in today's schools by examining the set of instructions the Department for Education (DfE) has given teachers for how to make sure that the expected learning happens. Today's teachers need to be aware of cognitive science, to focus on memorisation and to make learning long term and useful, removing barriers to the central learning content.

Evidence-led Practice

The aim of learning theory is to understand how pupils come to know, and become able to do. You should be able to rationalise (give reasons for) your lessons – not only what are you doing but why you are doing it. Of course, the pupils may not care less about such a rationale but your Training Provider does, and so should you. In the case of teaching, everyone can give advice, and there are plenty of 'experts' (often self-named) who believe they are more 'right' than anyone else. Teaching is not the only area for which this is true; it is also the case for another much-studied area, the science of sleeping. Experimental studies undertaken by 'experts' state that these three ways work best to ensure a good night's sleep: have a warm bath two hours before going to bed; keep the room cool; wear socks in bed to lower your body's core temperature. If you do all of these, experts claim, you will sleep. On the other hand, if your mind persists in racing about a lesson you have not prepared adequately, you might end up as a wakeful, clean, cold person wearing socks in bed. It is much the same with the theory of learning – it may work for you, and it may not. Nevertheless, it is certainly worth knowing.

The sheer quantity of theoretical ideas about learning is a particular problem, as Julie Allan notes:

> Theory lurks within the educational terrain as a malevolent and shadowy figure, hidden behind 'what works' and evidence-based practices. . .what is presented to educational policymakers as theory, by an often complicit research community, is ill-formed and inappropriate. (2014: 322)

Allan goes on to quote Thomas's (2007: 1) description of learning theory: 'junksculpture...a cacophony of incompatible explanations'. We have certainly both been guilty of sessions of 'theory junksculpture' – giving training teachers a mishmash of ideas about how best to teach to ensure learning, which leaves the poor souls rather confused about whether they should tell, show, or go to the staffroom and have a cup of tea while the class completes the given task. Fortunately, if you like a simple life, at the time of writing this book, learning theory has been seriously stripped down by the Department for Education (DfE) in the Initial Teacher Training and Early Career Framework (ITTECF) resulting in an age of what might be accused of being 'transmission teaching' or 'learning by rote'. Daniel Willingham, an author included twice in the ITTECF, which instructs Training Providers what to teach trainee teachers, advised 'inflexible knowledge', stating that, 'On the surface it may appear rote, but it's not' (2002). Kirsten Mould (2020), the Senior Content Manager of the Education Endowment Foundation (EEF), advised 'explicit instruction' and stated that this is not just 'teaching by telling' or 'transmission teaching'. If Willingham and Mould have to deny that something is something, then it must have a lot of similarities. We can settle with Mould and call today's dominant learning theory 'explicit instruction', because that is what another key influence on contemporary practice in schools, Barak Rosenshine (2010) calls it... and anyway, does it really matter what it is called? Explicit instruction promotes a rather simple process:

- Get the pupils to recall prior knowledge.
- Tell the pupils what they need to learn.
- Build up knowledge in a manageable way.
- Model learning to the pupils.

Critical to the current mode of thinking about learning is the idea that knowledge is held in mental schemas. A **schema** is an established structure of neural connections and pathways. For example, a child having learnt that balls rotate, can extend this knowledge by exploring different ways of rotating them, such as spinning them, and move on to exploring the impact of an object when it hits the ball. Each time, the schema about 'ball rotation' gets extended. This knowledge can then be developed in Physical Education when teaching about a golf swing, for example - back straight, bottom out, legs bending at the knees, eye on the ball, arm straight pulled back over the head and then keeping those arms straight swing around to hit the ball which your eye has never left (and whoosh, in our case, the ball hits a tree). A schema can be built by adding something new (this is called 'assimilation'). A schema can also be altered when new information which contradicts what is contained in it, is accepted (this is called 'accommodation'). Take the example of King Henry VIII; let us presume the class already knows who this person was but now needs to add the knowledge that he lived from 1491–1547 (and no, we are not going to reference our Wikipedia learning source). How can the pupils learn (or assimilate) this new knowledge? We could get them to explore the life and times of the king independently, get them to take part in a drama production of Henry VIII, get them to learn a song which went something like 'Grumpy old King Hen-ery was born in 1491 and died in 1547' (not very catchy, we know). We could get them to design his mausoleum with the dates on. Would this teach them it? Possibly. It is time-consuming, though. Why not just tell them? Why not tell them, then repeat it, repeat it, repeat it, get them to repeat it and repeat it some more? Would this work? In the end, yes...probably. This is the explicit instruction approach.

Explicit instruction is in fashion in schools at the time of writing this book but neither of us can be accused of being victims of current trends when it comes to clothes – we are at the life stage where our trousers are often older than our trainee teachers. What we are victims of is a changing fashion in teaching theory. Picture us, 15 years ago: younger, yes; same trousers, yes; more energy-filled, certainly. We were then also armed with some strong learning theory as to how trainee teachers should do the following: differentiate for every pupil; differentiate lesson outcomes; address multiple ways of learning; address multiple intelligences; engage all learners in practical activities and regulate teaching so that it met a hierarchy of learning needs. In terms of teaching styles, we were recommending that trainee teachers use: experiential learning (get the pupils to go through an event); pupil-led learning (let the pupils decide on lesson content); situated learning (take the pupils to a place where the learning knowledge will be needed); interactive learning (focus on classroom discussion and group work); project-based learning (extended task involving problem-solving). The DfE's (2024) Initial Teacher Training and Early Career Framework (ITTECF) has since determined what is 'best practice' – and by this term, we mean someone somewhere has decided this approach works better than other ways of teaching and learning. The ITTECF gives the minimum content in terms of theory, and gives some theory the label 'evidence-informed'. Other aspects of theory have been found guilty of being 'misconceptions' (DfE, 2019). Some people may have previously thought these aspects of theory to be important to teaching, but current fashion seeks to dismiss and debunk them as 'neuromyths' as they have insufficient evidence behind them.

'Evidence' might come from a collation of other research on a topic (Rosenshine's (1986) 'synthesis of explicit teaching', for example). It seems as though as long as the so-called evidence is in numerical form and conforms to the idea of explicit teaching, it is not considered to be a misconception. Black and Wiliam excelled at providing numerical data and so it is no surprise to see them in the ITTECF. To give a flavour of their output, Black and Wiliam (1998a) used numbers 57 times in one journal article and this is not including dates, such as '681 publications...47 different labels...2.4 labels per reference' and their conclusion that the 'typical effect sizes of the **formative assessment** experiments were between 0.4 and 0.7' (1998b) leaves us wondering what this means in the real world. There is a pleasing and reassuring certainty to numbers, especially in meta-studies which collate the findings from sometimes hundreds of different journal articles. In the end, though, these journal articles were still often based on studies from individual classrooms and (whisper it) relied on the experimenter interpreting the results and (whisper it even quieter) often this was using qualitative research – words not numbers. The government likes numbers, and is rather like the Deputy Head one of us witnessed, waving a book on cognitive science and boldly stating: 'We didn't used to know how people learned and now we do!' This was said just before one of us was about to present a session on the limits of cognitive science, which that Deputy Head, unsurprisingly, sat through scowling. In this world of datafied evidence, computer readings of brain activity seem to provide the most solid kind of 'proof'. Some might be tempted to conclude that developments in neuroscience have provided, for the first time, evidence to support the biological basis of learning, but it is still not possible to 'read' the mind on a computer. Nevertheless, there is inclusion in the 'How Pupils Learn' section of the ITTECF (DfE, 2024) of Baddeley's (2012) study of neuroscience and Simonsmeier et al.'s (2018) studies of brain domains. To give an idea of how complex the brain is compared to the way it is depicted on a screen, there are around 100,000 neurons (brain cells) per square millimetre of the brain and a single pixel on a screen represents over 5 million of them, and 22 kilometres of axons (linking pathways between groups of cells) (Kenning, 2008: 47). Neuroscience offers us a limited (though still useful) understanding of what is happening in the brain but it does not provide proof of how we learn and, anyway, too much focus on the brain can forget that we are also feeling, experiencing bodies.

We cannot 'input' information into people, because the brain does not work like a computer. The linguist and philosopher Noam Chomsky (1980) called the brain a 'mental organ' and, like the other organs such as the heart, it works as part of a whole and cannot be divorced from the 'self'. Chomsky separated this organ into two – 'the brain', a constructed and reconstructed set of cells, and 'the mind', the thinking, conscious self. It can be tempting to think that in the classroom we are altering brain cells, but it is the mind that we should be developing, and this is complex and rich with experience, and feeling, and dreams, and desires, and purposes, and beliefs and so on. Learning theory is particularly problematic if we start to think of the brain acting like a computer or Artificial Intelligence (AI). The brain is no more like a computer than like a clock working with cogs (as it may have been envisioned in the 19th century), partly because it is connected to an organic body. Language terms such as 'working memory', 'retrieval' and 'intrinsic load' (Sweller, 1988) evoke a computerised form of memory and schema. Steven Pinker rather dryly discounted the metaphor as not a useful one:

> Computers are serial, doing one thing at a time; brains are parallel, doing millions of things at once...Computers have a limited number of connections; brains have trillions. Computers are assembled according to a blueprint; brains must assemble themselves. Yes, and computers come in putty-coloured boxes...and run screen savers with flying toasters. (Pinker, 1999: 26)

There is a 'tell don't show' mantra in schools at the time of writing this book and some learning theory is prioritised above others. Teaching is just not that easy. The educational thinker Richard Pring (2011: 158) explained what has been happening with educational theory as it became simplified in order to control the mechanisms of schools:

> One needs to know 'what works', and then to ensure that schools and their teachers 'deliver what works'. That, in turn, requires the close specification of what it means for the educational system to work, and this is duly done in the setting of precise

targets and the measurement of these. A system of testing, of publication and league tables of results, of financial incentives and of 'customer' choice of provider becomes the machinery for making educational provision effective and thereby overcome the disadvantages which previously had been seen to be insuperable.

Pring (2011) went on to cite the studies of Diane Ravitch which concluded that testing, choice, targets, performance indicators, measurement and incentives are: 'impoverishing what it means to educate' (157). That is the problem in a nutshell. When we use the instruments by which we can measure education's success to discover what is successful for passing exams, we end up with direct instruction and constant testing, and these are not good enough to prepare a generation for the future. The rationale for explicit instruction is not always plausible, but Barton (2018) tried:

> What damage is being done in our desperate quest for them to say exactly what we want – what we need – them to say? If there is one particular response I have in mind, why on earth should I play a game of 'guess what is in my head' with students, with each swing-and-a-miss potentially causing more confusion? Why not just cut out the middleman and deliver the explanation myself?

In the same way, Riches (2019) points out that:

> When I do training on modelling, I often use the analogy of drawing a tree. My instruction is to draw a tree: one person draws a palm tree, one draws an oak, and two draw a tree with no branches. Now I have a problem – all have followed the instruction, but what kind of tree was I expecting? Without a clear model of expectation, how is a student going to do exactly what you want of them?

There is a sense that learning can somehow be given or created in a collective schema, but all we can do is access the individual's current understanding and feelings, and how what is there currently links to the sense of self. In other words, the pupil needs to know what the knowledge and skills 'means to me'. If it does not mean anything to the pupil, then the connections to the schema may grow quickly into disuse; much as a pathway, which is rarely trodden on, becomes so covered in weeds and plants that eventually no one remembers that it ever existed.

Cognitive Science

Cognitivism is an approach to understanding human psychology that became popular in the 1960s. It focused on brain development and developed, itself, from the work of Lev Vygotsky and Jean Piaget among others. In the ITTECF, there are 27 mentions of 'cognitive' and it became the go-to approach for those who advise Training Providers about 'best practice'. One example of cognitive science is John Sweller et al.'s (2011) **Cognitive Load**

Theory which came out of studies of sensory input in classrooms. The conclusions were that it was important to reduce the cognitive 'load' on pupils. This load includes both the input – the learning objectives of the lesson (part of the 'intrinsic' load) – and that which is a by-product of the complex interactions and environment of the classroom (the 'extraneous' load). Sweller et al. argue that the extrinsic load should be minimised to avoid competition for working memory resources; we can minimise the extrinsic load by simplifying instructions, clearing away the clutter of the classroom, **scaffolding** tasks, etc. We also need to focus on limiting the intrinsic load by establishing ready recall of knowledge and skills in the long-term memory so that pupils can access complex information quickly and easily. Once a topic has been learnt, the pupil's brain will naturally 'fire' a response on the topic and be in a position to learn something more about it. Sweller et al.'s (2011) study somehow managed to avoid any mention of the founder of the idea that the brain organises knowledge in schemas, Jean Piaget (although schemas are mentioned 105 times) nor does this study reference Piaget's work (although Sweller gave himself 98 mentions). Cognitivist Jean Piaget is the mind behind the original theory (with much help from the work of Lev Vygotsky).

Harvard University (n.d.) called Jerome Bruner the Father of the Cognitive Revolution but even he does not get a mention in the ITTECF, although Bruner's term 'scaffold' gets 10 mentions in various forms. 'Scaffold' means that support is given so that pupils who are at different levels of knowledge can access the lesson's main topic. You might, here, be looking at these names and thinking: 'Hang on! Jean, John, Jerome, Lev, these are all men...and so are you two!' and this would be a thoughtful observation. It tends to happen to white, ageing males who work in large universities (mainly American). When boiled down, in terms that can be used practically in the classroom, their theories tend to be metaphors for learning. For example:

- Sweller: load – an image of a computer-brain trying to download too much, resulting in Error Code 404.
- Bruner: scaffold – an image of metal scaffolding which gives support on a temporary basis.
- Piaget: schema – a plan, diagram or organised set of instructions which simplifies complex ideas (a scheme of work, for example).

While it is useful to have these metaphors, we are not convinced that without the contributions of cognitive science, we would not have known this. We cannot imagine prehistoric cave-dwellers not knowing that children need to be told information a few times, that they cannot absorb everything in one go, that it is best to stop distractions when a child is learning something, that they need to master one skill before they can move onto another.

Having made sure that the memory and retention practices of Rosenshine are in place and reduced the 'cognitive load', as Sweller advocates, you can try exercising Jerome Bruner's (1960) **spiral curriculum**. This means that you need to keep returning to the same topic, each time adding more. Having made sure all of these steps are in place, you can think about the 'primacy effect', which means that you are more likely to recall information presented at the start of a learning episode, and the 'recency effect', which means that information presented most recently is more likely to be recalled. The Spaced Learning Effect was first identified by Hermann Ebbinghaus in 1885; Ebbinghaus advised on the positive effect of repeated relearning of material, spaced at intervals of several weeks, on the amount of information retrieved. With successive revisions, the proportion of material recalled and the length of time for which it is successfully recalled increase as stable long-term memories are formed. This effect supports the now common strategy of retrieval practice at the start of lessons. There should be a voice in your head that asks these questions:

- What is the purpose of this lesson?
- What do I need the pupils to have learnt by the end of it?
- How will I know they have learnt?

You will not be able fully to plan your next lesson without gauging what has been learnt. Some pupils will learn more than others; you need a record of their learning and a strategy to allow their imaginations to be probed enough that they want to know more and have the mechanisms to do so.

Barak Rosenshine (Male? Yes! Worked at major US university? Yes!) summed up this process very well. He created a very useful set of principles and – partly due to the influence of educationalist Tom Sherrington – these are fast becoming the template for many lessons across the land. Rosenshine's principles happen to incorporate many cognitive science theories so might seem to make an ideal solution to any lesson. You may well find yourself being told to:

1. 'Begin each lesson with a short review of previous learning'.
2. 'Present new material in small steps with student practice after each step'.
3. 'Ask a large number of questions and check the responses of all students'.
4. 'Provid(e) students with models and worked examples can help them learn to solve problems faster'.
5. 'Guide(e)... students' practice of new material'.
6. 'Check... for student understanding at each point can help students learn the material with fewer errors'.
7. 'Provide... students with temporary supports and scaffolds to assist them when they learn difficult tasks'.
8. 'Require and monitor independent practice.'
9. 'Engage students in weekly and monthly review'.

(taken from Rosenshine, 2010: 13-19)

If you put these principles into place, in theory, your class learns. On the other hand, if the class has just had a two-hour assessment in another lesson, not much lunch, and it is a wet and windy Wednesday afternoon in October, you perhaps do not stand much chance of success, no matter how many of Rosenshine's principles you follow. Recognising that human dynamics, the flexibility to adapt the lesson, as well as systematic organisation is important. It is also important to stop the lesson if, on fulfilling the sixth of Rosenshine's principles, there are no correct answers!

Conclusion

Cognitivism and cognitive science have illuminated our understanding of how learning happens. The pioneers who tried to discover what happens in the human mind are like space explorers, to us - heroic investigators of the natural world. It may well be that some of the theory is the plainly obvious, given a veneer of credibility by numbers, but it still made the processes of learning explicit, and the process of learning something we can be conscious about. It is possible that good teachers have always been breaking knowledge down to manageable 'chunks', making sure the pupils know which area of prior knowledge it belongs to, and striving to provide support for everyone in the class; nevertheless, the move to make these ideas essential to all shares good practice. No one wants your lesson to be boring, and just because it is split into predetermined steps, there is plenty of freedom to adapt the content, resources and timing. Fashion, by its very nature, changes. The current trend for explicit instruction will move on. (And who knows, by the time you read this you could be being informed, as in times gone by, of the importance of multiple learning styles, moving pupils up the hierarchy of Bloom et al.'s (1956) knowledge taxonomy and ensuring that the lesson takes into account the hierarchy of needs explored by Abraham Maslow, who was, yes, male and yes, worked in a top United States university). Education theory is like a pendulum. It goes in one direction, then this is seen not to be the best way, so moves in the other direction. Fashion is, as the musician David Bowie once observed, about turning to the left, then turning to the right. We will close this chapter with the wise words of one of the founders of the discipline of psychology - which encompasses cognitive science - William James (1878-1958):

> You make a great, a very great mistake, if you think psychology... is something from which you can deduce definite programmes and schemes and methods of instruction for immediate schoolroom use. Psychology is a science and teaching is an art. (James, 1899: 14)

···**REFLECTION**

Remember your experience of being in a class, maybe sitting by a window worrying, perhaps grieving, working out how you will avoid this or that person for the rest of the day, or thinking about what you will eat and do for lunch, scheming, or dreaming. Your pupils are active humans with minds that desire something. This 'something', sadly, is possibly not what you are offering. Think about a lesson you have planned, or are about to plan, and how you can move these active minds around to the topic in hand. What are they interested in, and how can you bring the topic you need to teach to them and their interests?

···

.... **ACTIONS**

Read the ITTECF's 'How Pupils Learn' section to get a sense of the learning theory you need to know. Consider what 'evidence' is, take what you can from each theory and be open-minded to other ways of learning as it gets introduced. Because, everything will change – that is the nature of fashion.

....

Case Study 6

Luke Amos is now Deputy Head of an English department in a large mixed comprehensive school. Since his Post Graduate Certificate of Education (PGCE) year, he has taught in the same school for five years. The restrictions of the ITTECF might seem to have limited what teachers can do in the classroom but Luke explains how, although there are some aspects of control over his lessons, he still has much creative freedom.

> One of the greatest joys of my job is lesson planning. I like to do it 'from scratch'; that is, to think of what needs to be learnt and decide how it would be best approached. If I cannot think of what to do, I get the lessons from the school intranet, which I can pick up and run with and adapt how I like. I had two placement schools and now my current one and it has always been the same approach. I did go to an interview at a school where they explained that lessons were given to the teachers, and I walked away from it halfway through, because I knew that this would not work for me. When we have trainee teachers, they sometimes come from a first placement where the lesson has been given to them, but I think that they need to have the opportunity to make their own lessons and resources as well as change the lessons of others for delivery and adaptation.

> There are restrictions, of course, from those who run the school. One is that I have to start with a retrieval point and it has to be called DNA or Do Now Activity. This can be done in any way, so I might show a video and ask questions, or do a quiz, do a card sort, or whatever. This DNA must last 5-10 minutes. I have to put up the learning objective and the pupils have to write this in their books. Once a term, the pupils have to do an extended writing task. We have to model part of the answer, but not in every lesson, and only when it would help. I have to do red pen activities, where I go round and 'live mark' the work for errors but, perhaps only every other week. Four times a term, I have to do what we call a 'vocabulary lock' where new words are introduced and investigated – all subjects do this across the school. Questioning has to be 'cold calling' rather than hand-up for volunteers and this is also across the school. Recently, the 'pose-pause-pounce-bounce' initiative has been introduced, because questions were being asked of pupils and answers received but they just lay there unexplored. Now, we have to ask a question (pose), wait to give

thinking time to all (pause) then choose a pupil to answer (pounce) and choose another to explain and expand on the answer (bounce). We have visualisers in the rooms and sometimes use them, mainly to give positive feedback to pupils by putting their work on the screen. I have to use mini whiteboards in some lessons at some point. Rosenshine's theory of education is seen as an ideal model in terms of explicit instruction.

I am not overly monitored. Senior leaders will come round unexpectedly on a 'walk through' for 10 minutes of the lesson, so they don't insist on checking every aspect of the lesson. I am pretty sure that if our examination results were not improving year on year, we would, ourselves, be given more explicit instructions about using certain methods, but our success protects us. Regurgitating information is the 'name of the game' in terms of the exams, but we have had training from the examination board and the pupils getting top responses have their own opinions, their own conceptual ideas, and do more than repeat what we have told them. So, we always 'stretch and challenge' the pupils, and push them further. I asked a Year 11 pupil what they had learnt recently, and he answered, "To think in different ways," and that seemed a very satisfying answer. Our school is part of a large organisation which runs many schools across the country but they do not over-impose authority from the top of the organisation. We do meet up with teachers from our MAT's schools in the region, and that can lead to some good sharing of practice.

I am allowed to introduce new ideas and offer them to the department, though teachers are free to adopt them or not. One of the initiatives I have introduced is a class reader; while we are enjoying the fiction story, we also study some non-fiction texts on the same themes. I have drama in my classroom where the tables are moved to the side, chairs set out in a semi-circle and there is space to act scenes from *The Tempest* or *Romeo and Juliet*.

As teachers, we are not robots, and many of us are parents, so we see our pupils from different angles. They know they get taught well and we offer variety. I am not abandoning PowerPoints but do not focus much on the slides. I do not do booklet learning because I find them restrictive. What matters for me is that the pupils are really enjoying the lesson. I love my job still five years on, the same as ever. Some days, and some classes, are better than others of course, but the sense of fun in front of me is an everyday pleasure and I am in a school which gives me the opportunity to make enjoyable, purposeful lessons.

.... WHAT TOOLS ARE IN YOUR TOOLKIT NOW?

- Greater understanding of the nature of brain change and how schemas develop.
- Greater understanding of the importance of recall and revision to strengthen memory retention.

(Continued)

- Greater understanding that learning theory was not created by ageing male university lecturers. Social Learning Theory does not belong to Bandura (1977) just because he did some experiments on children copying adults, for example. It belongs to each mother and father throughout humanity, who realised that children copy what they do far more than what they tell them to do.

Places to Get More Tools for Your Toolkit

Muijs, D. and Reynolds, D. (2017) *Effective Teaching Evidence and Practice* (4th edn). London: SAGE.

A clear summary of some of the main learning theories popular in schools today.

Glazzard, J. and Stones, S. (2022) *Evidence Based Teaching in Secondary Schools*. London: Learning Matters.

This book provides a digested guide to the key ideas of cognitive science in a thoughtful manner.

References

Allan, J. (2014) Making a difference – in theory – in Sweden and the UK. *Education Inquiry* 5 (3): 319–335.

Baddeley, A. (2012) Working memory: Theories, models, and controversies, *Annual Review of Psychology* 63: 1–29.

Bandura, A. (1977) *Social Learning Theory*. New Jersey: Prentice Hall.

Barton, C. (2018) *How I Wish I'd Taught Maths: Lessons Learned from Research, Conversations with Experts, and 12 Years of Mistakes*. Woodbridge: John Catt Education Ltd.

Black, P and Wiliam, D. (1998a) Assessment and classroom learning, *Principles, Policy and Practice* 5(1): 7–74.

Black, P. and Wiliam, D. (1998b) *Inside the Black Box*. Available from: www.kappanonline.org/inside-the-black-box-raising-standards-through-classroom-assessment/

Bloom, B. Engelhart, M., Furst, E., Hill, W. and Krathwohl, D. (1956) *Taxonomy of Educational Objectives: The Classification of Educational Goals. Handbook I: Cognitive Domain*. New York: Longmans.

Bruner, J. (1960) *The Process of Education*. Cambridge: Harvard University Press.

Chomsky, N. (1980) *Rules and Representations*. New York: Columbia University Press.

DfE (2010) *The Importance of Teaching. The Schools White Paper*. Available from: www.assets.publishing.service.gov.uk/media/5a7b4029ed915d3ed9063285/CM-7980.pdf

DfE (2019) *Core Content Framework*. Available from: https://www.gov.uk/government/publications/initial-teacher-training-itt-core-content-framework

DfE (2024) *Initial Teacher Training (ITT): Criteria and Supporting Advice*. Available from: https://www.gov.uk/government/publications/initial-teacher-training-and-early-career-framework

Ebbinghaus, H. (1885) *Spaced Learning*. Available from: www.td.org/insights/spaced-learning-an-approach-to-minimize-the-forgetting-curve

Harvard (n.d.). *Jerome Bruner.* Available from: http://www.psychology.fas.harvard.edu/people/jerome-bruner%20-%20:~:text=Jerome%20Bruner%20was%20a%20leader,the%20center%20of%20the%20field

James, W. (1899) *Talks to Teachers on Psychology.* Available from: www.gutenberg.org/files/16287/16287-h/16287-h.htm

Kenning, P. (2008) What advertisers can and cannot do with neuroscience, *International Journal of Advertising* 27(3): 472–473.

Mould, K. (2020). *EEF Blog: Five Evidence-Based Strategies to Support High-Quality Teaching for Pupils with SEND.* Available from: www.educationendowmentfoundation.org.uk/news/five-evidence-based-strategies-pupils-with-special-educational-needs-send

Pinker, S. (1999) *How the Mind Works.* London: Penguin.

Pring, R. (2011) Can education compensate for society? *Forum* 53(1): 153–162.

Riches, A. (2019) *Effective Teacher Modelling.* Available from: https://www.sec-ed.co.uk/best-practice/effective-teacher-modelling

Rosenshine, B. (1986) Synthesis of research on explicit teaching, *Educational Leadership,* 43(7): 60–69.

Rosenshine, B. (2010) *Principles of Instruction: Research-Based Strategies That All Teachers Should Know.* Available from: www.teachertoolkit.co.uk/wp-content/uploads/2018/10/Principles-of-Insruction-Rosenshine.pdf

Simonsmeier, B. A., Flaig, M., Deiglmayr, A. and Schalk, L. (2018) *Domain-Specific Prior Knowledge and Learning: A Meta-Analysis Prior Knowledge and Learning.* Available from: www.psycharchives.org/handle/20.500.12034/642

Sweller, J. (1988) Cognitive load during problem solving: Effects on learning, *Cognitive Science,* 12(2): 257–285.

Sweller, J., Ayres, P. and Kalyuga, S. (2011) *Cognitive Load Theory.* New York: Springer.

Thomas, G. (2007) Theory and the construction of pathology. Paper presented at the *American Educational Research Association* (pp. 24–28). New York, March.

Willingham, D. (2002) Ask the cognitive scientist. Inflexible knowledge: The first step to expertise, *American Educator* 26. Available from: https://www.aft.org/ae/winter2002/willingham

7

Running a Lesson

What this chapter will cover

- Planning for teaching
- Pitch, engage, scaffold and stretch
- Technology
- Behaviour management

Introduction

Apart from your pupils being safe, nothing matters more than how you use that precious lesson time for teaching them. If you get this right, we find, much else is forgiven. In fact, when we hear that a trainee teacher is 'good in the classroom' it is usually a euphemism meaning that other parts of the trainee teacher's practice are not as good as they should be, but that this has been forgiven because 'getting it right in the classroom' is critically important. In this chapter, we explore how to plan a lesson, and some of the problems of trying to teach one. We will be recommending that there is a focus on the people-dynamic of a lesson, rather than technology, which should be used with discernment. There will be tips about pupil engagement and the way lessons are typically structured, then some words on the theory of behaviour management.

Planning for Teaching

Imagine that you are a builder of houses. You cannot just go ahead and put a sink in the ground and build around this, because the plumbing needs to be in place, apart from anything else. In the same way, before you start the lesson, you need to know what the foundations are like, check the materials you have, and know what the people who ordered the house want it to look like: in other words, have a plan in place. Where this house-lesson building metaphor 'falls down' as it were is that we are dealing with children and if ever there was an unpredictable material to work with, they are made of it. What you put into a lesson, what you want to get out of a lesson, and what you do get out of a lesson, can be different things. If the pupils know no more about the taught subject at the end of your lesson than they did at its beginning, there is no point at all in your lesson - none at all - and furthermore, you have wasted a precious hour of their lives (and your own!). When you come to teach a lesson, you should be re-enacting one you have planned, rehearsed and taught in your imagination. Eventually, you will be repeating lessons and will know how they might go - but for a first run-through, plan everything: your words, your questions, even your ad libs. One of us used to even rehearse our jokes, such as the one where we'd tell the class that the egg we were using as a visual metaphor for a learning point was 'free range' when it moved around on the table. Lessons are like bad jokes - fully recyclable.

There was a time when the lesson plan was expected to be completed for every lesson, and it would include:

- Learning objectives: what you hope the class will learn.
- Learning outcomes: checkable learning.
- Resources.
- Seating plan.
- Questioning schedule: what you will ask, and to whom.
- Timings.
- **Special Education Needs and Disabilities** (SEND) provision: targeted support for those who need it.
- Risk assessment: health and safety check.

Lesson plans may not be the 'big deal' they once were because lessons are often taught using existing plans and resources including presentation packages such as PowerPoint. Whatever form your lesson plan takes, there is no need to plan a lesson 'from scratch'. Why would you, when your lesson subject has been taught thousands of times by thousands of different teachers? There should be resources in your school, with your placement colleagues, and with your Training Provider. If not, The Times Educational Supplement website alone has around a million resources (TES, 2024) for lessons which should see you through until Thursday lunchtime, at least. Your school should provide you with a Scheme of Work (SoW), resources and lesson plans for each topic. The SoW is a plan of topics and timings, usually created by the Head of Subject based on the subject curriculum (which may be the National Curriculum, a school's alternative, or guidance from professional bodies). At **Key Stage** 4, this SoW should also be mapped to Assessment Objectives (AOs) which are created by government-funded subject experts who advise exam boards on how to test knowledge in each subject.

As well as existing lesson plans and resources, there are plenty of structures you can rely on for your plan. Rosenshine (2010) believed that the following four processes help memorisation:

- Sequencing: position new learning so that it builds on prior knowledge.
- Modelling: show how the new learning can be put into practice.
- Questioning: assess whether the new learning is in place.
- Reviewing: remind the pupils what the new learning is.

The above is just one structure. Here is another to try:

- Already know – check what has been learnt on the topic.
- Get attention – find something about the subject which might 'hook' them in.
- Relevant – show how the subject will affect their lives.
- Model – demonstrate what a good response is.
- Teams – let pupils work together.
- Goals – give them an immediate purpose and challenge.
- Visuals – use images as well as words.
- Think and talk aloud – get the pupils to express ideas to each other.
- Mnemonics – find a memory aid to simplify the learning.
- Note taking – make sure there is a written record of the learnt topic.
- Closure strategies – such as telling a partner what has been learnt.

(Adapted from Fulk, 2000 cited in Sousa, 2001: 34)

Pitch, Engage, Scaffold and Stretch

In baseball, you pitch the ball at the batter and hope that they cannot hit it. The reverse is true of you as a teacher: you need to pitch the lesson content appropriately so that it is accessible and attractive and all pupils can hit a home run. In order to get your **pitching** right, you need a sense of what a Year 7 lesson (for instance) would look like, and also a

Year 8 one... but then some Year 7 groups may feel more like they are achieving as Year 8, so you cannot merely rely on expectations of age. The challenge is that, with 30 children in your classroom, it can seem like trying to pitch to 30 batters in the hope that even one of them might be able to hit it. Before you pitch, therefore, you need to diagnose what your pupils know already. When you go to a doctor with a series of symptoms, the doctor diagnoses your problem. This cannot be done in isolation, nor online – as one of us found when a doctor seemed to be putting our symptoms into the equivalent of a medical Wikipedia and incorrectly diagnosed Lyme disease. You will need to talk to the current class teacher, who will know what they have been taught already (bearing in mind that being taught it does not necessarily mean it has been learnt). From here, in addition to checking with the teacher whose class you are currently borrowing, you will need to ask the pupils what they have learnt, and if they have already learnt the planned lesson then you need something 'up your sleeve' – which is often the next lesson, so aim to plan and prepare at least one lesson ahead.

Your first task is to get the pupils to engage with the lesson. In 1981, media researcher David Morley observed that the audiences of television news programmes engaged with these programmes in four ways: (1) Dominant – they accepted the messages and interpretations offered in the programme; (2) Negotiated – they reinterpreted some messages, but accepted the main messages in the programme; (3) Oppositional – they rejected the messages in the programme; and (4) Critique of Silence – they did not engage at all with the programme. The Critique of Silence occurred when viewers did not perceive that the news programme had anything to do with them. This particularly happened when someone was watching who was not part of the white British majority (in those days, the people shown on the screen often did not represent a range of ethnicities nor the reality of the viewers' worlds). In your lesson, some pupils may listen and accept what you are saying and doing (Dominant); some pupils may filter it, and take in some of what you are saying and doing (Negotiated); some pupils may think that both you and your lesson are a waste of time and disagree with what you have said (Oppositional), and some pupils may not engage at all (Critique of Silence). In media terms, engagement is called attentioning; content creators ask how does something on the screen or speaker stop becoming 'just more noise' and start becoming something the audience wants to watch or listen to? How can you apply these ideas in a lesson? You can try:

- Reciprocal respect (Nicholson and Putwain, 2015) – the pupils will listen to you because you listen to them.
- Reward (DfE, 2019) – the pupils are motivated by trying to get it.
- Entertainment – a desire for fun can be motivating.
- Autonomy – giving pupils the right to choose what to do or how a topic is to be learnt.

A crucial point for getting pupils to engage with your lesson is at the start. Your lesson may start with a Do Now Activity (DNA). This is also known as a 'settler', or 'starter', and probably acts as both. A settler is designed to create a calm start to a lesson, and is typically something like free reading or a wordsearch. A starter is more focused on lesson content, and is a first activity which acts to introduce the main lesson learning point. You might also choose a 'hook' which is an idea which can make them think about themselves, or the topic, in a new way: a cognitive jolt. For example, one of us used to ask a class if they liked to drink cola – and they did – and we then asked what the ingredients were; pupils then realised that they did not actually know what they were drinking. This kind of realisation triggered something that they wanted to discover. The lesson involved 'blind' tasting and a series of similarly engaging acts, and left them full of caffeine. (If you are going to repeat this lesson, do not worry; it takes 40 minutes to 'kick in' so the class will have moved on to the next poor teacher by then.) You might undermine their belief that water boils at 100° with a multiple choice question that offers a selection of three temperatures, none of which is the expected one. You can 'stingray' them (as Socrates apparently advised) with a big statement such as: 'a whole kingdom is not worth a single horse' and let them question why this might or might not be true.

Having started, settled or hooked, you need to recall what the pupils ought to have learnt from previous lessons. Revisiting prior learning diagnoses the next steps in learning for some pupils; for others it teaches it for the first time. Imagine that you have a tin of sweetcorn that you put in a cupboard. Leave it there and it accumulates dust; you forget where it is, end up buying another, and the first tin gains a similarly dusty friend. Keep taking the tin out of the cupboard and it is easy to find. Bjork (2012) described this practice as 'using your memory shapes your memory'. Revisiting prior learning will help to diagnose those who need more support in the lesson, metaphorically referred to as scaffolding. One way you can scaffold is through modelling. You might even become the 'silent teacher' (Barton, 2018: 176–178) with students silently copying the example solution down in their books, before asking them to have a go at a problem question themselves. Tharby (2018) advocates the I-We-You 'Simple Approach To Modelling'. This three-step process can be understood as follows:

- I do – the teacher models how to do a certain skill/question/activity.
- We do – a similar skill/question/activity is then worked on collaboratively by the teacher and the class.
- You do – the pupils independently practise what they have just learnt while the teacher moves around the room giving guidance where it is needed.

'Stretching' a pupil always sounds painful, and it often is. It is not only physical activity – for example the tearing and repairing of muscles – that is a metabolic process; brain cells physically alter, and that is a metabolic process too. Here is a list of ways to stretch:

- Lateral thought – the ability to find connections between concepts and ideas and to resolve a problem in a new and creative way.
- Creative thought – the ability to invent, to make something new.
- Dialogic thought – the ability to consider a topic or event from different perspectives.
- Abstract thought – the ability to consider a world which is not physically present.
- Patterning – the ability to see and memorise connections and form new conclusions.
- Visualisation – the ability to mentally recreate or create scenarios which have not existed.
- Speed recall – the ability to access a range of knowledge instantaneously.

- Analysis – the ability to discover what lies behind concepts, words, actions and feelings.
- Inference – the ability to 'read between the lines' to see the hidden or less explicit message.
- Metacognition – the ability to consciously think about thinking.
- Emotions – the ability to control and moderate the self's and other's feelings.
- Critical consciousness – the ability to recognise how the structures around us force actions or thinking.

To take one example: lateral thought. Edward de Bono (2016) is the king of it, if you want to read more widely. You need to use lateral thought to solve maths puzzles like this:

A woman reads 30 pages of a book on Monday. On Tuesday she read a quarter of the book. On Wednesday she read an eighth of the book and finished it. How many pages did the book have?

We also see lateral thought in humour. Here is a joke:

Hearing a knock on the door on Christmas Eve, a man answered. Looking down, he saw a snail who sang, "We wish you a Merry Christmas; We wish you a Merry Christmas". The man kicked the snail to the end of the garden path, saying, "Get out of here!" At Easter, there was a knock on the same door. The same man answered it. The same snail looked up at him and said, "That wasn't very nice".

And here is another:

A man walked into a doctor's room and said, "I keep thinking I'm a moth". The doctor looked sympathetic but said, "I am a GP and you need a psychiatrist, I am afraid." The man replied, "I know, but your light was on."

We could regale you with more (yes, the winter nights do fly by. . .). What connects all of these is a lateral connection between what was expected and something new. Lateral thinking disrupts logic and requires the pupil to find a new explanation. It often asks for a link to be made from one schema to another and develops cognitive flexibility, which is perhaps why a sense of humour is often linked to perceptions of intelligence. It encourages pupils to spend time working on a problem as they would in 'real world' jobs, and to find solutions such as – in the case of the maths puzzle above – 48 pages.

Technology

Quite soon after PowerPoint became the most popular presentation resource, the phrase 'death by PowerPoint' became commonplace; it sounded like the title of a particularly dull Agatha Christie story. We are over-tired of the over-use of PowerPoint, and we suspect the pupils are too. Technology means 'tools', and the philosopher Ernst Kapps (1808–1896) described these tools as (no laughing at the back of the class): 'organ projection'. The organs which can be projected include our ears, eyes, brain, mouth, nose and legs. There are other engaging ways to integrate technology into your lesson beyond the presentation slides. The teaching profession has been stunningly slow in adopting interactive technology into lessons. In the 1960s, Marshall McLuhan wrote that:

> Today's child is bewildered when he enters the 19th century environment that still characterises the educational establishment where information is scarce but ordered and structured by fragmented and classified patterns, subjects and schedules. (1967)

If this was the case in 1967, how much more so today? A time-travelling Victorian would understand little about how the modern world operates, but would still be comfortable in the average modern school environment with its formal classrooms, desks, teachers and instruction mode. These traditional systems persist, despite the mediated world that teenagers are operating in outside of it. Some schools are trying to adapt. DeFerrers School, for example gave all pupils an iPad and taught large groups with communication happening to and from a screen at the front of the room (DeFerrers, 2022). Some schools are sponsored by the computer giants Apple, such as Essa Academy (2022) and there are Microsoft Showcase Schools (2024) such as Chilton Trinity (2024). Other schools have brought computer games into the classroom (The Guardian, 2016). We would hope that you, as a trainee teacher who may well be a computer native (possibly brought up with the internet, phones and computers as an extension of yourself), will be able to find ways to use technology to engage and teach pupils in school and at home. We also hope that you will not forget the fundamental usefulness of long-used technology such as pens, papers, markers and whiteboards.

Artificial Intelligence (AI) and Large Language Models (LLM) are taking over societal operations. If you want to check this claim out, start talking into a 'smart speaker' about a topic you have no usual interest in – for example, try canal boating and you should then find the colourful elongated floating vehicles popping up on your computer. Then, at least you know that someone is listening to you. AI can write lesson plans, but AI cannot plan a lesson. You might input the data of a lesson into a Generative Pre-trained Transformer (GPT) to create documents; a computer will be able to offer a facsimile of something a human might produce. For example, if teaching Geography, you might input the data that you are planning a lesson about river meanders and the GPT will access the words and reproduce them in a lesson format (though it cannot visualise river meanders, or comprehend what they are, or feel a sense of wonder about them). If you then add that this lesson is for Year 9, the GPT will change this lesson plan to match the age group (though it will probably defer to the American interpretation of 'Year 9' and aim it at Year 10). A GPT knows what a lesson plan looks like, can access a world of knowledge (or the parts of it which have electric communication), and may even be able to complete the lesson plan form your Training Provider uses. But, by the time you have inputted the information into the GPT, you might as well have planned the lesson. At least then you would avoid going into the classroom spouting Americanised content. AI is not there yet even in terms of its ability to write students' essays. It is possible that it might have fooled us with an essay or two (after all, how could we know?) but we have found it easy to identify when students have used AI, and are now rather enjoying giving sarcastic feedback which praises the amazing consistency of the referencing, including umlauts on names – and the wonderful variation of sources, including the North Korean health service in-house magazine. Usually, one look at the references list makes it fairly obvious that the student has resorted to AI. We are also a bit fed up with being sent emails asking us if we are the author of the article *'Shell-seeking in Medieval Peru'* by computer bots which do not know what they are doing. AI has its limitations, but we would be hypocritical if we did not recommend that it is used, when appropriate, and with caution, to save time. When a trainee teacher, a long, long time ago, one of us used to use carbon sheets when we typed up our lesson plans (yes, that old, and so poor we could not afford a computer at the time) so they came out in triplicate. When we taught the same lesson again, voila! GPT cannot really construct effective lessons for you. But it can save you some time, in some ways. It might:

- find a film clip to use in your lesson;
- put information into a particular format;
- fill in your personal details;
- update dates on a document;
- find a quotation;
- stop 'blank page syndrome' when you do not know where to start; and
- create some of your resources: for example, if you were teaching haikus in a school in Sandiacre, it can make one up about that particular town.

Behaviour Management

The behaviour of pupils can be a shock to some who come from other countries where teachers are more respected and classes are obedient. Without behaviour management, nothing (at least, nothing purposeful) happens, including learning. It is possible for a school to create an environment where a breach of rules results in an inevitable punishment. The Michaela Community School in London has put a non-negotiable system in place whereby a single rule-break means punishment or 'demerit' (Michaela, n.d.). All schools have rules but this one is ultra-strict about control and when a pupil challenged their ban of 'prayer rituals' they ended up in court (BBC, 2024). The school won the case, but it must have been costly and time-consuming, and the media attention disturbing – not least because of the impression it created of an intolerant school environment. At the other end of the scale is Summerhill, which allows the pupils to run the school. Summerhill has rules, or 'laws', made up by the pupils and debated constantly. Here is an extract from the school website:

> We believe in freedom but not licence. This means that you are free to do as you like – but you must not interfere with somebody else's freedom. You are free to go to lessons, or stay away, because that is your own personal business, but you cannot play your

drum kit at four in the morning because it would keep other people awake. Within this structure we probably have more laws than any other school in the country – usually around 250. (Summerhill, 2021)

It may seem ironic that a school which calls itself 'the original free school' (Summerhill, 2021) should have so many rules. This perhaps informs us that children need to feel safe, protected against others and against self-destructiveness. Freedom to do anything you like can be scary, especially when you do not know how to control your feelings or actions and are just learning to make sense of the world. In our view, a good teacher will give children – as a priority – the gift of safety.

In order to exercise control in your classroom, you might try Doug Lemov's approach: 'seek not only to be both warm and strict but often to be both at exactly the same time' (2015: 438). This means being Janus-like in the classroom. Janus was the Roman god of doors (we wonder whether the Romans had a god for every household feature) and therefore of transitions, so Janus was symbolised by a two-headed person, each with a different expression. In the classroom, there is no reason to be grumpy with a good class of working pupils, but if the class transgresses, or if one pupil does, then the other 'you' can come out. The ability to switch, dependent on the class's behaviour, is a powerful weapon.

Rather than pathologising pupils' 'poor' behaviour as something that needs to be eliminated, you could view behaviour as an effort to self-express, which could be harnessed towards the lesson's aims. We suggest that you try to become a skilled influencer of positive behaviour, rather than expecting instantly to control restless adolescents, who have their own motivations and agendas. The work of Bill Rogers (2015) becomes a life-saver in the classroom, we think. Rogers tells us that it is to give a pupil some time to think, and the choice to act differently. It is fine to allow the pupil to complain about you, and the consequences you have threatened. Rogers's advice is as follows:

- Give positive instructions: 'I want you to look this way'.
- Pause: use silence to gain the class's attention and focus them.
- For those not following a direction, repeat it but do not name individuals who are not complying.
- State the consequences for those not following the direction, and offer it as a choice: either follow it or choose the sanction.
- If necessary, apply the sanction.

The offer to the pupil which allows them the choice of continuing to disrupt and face the sanction, allows time for them to calculate whether it is worthwhile. If, as most often happens, the pupil chooses to follow the rule, rather than take the sanction, the pupil may start to complain. Rogers advises that you do not respond to this secondary disruption. As long as the original direction gets followed, then that is all you want.

For Eddie McNamara (2012), the route to successful classroom management is as easy as ABC: A is for Antecedents; B for Behaviour; and C for Consequences. To manage B, the A needs to be understood and C applied. There is a need to understand the A – the context of disruption. Asking a pupil 'why?' is a good idea, as is using a phone call home as a way to try to increase understanding, rather than to admonish. The parent/carer who receives several phone calls a week informing about how awful their child is will soon become resentful and the act counterproductive. One of our colleagues had a teacher on the phone at the end of the first school day telling her how dreadful her daughter had been. The teacher did not know that the daughter had Attention Deficit Hyperactive Disorder (ADHD), nor that the daughter was sleep-deprived, having spent the night in the cupboard, which had then felt like the only place of safety. We recommend that you ask a parent/carer for help, and find out what the child's life is like out of school, and try to understand it, so that you can support the pupil.

Tom Bennett (2019) advises the following:

- Be proactive: introduce rules early, show what behaviour leads to success and be 'concrete' with instruction so there is no ambiguity.
- Language: use words that normalise good behaviour – for example, 'In this classroom, we. . .'
- Establish routines: entry to and dismissal from the classroom, corridor behaviour, transition between activities and silence.
- Sanctions, from mild to severe, are to be consistently applied: 'Their certainty is far more important than their severity'.
- Reward good behaviour: extrinsic (e.g. prizes) and to fulfil intrinsic needs (e.g. by giving praise).

Systems and routines work for Bennett. He stresses the need to create an environment that makes misbehaviour abnormal. For Bennett, the classroom should be a non-negotiable, controlled place where a dynamic of positive learning inhibits any desire to disrupt. Bennett implies that if the teacher does their job properly, then the class will behave. It sounds beguilingly easy, but the challenges faced in schools over decades and the experiences of all new teachers suggest otherwise. Nevertheless, Bennett's approach is popular with schools – possibly because it allows schools to blame the teacher if the pupils are unruly (although we are sure that Bennett did not intend this). Possibly it is also popular because it can work: children may well conform to fair and clear expectations of how to act. Rebellion takes effort and it is easy to go along with routines in school – we find that most pupils (and teachers, for that matter) do.

At the heart of Rogers's, McNamara's and Bennett's ideas are school 'rules' – rules, which if they are not obeyed, can be sanctioned (Bennett), investigated (McNamara) or offered as a choice whether to obey or take the punishment (Rogers). These are all 'tools' for the 'toolkit' as you can move between them, according to what your class is like. In most schools, there is a system of rules that the teacher expects to enact. Masden et al. (1968) 'rules rules' are helpful:

- few in number;
- simple;
- described positively; and
- consistent with school policy.

'Described positively' is particularly useful as this phrase avoids what Masden et al. (1968) called 'the criticism trap' – the teacher who falls into this trap gets caught into delivering a series of negative comments, often to increasingly disinterested pupils.

The explicit control methods of shouting commands and issuing threats may well receive a response like: 'No!...I don't care!' The teacher who understands the importance of body language goes into a classroom armed with a means of power and control which operates on a subconscious basis. Pupils recognise the meanings in body language but not at the conscious level which allows them to challenge it directly. The popular theorists behind body language are Desmond Morris (2002) and Alan and Barbara Pease (2017). Desmond Morris's (1978) *Manwatching* is a classic book that popularised the pseudo-science of body language – an inborn communication system that works beyond words. The teacher in the classroom can employ body language signals to great effect:

- Tight upper lip – I am angry.
- Staring into eyes – I am dominant.
- Palm down – be calm.

The teacher can also be aware of the body language of the pupils to find out what they really want to communicate about your lesson on a scale of lack of engagement: yawning, chin resting on hand and head on desk (at this point you had better intervene). Space is a major signifier of how we are feeling. In lesson observations, we notice where teachers stand in the classroom. Someone nervous will employ barriers such as a desk to protect them. If they manage to move from behind the desk, arms and legs are folded or crossed to protect them from the pupils. A teacher needs to over-ride such defensive mechanisms by opening up the torso, the chest area. This gives a non-verbal message that the teacher is not afraid of the group. We are programmed to move away from danger, but a teacher might try to deliberately move towards a pupil. Invading space is normally rude but, in a classroom, it can be a necessity. Caswell and Neill (2003: 26) pointed out:

> one sign of your control. . .is that you always have the freedom of movement so you can adjust your distance and. . .invade their personal distance if you want to, whereas you often deny them freedom of movement.

Even the feet matter. Watch a group of people and look only at the feet. When a group is in harmony, the feet will be splayed out to point at each other. When someone does not want to accept another person, their foot will not point to that person. Body language can also be used to communicate a lack of confidence. The teacher who pulls at a shirt collar, brushes down clothes or tugs at the sleeve of a top, or jacket, is informing the class that they are nervous. Hands need to be used purposefully. Try the palm grab (cup the hand and pull it towards you) to bring the class to attention, and learn all you can about ways to control through the body; they can be so much more effective than verbal communication when convincing a class that you are in control.

We can also use the prosodic features of our voices – the ways of communicating which go beyond the words spoken. Our voices have four elements beyond words to communicate:

- pace,
- pitch,
- pause, and
- intonation.

Pace is the speed with which we speak and, if there is a typical trainee teacher issue, it is speaking too fast. When we meet ex-trainees, their use of voice is a notable change in them, we find, as it has typically got two octaves lower and 20 decibels louder. Before you get to this stage, you have to learn to control your voice. Your mind might be going at a terrible speed when you are nervous in front of a group of people; consciously slowing down can be difficult, so it is a good idea to take a breath at the end of every sentence. This gives the pupils' minds time to catch up with the content. Some teachers shout their words, some-times because they are trying to overcome the noise in the classroom. Early in our careers, one of our mentors told us, 'Calm voice, calm class'. Speak quietly so pupils have to listen, especially if you are likely to say their name; directing something to a specific individual can be effective. Staying at a single level of loudness (mono-pitch) may mean that the pupils 'zone out', so you need to vary the loudness of key words. Equally, a powerful message of control comes with those who have a powerful booming voice; we advise those lucky people to use it when being positive with the group. Shout out how great they are and how pleased you are with them and name a pupil while you are there. This sends a powerful message about classroom control and gives a subconsciously received warning that if the pupils do not attend to the lesson, this voice weapon might be used against them. Intonation is necessary in a classroom because if you are monotone, the class may not attend to the particular musical note you are speaking on, and so miss the content. Learn to 'sing' your words and go through the octave (although not in a crazy way). Emotions are communi-cated through such means: you can go higher for the positives and stay low for the serious matters. Finally, and one of the best ways of getting attention is to pause before the key message, or to stress something, as you would if you wrote: best, lesson, ever!

Babad (1992: 171) observed that

> teachers often have negative affect toward low-expectancy students. . .which is reinforced by these students' problems in learning and social conduct domains.

When Babad mentions 'affect', he means the emotional cues of acceptance – positive eye contact, smiles and body positioning – and these are read on a subconscious level by the pupil. Some pupils do not need control mechanisms but, rather, support and care. They may, in general, not receive many smiles and positive eye contact, and this lack of positive signals reinforces their feelings of low self-worth. There can be no beating a smile at a pupil who is normally badly behaved, given by a trainee teacher in a corridor or playground. In this setting, the pupil is not disrupting your lesson, so why would you not greet them positively?

Conclusion

We would like to tentatively pose a few possibilities about planning and running a lesson:

- Some pupils will find your lesson more interesting than others.
- Some pupils will not respond to you.
- Some pupils are bored of school.
- Some pupils cannot understand the topic, because the groundwork was never in place to allow them to comprehend the concepts discussed.
- Some pupils are looking out of the window when you speak.
- Some pupils have other things to worry about during your lesson rather than you 'droning on' about the importance of, for example, matrices.
- Some pupils are so scared by an inner panic that they can hardly breathe, let alone do multiple fractions.

All pupils can have reasons not to attend your lesson or access it. It is your job to put in place whatever you can to overcome these issues. In the words of Jerome Bruner (1966: 72):

> We teach a subject not to produce living librarians on that subject but rather to get a student to think...to consider matters, to take part in the process of knowledge-getting. Knowledge is a process not a product.

Engagement is a key to success and you should view learning not as a one-shot exercise, but an ongoing process, which each lesson contributes to.

It is unlikely that much learning will be done if the classroom is in chaos. In this chapter, we have examined ways of managing behaviour – but there are problems with viewing behaviour as something that can be managed. One problem is that some pupils do not want to be controlled or to be 'good', and no amount of understanding, consequences or offering choice will influence their decision. Rebellion is a natural human state. We observe it in ourselves when our better self knows that something should be done, but our rebellious self refuses, as Paul Willis observed:

> the most basic, obvious and explicit dimension of counter-school culture is entrenched, generalised and personal opposition to "authority." (1977: 11).

We should always be ready for the human in the child, and that includes the impulse to rebel against the teacher as the holder of authority and school rules. Getting angry with pupils will probably not help in the long term:

> Thus, while there is an immediate cessation of the behaviour, in a longer time the behaviour occurs more frequently. This analysis explains why some teachers persist in using negative control techniques when they patently don't work. (McNamara, 2012: 13)

If you have not got a strong presence in the classroom and cannot use your voice and body, you may well find no one attends to you. If you cannot gain the attention of the class, then your lesson, no matter how well planned, is unlikely to result in learning. If you have not planned your lesson, all the technology in the world will not save you. These factors show how all the Teachers' Standards (DfE, 2011) are related. You have a lot to learn or master in a short time, and it is best to take it step by step, and be guided by a mentor. This often means working on one area one week, and another area when the first has been achieved.

.... **REFLECTIONS**

Rebellion comes in many forms and we would be surprised if you had gone through the secondary school years without it. It may have come in the form of disruption, refusal or truancy. Think hard, and back to yourself as a teenager, and what you went through, and it will help you to empathise with the children in the class. They are going through a lot of mind and body changes, and these changes can be exhausting and bewildering. The adult in the room is you, so you need to bear that in mind in how you respond. One of our trainees once told us that, "Poor behaviour is a need unmet," and this idea is certainly worth reflecting on.
....

.... **ACTIONS**

- Observe successful teachers and try some post hoc planning – write the lesson plan you think they were following.
- Practise positive body language.
- Practise voice control of pitch, pause, intonation and pace.
- Talk to pupils about their perceptions of classroom management in the school.
....

Case Study 7

Alex Harden demonstrates there are many types of schools. He is currently an English teacher working at a girls' grammar school, and he worked at a mixed Church of England school for a year, and before that a free school. He trained at two mixed-sex academies. Here, he recalls the different approaches to behaviour management.

> I have been in five schools, two as a trainee and three as a teacher and all of them have hugely different experiences, giving me a broad scope of how schools work and that what works well in some schools, does not work at all in others.
>
> In the first school, shouting was king. I remember one of the younger male teachers giving me advice that suited the school, when he said that I should make the person who is in control undeniable from the very start of the year by crushing the first person to try to disrupt the lesson. It was very authoritarian, very discipline-focused

and behaviourist: if a pupil did not read 50 pages in a week, for example, they got a detention - which is a great way to get pupils to hate reading.

There was no such strictness about the second placement school. Behaviour was not good in the school generally, but in the department I was in, it was fine, leading me to learn that you never can tell with a school; it might be a rough place from the outside but the teachers and department might be successful at managing it.

My first teaching school was hard work because there was no workable behaviour policy in place at the time. The pupils were unruly and while I managed as well as I could, the learning of the pupils suffered as the focus was on getting pupils in and keeping them calm: all I did that year was tried to stay afloat. My second school was a great relief. It was a mixed comprehensive school with an ethos the pupils supported, a department who were friendly and welcoming but, unfortunately, it was a maternity cover placement, so once I began to put roots down, it felt as if it was being taken away from me. What I learned and what I continue to learn is that schools are all very different. I learned a lot from this school, but the vast difference between schools means what works in one, might fail in another.

I ended up at a girls' grammar school with a permanent contract, and this is the school where I have been for two years. The pressures are different here as there are no behaviour issues. You can actually teach here, and the pupils want to learn. However, there has been a lot of pressure on me, and sometimes it has been a challenge to cope with. But while it has taken time to settle in, I finally feel I know what I am doing - but the strategies at my previous schools have not worked well. I have had to re-learn a lot, and ask a lot of questions.

Another thing which helped me to improve my approach to teaching was a book, *Atomic Habits* by James Clear - which the Head Teacher read and introduced me to. It states that, instead of giving goals and targets, which are not particularly helpful, you create systems which can achieve an aim. For example, the school implemented a system for lesson starts to get an ordered classroom: I stand in the doorway with one foot either side of the threshold, and greet the pupils as they come in in silence, then read for the first 5 minutes of every English lesson. I do the register in this time, and the result is a calm and ordered group of pupils. My embedding of this system got me noticed for the right reasons, leading to an observation of one of my classes from six guests to the school, to see how well that strategy was working.

In less than five years, I have been in a school with a severe discipline policy and been in one with practically none. I have worked in a school which had all of the typical problems of a mixed comprehensive school and had great approaches to learning which worked for that cohort, but not for other schools. I have worked in a school with a depressed, crushed staff culture and in one where the staff had so much fun and loved being there. I would advise that what works in one school may not in another and that there is no such thing as the typical school so if you end up in one you do not like, wait for the next; it takes some 'shopping around' but teachers can find their matched school in the end – just make sure you work out what works best in that school, as it may not be what worked for you previously.

.... **WHAT TOOLS ARE IN YOUR TOOLKIT NOW?**

- Ways of starting your lesson to engage the class.
- Putting in place rules that are described positively.
- Giving pupils the choice between the sanction or the disruptive act.
- Understanding of the antecedents to disruptive behaviour and how to mitigate them.
- Being proactive in creating an environment that expects good behaviour.
- Practising the body language of control and support.
- Knowing to use your voice's range purposefully.

Places to Get More Tools for Your toolkit

Bennett, T. (2019) *The Trainee Teacher Behavioural Toolkit: A summary.* Available from: www.gov.uk/government/publications/initial-teacher-training-itt-core-content-framework. Bennett's ideas are a staple ingredient for every school. The advice is clear and may help to put in place a no-nonsense approach to a routinised classroom.

Rogers, B. (2015) Classroom Behaviour: A Practical Guide to Effective Teaching, *Behaviour Management and Colleague Support.* London: SAGE. Published by Sage and as sage as you will get. Rogers focuses on negotiation and mutual respect and advises ways of coping with rebellion.

Dix, P. (2017) *When Adults Change, Everything Changes.* Carmarthen: Crown House Publishing. Gives a revolutionary approach to behaviour management focusing on how grown-ups can model conflict resolution through restorative justice approach.

References

Babad, E. (1992) Teachers' nonverbal behavior and its effects on students. *Higher Education: Handbook of Theory and Research* 22: 219–279.
Barton, C. (2018) *How I Wish I'd Taught Maths: Lessons Learned from Research, Conversations with Experts, and 12 Years of Mistakes.* Woodbridge: John Catt Education Ltd.
BBC (2024) *Michaela School: Muslim Student Loses Prayer Ban Challenge.* Available from: www.bbc.co.uk/news/uk-england-london-68731366

Bennett, T. (2019) *The Trainee Teacher Behavioural Toolkit: A Summary*. Available from: www.gov.uk/government/publications/initial-teacher-training-itt-core-content-framework

Bjork, R. (2012) *Memory*. Available from: www.youtube.com/playlist?list=PL7bq3cDfbRs4-d19Tsg9T2Tg8bR0bs7xW

Bruner, J. (1966) *Towards a Theory of Instruction*. Cambridge, Massachusetts: Belkapp Press.

Caswell, C. and Neill, S. (2003) *Body Language for Competent Teachers*. London: Routledge.

Chilton Trinity (2024) *Ambition, Engagement, Resilience*. Available from: www.chilton-trinity.co.uk/

de Bono, E. (2016) *Lateral Thinking: a Textbook of Creativity*. London: Penguin.

DeFerrers (2022). *About*. Available from: www.deferrers.com/about

DfE (2011) *Teachers' Standards*. Available from: https://www.gov.uk/government/publications/teachers-standards

DfE (2019) *ITT Core Content Framework*. Available from: https://assets.publishing.service.gov.uk/government/uploads/system/uploads/attachment_data/file/974307/ITT_core_content_ framework_.pdf

Essa Academy (2022). *Welcome to Essa Academy*. Available from: www.essaacademy.org/

Lemov, D. (2015) *Teach like a Champion 2.0: 62 Techniques that Put Students on the Path to College*. New Jersey: John Wiley and Sons.

Masden, C., Becker, W. and Thomas, D. (1968) Rules, praise and ignoring: Elements of elementary classroom control, *Journal of Applied Behavior Analysis* 1(2): 139–150.

McLuhan, M. (1967) *The Medium Is the Massage: An Inventory of Effects*. California: Gingko Press.

McNamara, E. (2012) *Positive Pupil Management: A Secondary Teacher's Guide*. Abingdon: David Fulton.

Michaela (n.d.) *Michaela Community School Behaviour Policy*. Available from: www.michaela.education/wp-content/uploads/2022/05/Behaviour-Policy-V2.pdf

Microsoft (2024) *Microsoft Showcase Schools*. Available from: https://www.microsoft.com/en-us/education/school-leaders/showcase-schools

Morley, D. (1981) The Nationwide audience: Structure and decoding. *BFI Television: Monograph Number* 11.

Morris, D. (1978) *Manwatching*. London: Triad.

Morris, D. (2002) *People Watching: The Desmond Morris Guide to Body Language*. London: Vintage.

Nicholson, L. and Putwain, D. (2015) Facilitating re-engagement in learning: A disengaged student perspective. *Psychology of Education Review* 39(2): 37–41.

Pease, A. and Pease, B. (2017) *The Definitive Book of Body Language: How to Read Others' Attitudes by Their Gestures*. London: Orion.

Rogers, B. (2015) *Classroom Behaviour: A Practical Guide to Effective Teaching, Behaviour Management and Colleague Support*. London: SAGE.

Rosenshine, B. (2010) *Principles of Instruction: Research-Based Strategies that All Teachers Should Know*. Available from: www.teachertoolkit.co.uk/wpcontent/uploads/2018/10/Principles-of-Insruction-Rosenshine.pdf

Sousa, D. (2001) *How the Special Needs Brain Learns*. California: Corunia Press.

Summerhill (2021) *A Better Way to Educate*. Available from: www.summerhillschool.co.uk

TES (2024) Available from: www.tes.com/teaching-resources

Tharby, A. (2018). Available from: www.classteaching.wordpress.com/2018/12/05/i-we-you-a-simple-approach-to-modelling/

The Guardian (2016). Available from: https://www.theguardian.com/education/2016/feb/05/tomb-raider-ian-livingstone-open-free-schools-digital-focus

Willis, P. (1977) *Learning to Labour: How Working Class Kids Get Working Class Jobs.* Farnborough: Saxon House.

8

Recognising and Responding to Diversity

What this chapter will cover

- Teaching for equity
- Physical and sensory needs
- Neurodiversity
- English as an Additional Language
- **The Pupil Premium**
- Race

Introduction

Responding to diversity is not about mechanically altering your teaching or resources based on common preconceptions of this or that condition; it is about responding to the individuals in your classroom. Each pupil is unique. Adaptations of lesson content, and delivery, need to be made to ensure equity of provision, and, therefore, equality for all; these concepts will be discussed in this chapter. English as an Additional Language (EAL), Special Education Needs and Disabilities (SEND) and Specific Learning Disabilities (SpLD) will be considered in this chapter, with a review of best practice and of places to go to learn more. The chapter will end by reinforcing the message to teach holistically, to recognise the teacher's child development role, and to understand how schools act as moral, social, spiritual, and cultural forces for good. It is not possible for any teacher to be a wholly neutral and objective presence in the classroom, however hard you might try; you go into it as you, with all of your cultural prejudices, acknowledged or not, and you go in, whether you like it or not, as a coded message about normality, control and social power. It helps if you also bring awareness of institutional and personal prejudices.

Teaching for Equity

The meanings of, and difference between, 'equity' and 'equality' actually matter much less than the requirement that you take practical steps to reduce inequity and inequality as much as possible. The difference between these two words is perhaps best explained by the popular image of three children of differing height trying to watch a sports match over a fence which is preventing their view of the stadium. The three children are all given the same box to stand on, but the smaller child still cannot see over the fence. Equality means everyone gets the same. Equity means that changes are made for individuals, so that everyone has an equal chance of success. To be equitable, each child should be given a box to stand on, the size of the box varying according to their individual needs, with the result that all the children can see. In a lesson, equity means ensuring that every pupil's individual needs are accommodated so that every pupil has the same chance to access the lesson content. In order to put the boxes up, as it were, trainee teachers adapt the lesson to fit the individuals in the class. This can be by means of adapting resources, environment, seating, your position in the room, pace, when subjects are taught, and so on. You can ask yourself the following questions:

- Have you made your lesson equitable by giving extra support to those who need it?
- Have you recognised particular SpLDs, such as **dyslexia**, **dyscalculia** and dyspraxia, so that over the course of the year you learn some strategies to help to mitigate those barriers?
- Have you learnt how to support pupils with SEND, for instance with Attention Deficit Hyperactivity Disorder (ADHD), or Social Emotional and Mental Health (SEMH) issues?
- Have you discussed pupils' needs with colleagues in school?

- Have you co-planned lessons with your mentor or experienced teacher?
- Have you made sure those pupils who may already know the lesson content have work which can extend or 'stretch' their understanding?

Training Providers, who run Post Graduate Certificate of Education (PGCE) courses, will follow the Initial Teacher Training and Early Career Framework's (ITTECF) lead and refer to the act of making a lesson equitable for all as 'adaptive practice'. You may hear the word **'differentiation'** in school. Differentiation was a popular approach to responding to diversity about for about 15 years, and so the term stuck and is still widely used, although it has become rather outdated. Differentiation meant that teachers provided different instructions, resources and expected the outcomes to vary between individuals. Typically, it was based on an: 'all will achieve, most will achieve, and some will achieve' scaling of expectations. Sometimes, the pupils were even named as to the outcomes expected on the lesson plan. Differentiation was part of a move to individualise the curriculum which could be summed up by the title of the government initiative to focus on child welfare: **Every Child Matters** (2003). In 2003, children were no longer to be taught 'en masse' but personally diagnosed, assessed, and given what would have be called in those days 'a learning journey' to suit their need. Differentiation was very much in 'full swing' in 2003 with pupils being given Individual Learning Plans (ILP) responding to preferred learning styles that best fitted them. Ofsted (1999) promoted differentiation, the Teachers' Standards (DfE, 2011) insisted on it (they still do!). One exasperated teacher echoed the complaints of many teachers who were expected to address 30 individuals in a room: 'differentiation in practice is harder to implement in a heterogeneous classroom than it is to juggle with one arm tied behind your back' (Delisle et al., 2015).

Around 2017, the approach recommended in policy changed from using the word 'differentiation' to 'inclusion', guided by the United Nation's Educational, Scientific and Cultural Organization's (UNESCO) document *A Guide for Ensuring Inclusion and Equity in Education* (2017). This policy language change discouraged teachers from individualising the curriculum but instead to ensure that all pupils could access the same lesson, and to make sure that all pupils learnt what was required. By 2019, the word 'inclusive' turned to 'adaptive' when it was realised that the 'inclusive' approach could lead to rigid 'one provision for all' lessons. By teaching a single lesson and expecting everyone to achieve (and, in theory, if they did not then they would have to complete extra work at home), it set unrealistic expectations of what could be done in a state system where classes were often consisting of more than 30 pupils. Instead, a lesson should be a self-contained, dynamic event, between the teacher and pupils who all work to make the lesson meaningful and purposeful. In adaptive teaching, the whole lesson is organic – and you, the teacher, are part of this organism, and a key part of the creation of its dynamic. The Educational Endowment Foundation (EEF) explains adaptive practice like this:

> Having a full understanding of every child is extremely important in adaptive
> teaching. Time needs to be diverted to identifying reasons for learning struggles, not
> just the struggles themselves. As such, pupils' physical, social, and emotional
> well-being, including their relationships with peers and trusted adults, are
> fundamental. Schools need systems that ensure regular communication between

teachers, families and the young people themselves to understand barriers and to share effective strategies. The success of adapting teaching also lies in careful **diagnostic assessment,** in order to avoid prescriptive and inflexible delivery. (Mould, 2021)

The words may have changed, from differentiation, to inclusion, to adaption but, in the end, it is still you, the teacher, making changes, as required, to allow all pupils to access your lesson. Here are some ways you can adapt your lesson so that everyone can access it:

- Task – include extension tasks on the same subject for those who have advanced knowledge.
- Pace – change it according to the group.
- Support – for anyone who might be at risk of not keeping up with the group.
- Resources – adapted for individuals in the class.
- Grouping – used purposefully, for instance with one pupil supporting another.
- Roles – give responsibility to pupils; create different purposes for groups. A frequently disruptive pupil, for example, may be given the role of behaviour monitor (might be a disaster, but worth a try).
- Homework – use the Virtual Learning Environment (VLE) to target different learning goals.
- Dialogue (including questioning) – plan key questions and discussion points in advance, and develop a dialogic classroom which encourages oracy.

One aspect of adaptive practice is to make sure that every one of the pupils is noticed and feels like they belong in the room. When we were pupils ourselves, we both aimed to be invisible to the teachers, and were largely successful. One of us had the same form tutor for five years and by the end of the fifth year this tutor still didn't know our name; the other had a form tutor who could remember pupils' names in the morning but not always in the afternoon after the teachers' lunchtime pub visit. . . as you can see, it was all a long time ago. Nowadays, it is almost impossible to have such 'unseen children' because, apart from anything else, increasing management of schools using data means that a pupil will be recognised by their score, if not by their name and character.

Pitching is part of equity. Some teachers teach the topic at a high level and hope to bring the others up. It was Jerome Bruner's contention that you can teach any subject at any level at any age and as you repeat the lesson, over the years, it becomes comprehensible to all. But that approach relies on your being sure that what you are teaching will be revisited, and you cannot always guarantee this. His approach brings to mind some American politicians' fondness for the 'trickle-down effect'. In this way of thinking, politicians clear the way for the very rich to get very much richer and, in theory, this money finds its way down the social scale. The United States' former president, Joe Biden, said: 'My fellow Americans, trickle-down economics has never worked and it is time to grow the economy, from the bottom and the middle out' (CNN, 2021). In the same way, perhaps, aiming learning at the highest level may well not 'trickle down' to all. Words like 'bottom' and 'top' are fine when discussing economics but do not help in education, or rather they do not help those labelled as being at the bottom. This does not mean that you cannot 'teach to the top' as Sherrington (2017) advised as long as you follow Sherrington's other advice and 'scaffold', or support, those who might struggle. There is nothing wrong with high expectations, as long as they are for all. Sue Cowley (NACE, 2019) always has good, measured advice about such matters and advises the following.

- Check prior learning first. Those with advanced knowledge can be set additional tasks and activities or be released from the lesson (if there is a safe mechanism to do so) to continue their investigations.
- Encourage and equip pupils for wider learning. Lend books to pupils and 'feed the fire' of enthusiasm.
- Depth, lateralisation and abstraction are ways of working on cognition. Every subject has levels of learning which go up beyond the scaled qualifications, so move the pupils who need this to the next level.
- Give roles. Those who know can lead and teach others while developing (with your help) the empathy and communication skills needed.

In order to make learning accessible to all, try the following:

- 'Chunk' learning into mini-lessons so that each step can be taught and learning checked. Work backwards from the outcome you want from your lesson and think of it in separate stages. Teach a stage and check the learning. If it is okay, move to the next stage; if it is not, stop, and try again.
- Model answers. Show the pupils what a good answer might look like.
- Describe difficult concepts in different ways. Try to exemplify them. Use a range of definitions that are accessible, especially ones that the pupils might relate to.
- Give a checklist of steps to follow.
- Slow down. Watch an experienced teacher and you will find that they can modify voice and pace.
- Speed up. Go with the group; move pupils who are working hard and achieving onto the next task – which should always be presented to them as a reward, alongside praise.
- Give sentence starters to begin pupils' writing for them. There is a fine line between a 'scaffold' and a 'crutch'; some pupils rely on the latter to make life easy for themselves when they do not need it, so be aware of this, and challenge the individual to work without it. Flattery normally helps to motivate pupils to accept a challenge.
- Teach subject disciplinary language before using it. Have a glossary available, preferably one that the pupils have made themselves.

Physical and Sensory Needs

At the end of the acronym SEND is D for Disability. Disability is not a biological fact, but:

> occurs at the interaction of that person's unique profile of strengths and limitations and the demands of the environment. . .all people have differing profiles of strengths and limitations, and disability is not inherent to the person. . .an inaccessible aspect of physical environment is disabling. (Shogren et al., 2018: 33)

If we approach disability as the problem of the environment, rather than the person, we can see practical steps needed in each school and lesson. One of us recalls, with joy, the way a paraplegic university student used to ram the door barriers with his wheelchair – and, with shame, that on one occasion an inaccessible venue was booked, so that this student had to be carried upstairs as there was no lift. Disability should not be seen as the province of the pupil, but of the school and the classroom. Does your classroom enable wheelchair access without fuss? Does your lesson include a hearing loop? Have you copied your resources in large print and made them available in advance to pupil and parents? Or, are you standing in front of a PowerPoint presentation, on a screen several metres away from the pupils, mumbling your instructions, in a way which prevents them from hearing, seeing or comprehending?

For pupils who have physical and sensory difficulties, adaptations to the environment are necessary. These adaptations might be indicated on a seating plan using the following codes:

- VI – Visual Impairments.
- HI – Hearing Impairments.
- PD – Physical Disabilities.
- MSI – Multi-sensory Impairments.
- SPD – Sensory Processing Disorder.

Talk to the class teacher and form tutor about what adaptations might be needed for the pupils in your class, and as you develop your work in the classroom, observe, and if possible talk to pupils. If any technical help is needed, such as the creation of braille worksheets, you should be given support for this, and the pupil will probably also have specialist software.

Neurodiversity

Every mind is unique, including yours. You are, therefore, part of a **neurodiverse** humanity. One aspect of neurodiversity is a variation in motivation to learn. Some minds think, 'I'm a good learner'. Other minds think, 'I love Geography'. Other minds think, 'I'm very good at sport'. Still others think, 'I learn quickly'. Some think, 'I am no good at Maths'. These ideas can "freeze" in us and help to make who we are. While we are all neurodiverse, some of us are labelled or label themselves as 'neurodivergent'. Perhaps you are too. In which case, perhaps you have diverged – in the sense of having moved away, or taken a different path. The word 'neurodivergent' is better than many alternatives, but it absorbed many of the connotations of 'disability' (the prefix 'dis' meaning 'the opposite of'). Neurological development differences such as ADHD and Autistic Spectrum Condition (ASC) have both dimensions and degrees. This means that those who have the condition will vary in terms of how it displays itself (dimensions) and there are levels to which they are affected (degrees). It is estimated that one per cent of the population of the United Kingdom will have ASC; of these 700,000, at least four boys to every one girl, are actually diagnosed (Department for Health and Social Care, 2021). People with ASC may find it particularly hard to: understand and interpret other people's thoughts, feelings and actions; predict what will or could happen next; understand the concept of danger; engage in imaginative play; prepare for change and plan for the future; and cope in new or unfamiliar situations. On the other hand, those with ASC might not struggle with some or all of these, or have additional strengths and weaknesses when it comes to learning. There can be a need for the security of routines and sensory over-sensitivity. Then again, there may not be. Jim Sinclair (1993), in the **Autism** Network magazine, wrote:

> Don't mourn for us. . .Autism isn't something a person has, or a 'shell' that a person is trapped inside. . .Autism is a way of being. . .It colours every experience, every sensation, perception, thought, emotion and encounter, every aspect of existence. It is not possible to separate the autism from the person – and if it were possible, the person you'd have left would not be the same person you started with.

One way of supporting pupils with ASC is to work on communication, targeting one or more of these specific areas according to individual pupils' needs:

- Speaking and listening: teach the pupil to learn 'conversational maxims', using and recognising paralinguistic features (the way we communicate beyond words), prosodic features (the emotional qualities of voice), and registers (different styles of speaking and writing according to audience and other contextual factors).
- Reading: help the pupil to understand inference, decode unfamiliar words from prior use, learn idioms or figurative language, read for meaning, and be explicit about possible connotations of words, as well as how these words can be 'anchored' by other words in the sentence.
- Writing: practise re-presenting information, understanding how text genre can provide the ingredients for a piece, and understanding of phonically irregular spelling.

Routines may help, as Dominque Dumortier (2004) noted:

> Many of my problems can be sidestepped by pre-planning. Schedules are very important to me. I need to know well in advance what is going to happen, how, who is involved and so on. . .Any change of plan leads to frustration, powerlessness, anger and anxiety. . .Being late causes difficulties, but so does being early, and people who leave earlier or later than planned also make me feel uncomfortable.

Another neurological condition which affects many pupils is ADHD. Here the D has not been changed to a C yet, and Hallowell and Ratey (Additude, 2024) offer up an alternative name:

> a more accurate descriptive term is "variable attention stimulus trait" (VAST), a name that allows us to "de-medicalize" ADHD and focus instead on the huge benefits of having an ADHD brain.

Until such a term becomes normalised in language, ADHD remains. John, aged 13 and diagnosed with ADHD, said: 'If teachers know you are ADHD as soon as someone does something they will blame you instantly' (ADDIS, 2005). To add some substance to this lament: 39% of children with ADHD have had fixed-term exclusions from school (ADDIS, 2005), and O'Regan (2009) reported that they were 100 times more likely to be excluded permanently. Experiencing difficulty with sitting still and concentrating because of the hard-wiring of your brain is, inevitably, going to have a negative effect on your learning in most school settings – and if the rather dated statistics quoted above are even partly accurate today, then we urgently need to do more to help pupils with ADHD. Licensed treatment of ADHD comes in the form of 'dates' or 'ines' including methylphenidate and lisdexamfet-amine, such as Ritalin, the most commonly prescribed drug for children. These drugs work chemically to calm brain activity, but they are not without consequences or side effects – such as agitation, nervousness, and stomach pain. We echo Simon Bailey's concerns (2014: 6):

> is the child the lowest common denominator, the powerless one at the bottom of the pile? Certainly it seems that others have authority over them. . .Yet they are also 'the centre of the game'. . .simple changes in a child's behaviour force these authorities to mobilise resources: time, energy, money, labour, in an attempt not just to control or quash this behaviour, but to shape it, through discipline, into something more socially acceptable.

Bailey, viewing ADHD through the lens of social control, noted how it is easy for those in power to label anyone who does not conform to the system they created as 'different', at best – and at worst, 'deviant', 'delinquent', 'You're ruining it for everyone else'.

Changing the system is not something you, as a trainee teacher, can do alone. But you can change your lesson. The tools below offer some approaches that may help pupils with ADHD and, indeed, all pupils.

- Attention: stand closer to an inattentive child; incorporate a child's hobby or interest into the lesson content; give clear timings so that the child knows how long there is before a change of activity; remove unneeded stimulation from the classroom environment; use names regularly.
- Voice: slow down or pause your speech to gain attention; use a calming tone of voice.
- Questioning: inform a child in advance that a question will be asked of them in the lesson; ask simple questions to inattentive children. Give them opportunities to contribute and achieve.
- Activity: shorten the lengths of activities and written work where you can; alternate between physical and mental activity; and increase the variety of activities in lessons.
- Instructions: repeat and clarify social rules and demands of the classroom; ask pupils to repeat your instructions.
- Teach: play listening games; teach how to regulate emotions through self-talk, and how to plan.

- Praise: prioritise accuracy over speed, and praise when the pupil takes time and care over work. Teach the importance of allotting the correct amount of time to a task which will ultimately help when examinations come.

Dyslexia can affect children in many different ways, to the extent that Doyle believed: 'It is illogical for a person to say, "My child cannot read because he is dyslexic"... It tells us no more than saying a person is bleeding badly because he has a haemorrhage or that someone has a high temperature because they are feverish' (1996: 69). Pumfrey and Reason (1998) identified 11 types of dyslexia; Rice and Brooks (2004) expanded the list to 40 (cited in Mortimore, 2008: 50). The several processing conditions that we collectively call dyslexia include the following:

- Auditory: difficulty processing sounds and making them into words.
- Dyseidetic (or 'surface'): difficulty processing words that have spellings that do not correspond to letter sounds.
- Semantic processor: delayed access to the meanings of words.
- Strephosymbolia: the brain reverses the shape of letters.

Trainee teachers should not expect to be provided with a single solution for a diverse range of conditions. Often, pupils with dyslexia are given coloured filters to read through, but these filters will only help those pupils who have a visual processing issue and, even then, the colour that would help varies from pupil to pupil. For pupils with dyslexia, we recommend that in your lessons you do the following:

- Write down the main points on a board/screen.
- Limit the expected amount of copying from the board/screen.
- Use pictures, flow-charts and mind-maps.
- Signpost topics and key points on handouts and the board/screen.
- Allow pupils sufficient time to absorb information.
- Use recording equipment and make them accessible using the VLE.
- If you have a Learning Support Assistant (LSA), make positive use of them by directing support in advance of the lesson.
- Give out pre-printed homework instructions.
- Use a font without serifs (squiggly bits on the ends of letters) such as Arial.
- Print copies of slides and worksheets on blue and cream paper (or another colour that helps the pupils in your class).

English as an Additional Language

What would you do if two pupils who speak English at a very basic level were put into your classroom at the start of a lesson with no notice or support – and, furthermore, it was a lesson you were being observed in? We have been there, observing such lessons – although, fortunately, these scenarios are few and far between. EAL is specifically mentioned as a learning need in Teachers' Standards 5. Part Two of the Teachers'

Standards states that teachers must specifically cater for 'pupils whose first language is not English' (DfE, 2011). One issue with EAL, as is the case with so many topics of education, is defining it. A pupil with EAL is identified as: 'exposed to a language at home that is known or believed to be other than English' (DfE, 2020: 4). This definition is not always particularly helpful; after all, there is no reason to presume that a child brought up by a parent/carer who speaks another language would have been greatly affected by that fact, beyond the benefits of bilingualism. Being exposed to more than one language, especially when young, brings many cognitive and cultural benefits; a child in this situation is hardly synonymous with a refugee child who has never spoken a word of English.

For the pupil who is new to English, everyday language that needs to be mastered to be able to function in school should come relatively quickly, but cultural and contextual expectations take much longer to learn and understand. One of our trainee teachers from Somalia recalled that, growing up in her home country, there was no cultural expectation to say 'please' and 'thank you'. On coming to England, she could not fathom why people thought she was rude. A pupil with EAL may have to learn not only a new language and set of cultural expectations, but also the specific language pertaining to each subject. Jim Cummins (1979, 1986) usefully separates the process of learning a second (or third or fourth in some cases) language into two stages – Basic Interpersonal Communicative Skills (BICS) and Cognitive and Academic Language Proficiency (CALP). BICS, Cummins suggests, will take up to two years to learn. CALP can take five to seven years to master, so the length of this process is likely to extend beyond the child's experience of school.

We recommend that you place explicit value on the child's background and home culture. Cummins warns against those who do not do so, or who consider the child to be 'starting from scratch': they are not. Other useful teaching strategies include:

- Using gestures to illustrate actions and activities (pointing, miming).
- Using visual cues (photographs, posters and pictures) to support the development of oral interactions.
- Displaying printed phrases on cards that are commonly used by teachers and children.
- Writing and speaking words and phrases the child can learn and use when looking for clarification – for example, 'Can you explain that again, please?'
- Simplifying texts.
- Encouraging the pupil to create bilingual glossaries.
- Putting up displays in the pupil's first language.
- Encouraging group work.
- Arranging or providing one-to-one workshops.

Any act of support for EAL children, any move towards the home culture and language, will make a positive difference to how the pupil feels, thinks and learns. The meta-message of care, concern, support and genuine interest in their life can have a powerful effect.

The Pupil Premium

For pupils whose family income is lower than average there is extra financial support known as The Pupil Premium, or PP for short. To respond to the extra funding, the school will be expected to put additional time, resources and support in place. In class, you will be required to adapt your teaching for those pupils whose parents have been identified as in receipt of PP. The PP initiative came in 2010, when the Conservative-Liberal government decided that the 'unseen children' of the day were those from low incomes and made them the primary focus of any financial support. One reason behind this thinking was that statistics showed that the majority of those pupils who under-achieved came from lower income homes. PP was a 'catch-all' mechanism for extra support – which representatives of those who are from a Gypsy, Roma and Traveller (GRT) background regretted:

> Between 2003, 2008, when Traveller Education was 'mainstreamed', there were coordinated policies involving central government, local authorities, schools, Traveller Education Support service and families...The Pupil Premium, which the Department of Education suggests meets the needs of Gypsies, Roma and Travellers does not deal with these situations and not all GRT children are eligible for Pupil Premium. Therefore, children are excluded, encouraged to home educate and allowed to drop out, with no-one having responsibility and skill to pick up the pieces. (The Traveller Movement, 2019)

Nevertheless, the scheme was expanded in 2014 to Pupil Premium Plus (PP+) which gives more money to schools for children in care or 'looked-after' children. In your classroom, you will need to use PP data and give the pupils so identified adaptations such as more attention, more questioning, and deliberate positioning in the room.

Race

The journalist Eddo-Lodge (n.d.) wrote the following, possibly as a cry of exhaustion:

> I'm no longer engaging with white people on the topic of race. Not all white people, just the vast majority who refuse to accept the legitimacy of structural racism and its symptoms...At best, white people have been taught not to mention that people of colour are 'different' in case it offends us. They truly believe that the experiences of their life as a result of their skin colour can and should be universalised...They've never had to think about what it means, in power terms, to be white...So I can't talk to white people about race anymore because of the consequential denials, awkward cartwheels and mental acrobatics that they display when this is brought to their attention. Who really wants to be alerted to a structural system that benefits them at the expense of others?...Worse still is the white person who might be willing to entertain the possibility of said racism, but still thinks we enter this conversation as equals. We don't...I don't have a huge amount of power to change the way the

world works, but I can set boundaries. I can halt the entitlement they feel towards me and I'll start that by stopping the conversation.

The book which followed, *Why I'm No Longer Talking to White People About Race*, extended this thesis, detailing event after event in UK history which points to a country which structurally and institutionally favours the majority 'white' population. We can bombard you with statistics and downward pointing line graphs – but, for now, we will focus on the fact that acceptance rates onto PGCE courses are 21 per cent lower for applicants from black and other minority ethnic backgrounds compared with acceptance rates for white applicants (Worth et al., 2022), and on the fact that 86 per cent of publicly funded schools in England have all-white Senior Leadership Teams (SLTs) (NFER, 2022). After these disturbing statistics, you might not feel able to bear any more. White 'privilege' brings responsibilities, including the possibilities of 'allyship'. An ally is 'someone who makes the commitment, and effort, to recognise their privilege (based on gender, class, race, sexual identity, etc.) and work in solidarity with oppressed groups in the struggle for justice (Harvard, n.d.). One aspect of allyship is taking an anti-racist stance in school regardless of your own personal heritage/ethnicity. This stance can be articulated in:

- Curriculum – making sure all ethnicities in the class are included in teaching and learning. Give 'the floor' to different voices and open the lesson up to the worlds the pupils inhabit at home.
- Representation – stopping the 'symbolic annihilation' which occurs when people of colour and from differing ethnicities are not included in the images and examples used in the lesson.
- Treatment – realise that we all carry prejudices, and consciously counteract these prejudices in the way we look at, treat and think about others. Reflect on such prejudices, and their effects on your pupils and your lessons.
- Yourself – the idea that you are the norm, the one others deviate from, is a power stance that should be avoided. Try taking a DNA test and see the mix of genes in your body; you might be surprised.

We can also consider the language we use in schools. Benjamin Zephaniah (Poeticous, n.d.) once pointed out the negativity of the word 'black' in English by writing that he had been 'whitemailed', 'whitelisted' and called a 'white sheep' and that he was going to write to the Black House to complain. Language and labelling both reflect and contain power. It is worth seeing if language can be used to protect and re-balance instead. Instead of calling some people 'ethnic' (we are all this) and some people a 'minority', try the term BAGM – Black and Asian Global Majority. Pupils who are third or fourth generations from their great-great-grandparents' homeland may understandably not have much connection to it. A cultural heritage is only of value to a pupil if the pupil wants it to be so, and their family may have abandoned it long ago. While Black History Month offers a chance to re-balance the curriculum, Paul Beatty's (2016) Booker Prize-winning novel, *The Sellout* reveals, in a darkly comic way, what a token gesture the month can be when its main character gets so tired of racist America that he turns a school into a black-only institution and instigates White History Month.

The importance of recognising the needs of all pupils is inscribed in Part Two of the Teachers' Standards (DfE, 2011). It is also part of Standard 5 (DfE, 2011): 'factors which inhibit pupils' ability to learn' and 'distinctive teaching approaches to engage and support'. *Black Lives Matter* and *I Can't Breathe* are global awareness campaigns, affecting pupils' lives and how they think about education, as well as enlightening us all about inequality. Schools should not be in 'bubbles' away from these debates and concerns – and particularly not 'bubbles' where white privilege is evidenced in the curriculum, the textbooks, and the racial profiles of those who are teachers and senior leaders. One of our trainees was teaching Charles Dickens and set homework to discover more about him. A pupil uncovered Dickens's negative views about slaves in America, and quite reasonably stated: 'Why should I want to learn something about a racist?' It is better to be aware of these issues and open up dialogue, rather than pretending that they do not exist.

To colonise can be a 'political, economic, cultural or psychological' act (Gardinier, 1968: 269), and in many cases all four of these. The 'taking over' of a group of people by imposition, whether it is by invitation or (as in most cases) force, usually involves working on the 'hearts and minds' of the colonised. The word 'decolonisation' in its original form means the 'retreat of the West from formal dominance' (Bogaerts and Raben, 2012: 2) and recognition of the violence of colonialism: 'The naked truth of decolonization evokes for us the searing bullets and blood-stained knives which emanate from it' (Fanon, 1966: 30). Unfortunately, the most important reform of education in the last two decades, the White Paper of 2010, mentions 'race' only in this line: 'we are in a global race'. The ITTECF does not mention 'race' or 'ethnicity'. Regardless, in some schools, and by some teachers, there is a 'postcolonial retaliation' (Derrida, 1998: 44) against the coded messages pupils have been receiving about parts of the world other than the United Kingdom. There is also a growing awareness that some aspects of the National Curriculum need to be decolonised. You can be part of it in your lessons by making sure that they are:

- Representative – think about who you put in the images you use in lessons, and which texts and topics you choose.
- Accessible – think about the pupils in your class and make sure that the coded message is not about white supremacy.
- Inclusive– include the views and perspectives of all, not just the powerful, in your lessons.

In practical terms, postcolonialism means, 'greater representation of non-European thinkers' (SOAS, n.d.). Why, for example, is the Greek Pythagoras's Theorem mentioned in school as a great and important mathematical concept, but the concept of 'zero' developed by Bharamagupta in India, hardly mentioned (Adam, 2004)? In English, for example, there is an explicit agenda to promote the country; Britain's 'literary heritage' is the primary focus of taught content (DfE, 2014). But, as Nelson-Addy et al. (2020) noted, this focus on the Elizabethan and Victorian eras can glorify the Empire, give the impression of a monocultural national identity, and isolate those who consider themselves to have a multicultural identity. We surely cannot have gone through the tragedy and collective pain of Stephen Lawrence's murder in 1993, and the investigation which revealed the institutional level of racism, without having learnt that we all need to make sure that the school institution is not contributing to, and reinforcing, racial inequalities in society.

Conclusion

Adaptation is about making sure there is equity in the classroom. It may be that most pupils in your class can work effectively with the same, or similar, provision; it may also be that there are two, three or four pupils who need particular support. They are an important minority, standing in front of the fence – if we think back to the analogy we used at the start of this chapter – and needing to see. For some aspects of your lesson, adaptations may not be needed. The more 'eagle-eyed' among you will have noticed that good practice for those pupils with disabilities and special education needs is often good practice for all pupils. Try to ensure that your adaption can be good for all. We quoted the Democrat President Biden in this chapter so, in the interests of electoral fairness, we will end with Republican George W. Bush, and recommend that you follow his stated principles:

> The president of the United States is the president of every single American, of every race and every background. . .Whether you voted for me or not, I will do my best to serve your interests, and I will work to earn your respect. (BBC, 2000)

.... **REFLECTIONS**

What are your disabilities, and how have you shown or hidden them? In the safe space of your thoughts, examine what disables you and examine your response to it. Have you always been able to manage the disability? Do you wish that you had acted differently? Could anyone have supported you better? If appropriate – how might your experience be communicated to the pupils, and used to help them?

Consider your privileges – of sex, of race, and of economics. . .? If you have achieved to the point of being able to train to be a teacher, you are likely to have been helped in some way. How many privileges were you born with, and how many have you accumulated that helped you to achieve? We can get trapped in the myth of meritocracy, that success is earned through endeavour, forgetting that life may have given us some 'boxes to see over the fence' along the way. Jo Littler (2018) writes eloquently about this myth, and suggests that it can hide inequality in society by pretending that we all have an equal chance of success from birth onwards. Recognising, and acknowledging, this myth enables us to start thinking about teaching for equity – to try to give others the benefits we may have acquired in our own lives.
....

.... **ACTIONS**

- Read more about strategies to create lesson adaptations for all pupils, and put them into practice.
- Look at the dataset the school provides you with, and consider what you can put into practice for each identified learning issue.
- Talk with your mentor about ways to allow all pupils to access the learning in your lessons.

....

Case Study 8

Gabriel Zanovello is Portuguese-born and lived in Brazil and the United States until he settled in the United Kingdom to train to teach in a secondary school. He speaks three languages and this has helped him to understand more about EAL provision in school – so much so that the school ended up asking him to deliver a Continuing Professional Development (CPD) session while he was at his second placement school. Below is an extract from his essay on the subject, written during his training year, which gives a 'flavour' not only of how to improve matters for EAL pupil but also the level of professional engagement you can engage in while on a PGCE course. He is about to start his Early Career Teacher (ECT) years at a mixed-sex academy.

In England alone, there are over 1.62 million EAL pupils representing over 360 different languages spoken; the percentage of EAL pupils is higher in primary schools (21.2%) compared to secondary schools (16.6%) (Costley and Leung, 2020). This transformation has led to the development of newer pedagogical approaches seeking more creative methods to improve EAL pupils' attainment not just by aiding cross-linguistic transfer (Cummins, 2008 cited in Lewis et al., 2012, p. 645), but also acknowledging their home language (L1) as a resource from which pupils can draw upon when learning English (L2), thus truly celebrating their linguistic heritage. Translanguaging first emerged as a pupil-centred pedagogical strategy of alternating language use in the classroom. The term was originally used by Cen Williams (1994 cited in Lewis et al., 2012, p. 641) in Wales, as a reaction to the traditional approach in Welsh education where both languages, Welsh and English, were kept in a perpetual state of separation. In the process of revitalisation for the Welsh language, translanguaging instances took place where pupils would alternate language use in the classroom between English and Welsh to develop their bilingual competence (Lewis et al., 2012, p. 644). This was deemed to be positive and particularly advantageous for pupils' communication, cultural and cognitive development. Translanguaging was later refined by Lewis et al. (2012, p. 641) as a process where: 'both languages are used in a dynamic and functionally integrated manner to organise and mediate mental processes in understanding, speaking, literacy and not least, learning'.

This theoretical foundation informs pedagogical translanguaging, a disruptive approach to the monolingual paradigm in education, where traditionally, a single language, often the dominant societal language, has reigned supreme in the classroom (Cenoz and Gorter, 2020, p. 1; Costley and Leung, 2020, p. 8; Coyle et al., 2021, p. 1033). This subtractive approach has led to languages being compartmentalised, commonly referred to as the 'two solitudes' by Cummins (2007 cited in Cenoz and Gorter, 2020, p. 1). Arguably, the traditional approach has viewed EAL pupils' home languages as obstacles to acquire English, the target language. This monolingual paradigm has been demonstrably ineffective, as it puts teachers in a position where they are unable to capture the extent of EAL pupils' linguistic repertoire, and subsequently to capitalise on the linguistic richness that EAL pupils bring into the English classroom (Cummins, 2005; Cenoz and Gorter, 2020; Dutton and Rushton, 2020). In contrast, pedagogical translanguaging innovates classroom language use and exists in a pedagogical - spontaneous continuum (Cenoz and Gorter, 2020).

Spontaneous translanguaging is when EAL pupils use languages in a fluid manner, switching from their L1 to L2 without any prompting or direction (Cenoz and Gorter, 2020). An example of cognitive benefits to spontaneous translanguaging has been noted where pupils who speak the same home language engage in collaborative discussions to negotiate meaning. Within lesson plans, teachers achieve this by getting pupils to use their home language to create bilingual glossaries that can be used throughout the school year (Cenoz and Gorter, 2020; Bosma et al., 2022).

My experience at 'School A' - a coeducational faith school for pupils aged 11–18 - proved to be a valuable learning opportunity, albeit in an unexpected way. My Year 8 class consisted of EAL pupils with Polish, Hungarian, and French backgrounds. At first, I was confused and unsure whether I could use translanguaging strategies in my classroom, since these EAL pupils displayed strong English proficiency, were generally confident with their language skills, and exceedingly keen to participate in lessons. Filled with motivation to try this novel approach, I organised a meeting with the class teacher and we had a positive discussion but it also revealed hurdles that needed to be overcome. For example, one major hurdle was the school's emphasis on standardised testing, and a curriculum demanding monolingual English use (Ticheloven et al., 2019; Safont, 2021). In practice, this meant teachers perceived translanguaging as a strategy that would deviate from curriculum goals or in other words, there was no room for experimentation - a conclusion that Costley and Leung (2020) also found. I also noticed that after numerous discussions, most teachers believed exposure was the only way EAL pupils could make any gains in their proficiency. Even when speaking with EAL pupils, I noticed hesitation, apprehension, and ambivalent views towards their home languages which may have been driven by strict family attitudes towards home language use (Wilson, 2020, p. 73). Consequently, I became discouraged and felt a lack of autonomy to experiment in the classroom as a trainee teacher.

In contrast, 'School B' – a mixed-sex comprehensive school with a greater number of EAL pupils aged 11–16, who spoke a wide variety of languages – offered a more encouraging environment for implementing translanguaging practices. Colleagues at 'School B' were more supportive, and had a more positive disposition towards implementing new strategies to help EAL pupils. Prior to setting up translanguaging strategies, during my first week, I identified EAL pupils who spoke a variety of languages – Arabic, French, Romanian and Turkish. Once I had identified EAL pupils in my class, I spent the rest of the week intentionally building relationships with them, to foster a warm classroom environment that welcomes and celebrates their home languages. I engaged pupils in discussions regarding their home language use, and this was an excellent awareness-raising opportunity. Over the course of one week, these discussions allowed me to gauge and improve EAL pupils' perceptions of their home language (Decristan et al., 2024). During my first week, I decided to change classroom seating arrangements so that pupils who spoke the same home language would sit together. I felt this would open space for what has been referred to as spontaneous translanguaging (Cenoz and Gorter, 2020) during think-pair-share moments in lessons. Secondly, I created dual language glossaries aimed to enhance EAL pupils' metacognition, by allowing them to leverage existing language skills to learn new concepts in English. I provided a blank template where pupils could add words they encountered in lessons alongside translations in their home language. This strategy proved particularly effective. For example, Pupil A, who spoke Turkish actively used the glossary during a reading comprehension activity, translating the word 'ordeal' into Turkish by writing it down on his glossary to grasp its meaning in English. For pupils who struggled with their English proficiency, like Pupil B, who spoke French, I adapted their glossaries by including the French translation using machine translation (Kelly and Hou, 2021). By providing a translation of the word 'ominous' in French, this might have activated Pupil B's prior knowledge in L1, which might have in turn, lessened the cognitive load associated with the task of gaining a full grasp of the vocabulary using their limited English knowledge (Sweller et al., 2011). Machine translation helped me create word lists in EAL pupils' home language and the use of technology had a positive impact on my practice.

Reflecting on pupil feedback from my experience at School B, several positive aspects emerged. Pupils who were previously hesitant to participate in English lessons used their home languages as a springboard to confidently express themselves. I was proud to see EAL pupils becoming actively engaged with resources, and displaying an increasingly positive attitude towards using their home languages. Collaborative translanguaging activities fostered a sense of community, where pupils engaged in sense making through conscious investment in their linguistic repertoires within the classroom, creating a more inclusive learning environment. One example worth mentioning was Pupil C and Pupil D who would speak with each other in Arabic to come to an agreement on what was English words meant in Arabic. Eventually, Pupil C was excited to share this information with me, and I took the opportunity to praise their effort to work so well across languages. Another advantage that I observed was that giving EAL pupils the opportunity to build dual language glossaries was particularly effective at enhancing their metacognition, as they leveraged their existing linguistic knowledge to consciously learn new concepts in English (Cummins, 2008 cited in Lewis et al., 2012, p. 645). By the end of my two-week experimentation in School B, I felt like I was building professional capital as a trainee teacher. I had a much greater sense of satisfaction and gained valuable insights that I will use in my practice. This experience made me aware of how empowering translanguaging strategies can be for supporting EAL pupils in the English classroom. Translanguaging strategies allowed them to build upon their existing linguistic repertoire instead of starting from scratch. In addition, it created a more inclusive learning environment that recognised and valued their diverse linguistic backgrounds.

.............................WHAT TOOLS ARE IN YOUR TOOLKIT NOW?

- Greater understanding of the words 'differentiation', 'inclusion' and 'adaptive teaching', and the pedagogies behind them.
- Strategies to support pupils with EAL.
- Strategies to support pupils with ASC.
- Strategies to support pupils with ADHD.
- Strategies to support pupils with dyslexia.
- Greater understanding of the need to contribute to a fair and equitable society, by re-evaluating the curriculum and how you will teach it, avoiding coded messages which perpetuate power in an unequal way.

Places to Get More Tools for Your Toolkit

Peer, L. and Reid, G. (eds) (2021) *Special Education Needs.* London: SAGE.
Each chapter is written by a specialist and will build up your knowledge, and therefore confidence, in giving all pupils a fair education.

Westwood, P. (2018). *Inclusive and Adaptive Teaching: Meeting the Challenge of Diversity in the Classroom.* London: Routledge.
A comprehensive volume looking at how you can adapt your practice to cater for children with a range of learning needs.

Katy Hessell's (2022) book *The History of Art Without Men* gives art teachers plenty of details for this discipline. And why not try *Gender Swapped Greek Myths* by Karrie Fransman and Jonathan Plackett (2022)? Women need to be given as much space in your curriculum as men; given the historical imbalance of power, this is difficult. Do what you can to recognise the women who were airbrushed out of history.

References

Adam, S. (2004) Ethnomathematical ideas in the Curriculum. *Mathematics Educational Research Journal* 16(2): 49-68.

ADDIS (2005) *A Report Based on Research Amongst Children and Parents Illustrating the Impact of ADHD on the School.* Available from: http://www.addiss.co.uk/schoolreport.pdf

Additude (2024) ADHD needs a better name. *We Have One.* Available from: www.additude mag.com/attention-deficit-disorder-vast/

Bailey, S. (2014). *Exploring ADHD: An Ethnography of Disorder in Early Childhood.* Abingdon: Routledge.

Beatty, P. (2016) *The Sellout.* London: Oneworld.

BBC (2000) *Bush Speech in Full.* Available from: http://news.bbc.co.uk/1/hi/world/americas/1069929.stm

Bogaerts, E. and Raben, R. (2012) *Beyond Empire and Nation: The decolonization of African and Asian societies, 1930s–1970s.* Boston: Brill.

Bosma, E., Bakker, A., Zenger, L. and Blom, E. (2022) Supporting the development of the bilingual Lexicon through translanguaging: A realist review integrating psycholinguistics with educational sciences, *European Journal of Psychology of Education* 38: 225-247.

CNN (2021) *Biden Delivers First Joint Address to Congress.* Available from: https://edition.cnn.com/politics/live-news/biden-address-fact-check-updates-04-28-21#h_b99259226c5a2b76db1d83d415bd5ebe

Cenoz, J. and Gorter, D. (2020) Pedagogical translanguaging: An introduction, *System* (92).

Costley, T. and Leung, C. (2020) Putting translanguaging into practice: A view from England, *System* (92).

Coyle, D., Bower, K., Foley, Y. and Hancock, J. (2021) Teachers as designers of learning in diverse, bilingual classrooms in England: An ADiBE case study, *International Journal of Bilingual Education and Bilingualism* 26(9): 1-19.

Cummins, J. (1979) Cognitive/academic language proficiency, linguistic interdependence, the optimum age question and some other matters, *Working Papers on Bilingualism* 19: 121-129.

Cummins, J. (1986) Empowering minority students: A framework for intervention. *Harvard Educational Review* 56: 18-36.

Cummins, J. (2005) A proposal for action: Strategies for recognizing heritage language competence as a learning resource within the mainstream classroom. *The Modern Language Journal,* 89(4): 585-592.

Cummins, J. (2008) BICS and CALP: Empirical and theoretical status of the distinction Jim Cummins the university of Toronto. In Street, B. and Hornberger, N. H. (Eds.), *Encyclopedia of Language and Education* (pp. 71-83). New York: Springer Science.

Delisle, J. (2015) *Differentiation Doesn't Work*. Available from: https://www.edweek.org/teaching-learning/opinion-differentiation-doesnt-work/2015/01

Decristan, J., Bertram, V., Reitenbach, V., Schneider, K. and Rauch, D. (2024) Translanguaging in today's multilingual classes – Students' perspectives of classroom management and classroom climate, *Teaching and Teacher Education* 139(1).

Derrida, J. (1998) *Monolingualism of the Other or the Prosthesis of Origin*. California: Stanford University Press.

DfE (2011a) *Schools, Pupils and Their Characteristics*. January 2011. Available from: https://assets.publishing.service.gov.uk/government/uploads/system/uploads/attachment_data/file/219064/main_20text_20sfr122011.pdf

DfE (2011b) *Teachers' Standards*. London: HMSO.

DfE (2014) *National Crriculum in England: English Programmes of Study*. Available from: https://www.gov.uk/government/publications/national-curriculum-in-england-english-programmes-of-study/national-curriculum-in-england-english-programmes-of-study

DfE (2019) *Ensuring a Good Education for All Children: Attainment Gap, Reception Baseline Assessment*. Available from: https://educationhub.blog.gov.uk/2019/09/26/ensuring-a-good-education-for-all-children/

DfE (2020) *English Proficiency of Pupils with English as an Additional Language*. Available from: https://assets.publishing.service.gov.uk/media/5e55205d86650c10e8754e54/English_proficiency_of_EAL_pupils.pdf

Department for Health and Social Care (2021) *The National Strategy for Autistic Children, Young People and Adults: 2021 to 2026*. Available from: https://assets.publishing.service.gov.uk/government/uploads/system/uploads/attachment_data/file/1004528/the-national-strategy-for-autistic-children-young-people-and-adults-2021-to-2026.pdf

Dumortier, D. (2004). *From Another Planet: Autism from Within*. Chicago: Lucky Duck.

Dutton, J. and Rushton, K. (2020) Using the translanguaging space to facilitate poetic representation of language and identity, *Language Teaching Research* 25(1): 105–133.

Doyle, J. (1996) *Dyslexia: An Introductory Guide*. London: Whurr Publishers.

Equality Act (2010). London: Stationery Office. Available from: https://www.legislation.gov.uk/ukpga/2010/15/contents

Education Week. Available from: https://www.edweek.org/teaching-learning/opinion-differentiation-doesnt-work/2015/01

Eddo-Lodge, R. (n.d.) Available from: https://renieddolodge.co.uk/why-im-no-longer-talking-to-white-people-about-race/

Eddo-Lodge, R. (2018) *Why I Am No Longer Talking to White People about Race*. London: Bloomsbury.

Every Child Matters (2003) London: HMSO. Available from: https://assets.publishing.service.gov.uk/government/uploads/system/uploads/attachment_data/file/272064/5860.pdf

Fanon, F. (1966) *The Wretched of the Earth*. New York: Evergreen.

Fransman, K. and Plackett, J. (2022) *Gender Swapped Greek Myths*. London: Faber and Faber.

Gardner, H. (1999) *Intelligence Reframed: Multiple Intelligences for the 21st Century*. New York: Basic Books.

Gardinier, D. (1968) Decolonization. In Dunner, J. (Ed.), *Handbook of World History* (pp. 268–272). London: Owen.

Harvard (n.d.) Available from: https://projects.iq.harvard.edu/antiracismresources/allies

Kelly, R. and Hou, H. (2021) Empowering learners of English as an Additional Language: Translanguaging with machine translation, *Language and Education* 36(6) 1–16.

Lewis, G., Jones, B. and Baker, C. (2012) Translanguaging: Origins and development from school to street and beyond, *Educational Research and Evaluation* 18(7): 641–654.

Littler, J. (2018) *Against Meritocracy: Culture, Power, and Myths of Mobility*. London: Routledge.

Miles, E. and Miles, T. (1990) *Dyslexia: A Hundred Years on*. Buckingham: Open University Press.

Mortimore, T. (2008) *Dyslexia and Learning Styles*. Chichester: John Wiley and Sons.

Mould, K. (2021) *Asses, Adjust, Adapt*. Available from: https://educationendowmentfoundation. org.uk/news/eef-blog-assess-adjust-adapt-what-does-adaptive-teaching-mean-to-you

NACE (2019) *Key Strategies for Stretch and Challenge*. Available from: https://www.nace.co.uk/ blogpost/1761881/334589/5-key-strategies-for-stretch-and-challenge

National Autistic Society (2020) Available from: www.nas.org.uk

Nelson-Addy, L., Elliott, V. and Snapper, G. (2020) Changing the narrative: New voices, new texts, new perspectives in the literature classroom. *Teaching English*, 23: 34–40.

NFER (2022) *Headship Summary Report*. Available from: https://www.nfer.ac.uk/media/ ytnjlaz4/racial_equality_in_the_teacher_workforce_summary_report.pdf

Ofsted (2014) *Overcoming Barriers: Ensuring that Roma Children Are Fully Engaged and Achieving in Education*. London: Ofsted. Available from: https://assets.publishing.service.gov.uk/ government/uploads/system/uploads/attachment_data/file/430866/Overcoming_barriers_- _ensuring_that_Roma_children_are_fully_engaged_and_achieving_in_education.pdf

Ofsted (1999) *Raising the Attainment of Minority Ethnic Pupils*. London: Ofsted. Available from: https://dera.ioe.ac.uk/4386/2/Raising_the_attainment_of_minority_ethnic_pupils_ school_and_LEA_responses.pdf

O'Regan, F. (2009) Persistent disruptive behaviour and exclusion. *ADHD in Practice* 1(1): 8–11.

Poeticous (n.d.) Available from: https://www.poeticous.com/benjamin-obadiah-iqbal-zephaniah/ white-comedy

Pumfrey, P. and Reason, R. (1998) *Specific Learning Difficulties (Dyslexia)*. London: Routledge.

Rice, M. and Brooks, G. (2004) *Developmental Dyslexia in Adults: A Research Review*. London: National Research and Development Centre for Adult Literacy and Numeracy.

Safont, P. (2021) '"In English!": Teachers' requests as reactions to learners' translanguaging discourse, *Language Culture and Curriculum* 35(3): 1–17.

Sherrington, T. (2017) *Teaching to the Top: Attitudes and Strategies for Delivering Real Challenge*. Available from: www.teacherhead.com/2017/05/28/teaching-to-the-top-attitudes- and-strategies-for-delivering-real-challenge/

Shogren, K., Wehmeyer, M., Martinis, J., Blanck, P. (2018) *Supported Decision Making* Cambridge: Cambridge University Press.

Sinclair, J (1993) Don't mourn for us. *Autism Network International Newsletter 'Our voice'*. 1(3).

Sweller, J., Ayres, P. and Kalyuga, S. (2011) *Cognitive Load Theory*. New York: Springer.

The Traveller Movement (2019) *A Good Practice Guide for Improving Outcomes for Gypsy, Roma and Traveller Children in Education*. Available from: https://wp-main.traveller movement.org.uk/wp-content/uploads/2021/09/Improving-Education-Outcomes-for-GTR- Pupils-2015-Briefing.pdf

Ticheloven, A., Blom, E., Leseman, P. and McMonagle, S. (2019) Translanguaging challenges in multilingual classrooms: Scholar, teacher and student perspectives, *International Journal of Multilingualism* 18(3): 1–24.

UNESCO (2016) *Reaching Out to All Learners: A Resource Pack for Supporting Inclusive Education*. Available from: http://unesdoc.unesco.org/images/0024/002432/243279e.pdf

UNESCO (2017) *A Guide for Ensuring Inclusion and Equity in Education*. Available from: http://unesdoc.unesco.org/images/0024/002482/248254e.pdf

Wiley, L. (1999) *Pretending to Be Normal: Living with Asperger Syndrome*. London: Jessica Kingsley.

Wilson, S. (2020) To Mix or Not to Mix: Parental attitudes towards translanguaging and language management choices, *International Journal of Bilingualism* 25(1): 58–76.

Wing, L. and Gould, J. (1979) Severe Impairments of social interaction and associated abnormalities in children: Epidemiology and classification, *Journal of Autism and Developmental Disorders* 9: 1–29. Available from: https://www.ethnicity-facts-figures.service.gov.uk/education-skills-and-training/11-to-16-years-old/a-to-c-in-english-and-maths-gcse-attainment-for-children-aged-14-to-16-key-stage-4/latest/

Worth, J., McLean, D. and Sharp, C. (2022) *Racial Equality in the Teacher Workforce: An Analysis of Representation and Progression Opportunities from Initial Teacher Training to Headship*. Available from: https://www.nfer.ac.uk/media/hxpdemc4/racial_equality_in_the_teacher_workforce_full_report.pdf

9
Knowing and Documenting Progress

What this chapter will cover

- Diagnostic, formative and summative assessment
- Datafied learning
- Reporting to parents

Introduction

This chapter examines the nature of assessment. It discusses the idea of 'progress' and the datafication of learning, where it is represented in numerical form. Examinations, marking and other summative and formative assessment will be outlined with advice offered. Data is used as evidence of learning for pupils' parents/carers and there is advice about reporting this.

Diagnostic, Formative and Summative Assessment

One of our favourite Gary Larson Far Side cartoons has a person tentatively knocking on a door with the sign stating 'Assertiveness Course', and a voice behind saying, 'Go away! You've failed'. Unlike in this cartoon, assessment is always to be done sensitively. Sue Cowley (2011) recalled an event in a school in which a child had drawn a picture of a sad girl and written: 'The girl is sad. She has no friends'. The teacher opened this up to the class to comment on her work and some said that she could have written more, others that she could have chosen a better word than 'sad,' and one classmate said: "I'll be your friend". The pupil had looked beyond the content and responded to the writer, which is what McCormick Calkins (1989: 120) reminds us of when assessing work: 'It is not my piece of writing. It belongs to someone else'. When you respond to someone's work, remember that there is a person behind it, and it is not yours to scrawl over and change. You are there to guide the next steps of their learning through feedback – some call it more precisely feedforward, as it is all about helping to ensure improvement in the next piece.

Assessment is not a necessity until the very end of school. Learning is not assessment and teachers are in the learning business. Assessment is the externalisation of internal processes, and the teacher and pupil use it to discover whether teaching and learning have been successful or not. There are good reasons not to assess pupils, including the stress of high-stake assessments (the ones where the results impact on their lives, such as deciding which set they will be in), alongside the effect they have on self-efficacy (belief in an ability to do something) and self-esteem (feelings about the self) from doing badly. So, why do we assess? Here are some benefits:

- It stimulates recall.
- It informs about the pupils' understanding.
- It challenges pupils to learn more.
- It informs about likely success, given the current work rate.

Assessment may be useful but it does not have to be the teacher who does it:

- Self-assessment – the pupil marks their own work.
- Peer-assessment – the pupils mark each other's work.

Each method (including teacher-assessment) has its benefits and a mix of all three not only shares the burden of marking, but opens the pupils up to the important act of meta-learning, where they are conscious about what they are doing in class in terms of not only what has been learnt, but how.

Assessment for Learning (AfL) can be defined as:

> The process of seeking and interpreting evidence for use by learners and their teachers to decide where the learners are in their learning, where they need to go, and how best to get there. (Broadfoot et al., 2002: 2–3)

The AfL Toolkit has been with us so long, it still contains some Microsoft Word's Clipart stick people in the graphics. It was compiled by Mike Gershon (n.d.) and includes many ways of formatively assessing work including:

- Two stars and a wish: assess their own or another's work with two good points and one not-so-good.
- One-sentence summary: all they learnt in a lesson in a sentence. Can be used as a 'pass out' from the lesson (necessary to get out of the door) and assessed in time for the next one.
- All you know: stream-of-consciousness, timed writing about a topic.
- Post-it notes: popular tool to assess, and gives an opportunity for the pupils to move in the classroom as they get stuck either on a board at the front, or in a particular place in the room.
- Show and tell: pupils get up, stand up, and present a topic to the class.

There are lots of ways of checking learning, so there is no need to YAVA (You Ask, Volunteers Answer). Hands-up is something people like us warn trainee teachers about, but it still persists. It is a bit like scratching an itch – never a good idea but happens all the while. Hands-up volunteering not only disrupts the lesson, it gets answers from the people who probably knew them before the lesson started. Not relying on YAVA is a central piece of advice to training teachers in the book *How to be a Brilliant Teacher* by Trevor Wright (2009). One of us worked with Trevor and repeatedly heard this advice being given to trainee teachers and yet, to his and our bewilderment, there are few lessons that do not have YAVA and, to this day, it thrives. Instead of YAVA, use questioning purposefully. This takes planning, which is why so many teachers may resort to YAVA which does not, but the results will be more ordered, interesting, and purposeful, and worth every minute spent.

Oracy in the classroom develops learning. Oracy is an 'acy', like literacy or numeracy and refers to advanced ability with speech. Robin Alexander's (2017) work on classroom talk opened a generation of teachers to the benefits of a dialogic classroom with the following advice that it must be:

- Collective: teachers and pupils learn together.
- Reciprocal: teachers and pupils listen to each other, share ideas and consider alternative viewpoints.
- Supportive: pupils express ideas freely without fear of being 'wrong' and help each other to common understandings.

- Cumulative: teachers and pupils build on their and each other's ideas and connecting into a coherent response which answers a question.
- Purposeful: teachers plan and facilitate dialogic teaching with particular educational goals in view.

As part of this move to a dialogic classroom, plan the discussions and control them. Consider the following:

- Who is to be asked a question? Plan whether you are going to target a pupil or ask all of them to respond. Be aware of 'blind spots' where you might be choosing the pupil who you know has the answer.
- What is the question achieving? Is it checking knowledge or opening up debate and alternative ways of thinking?
- How will they respond – on whiteboards, for example – or verbally?

Teaching through dialogue improves the pupils' ability to express and debate ideas. Through classroom speech we can ease the cognitive demand on pupils, as they do not need to reinterpret their thoughts into writing; speaking is a cognitively 'lighter' (Kellogg, 2008) way of generating ideas. Class talk can also act as a scaffold of support before writing. The initiative Voice21 (2024) has given fresh impetus to this act. It is very tuned into today's concerns and the language of datafied teaching. Its 'impact report' of 2022-2023, for example datafied the confidence of teachers in increasing oracy (30%-70%) and states (if you can work this one out) how proud they were that 69% of schools were in the top 40% for Free School Meals. Oracy is not a new concept – Wilkinson wrote of the importance of it in 1970 – but Voice21 allows schools to 'buy into' (literally, as it is a paid-for service) its importance. The language of schools permeates Voice21's outputs with their 'oracy benchmarks' as well as an 'oracy framework'. Because Voice21 is focused on targeted on evidencing progress through the initiative, it is clear about what oracy means:

- Physical Voice: pace of speech, tonal variation, clarity of pronunciation, voice projection, body language and posture.
- Linguistic: vocabulary choice, language registers (formal and informal English), grammar and persuasive techniques.
- Cognitive: choice of content to convey meaning and intention, building on the views of others.
- Structure: organisation of talk, clarifying, summarising, questioning and summarising.
- Reasoning: critically examining ideas and viewpoints.
- Self-regulation: maintaining focus.
- Social and Emotional: working with others, managing interactions, turn-taking, listening actively and responding appropriately.
- Confidence: self-assurance, liveliness and flair.
- Audience awareness: levels of understanding.

Once learning has been diagnosed, then improved through formative means, you are ready to summatively assess – to test what the pupils know in a formal manner. This can be ipsative, value added, norm-referenced or criterion-referenced. Summative assessment is what you do at the end of a period of learning. Teaching of the topic is finished and now you can reveal its success or failure, usually with a letter or number. You can do this ipsatively when you rate the performance against the pupil's usual standard. It is what athletes do to themselves when they aim for a 'PB', or Personal Best. In the end, they may be on the track trying desperately to see through all the dust their competitors are kicking up in front of them, but if they stay true to the PB philosophy, they only need to be disappointed if they do not achieve their own targets. Translate that into school and each pupil is allowed to learn at their own pace, and we can praise individual success. This is not a popular approach in the current system which expects everyone to achieve a certain level. 'Value added' seems more like a phrase you would see in a supermarket than a school and it has the same sort of meaning – 'more bang for your buck'. 'Value added' can even be applied to those for whom expectations are different because of factors such as sex, parental income or Key Stage 2 marks. If one sex group, on average, typically achieves at a lower level than another, then a higher-than-expected result for a pupil in this category has greater value. The value might even translate into an improved picture on the school's data dashboard which records value-added information. This does not translate onto the individual pupil who just gets the grade on their certificates, and there is no asterisk on these mentioning 'but they were male so did very well, really'. Instead, the pupil will receive criterion-referenced assessment meaning that there is a set of explicit expectations for the answer and it is just a matter of finding them in the answer or not. Norm-referenced assessment is what takes over from criterion-referenced marking in an official examination. Every year, results come in and they are put through an algorithm to make sure they follow the expected pattern of grades. If, for example, in a particular year, 90 per cent of the pupils got below a 4 at GCSE, then the marks are changed to reflect the difficulty of the exam. In 2017, on a particularly tricky mathematics GCSE exam paper, 8300H, 15 per cent would have got you a 4 (C-grade equivalent) (AQA, 2019). There is the presumption that everyone in a cohort of exam takers is equally able, and that the exam is to blame if the results do not follow the expected pattern.

Markers have to be assessed as well. Standardisation happens before marking and is a check, usually with sample scripts, that everyone is grading in the same way. You will be given something to mark and a mark scheme. This marking is usually done separately, then either sent to a central adjudicator who will check that the grades are similar to others, or get together and discuss them. Moderation happens after marking and is a check that there is agreement about grading. Teachers share their marked work with others and remark it. If there is disagreement about a mark, there is discussion first and, if no agreement can be made, a third marker is involved. Often, from our experience, this results in a verbal 'punch-up' as no one wants their grades to be lowered. It is important to learn from this process in school and the disagreements of markers show that it is never an easy process. Even with criterion marking, there will always be differences with the way that more complex answers are graded. Coursework is moderated by examination boards who get sent a sample by each school. If the marks of the teacher are not 'within tolerance' – the examination board marker thinks the teacher's marks were more than 10 per cent different – they get changed. If the marks are consistently too high or too low, all of the coursework gets reduced or increased. If not, the school will have to send the whole set of coursework in to be re-marked.

Datafied Learning

You may have been in the state school system from 2010 to 2014 and if so would have known whether you were a 4a, 6b or 7c in Maths, English and Science, because a scheme was in place called **Assessing Pupils' Progress** (APP). APP used grids with very specific learning topics and stages, and the pupil was graded according to whether they had fulfilled the criteria: just about (a), partially (b) or fully (c). In a rare show of unity, all the major teaching unions, the Qualifications and Curriculum Authority, and the Qualifications and Development Agency agreed that it was a 'good thing', and: 'has been shown to improve learners' progress' (QCDA, 2010: 10). Despite this, it was firmly scrapped four years later. Educational initiatives come in a blaze of glory to transform education then leave quietly by the back door and teacher John Dabell (2018) gave this one a firm kick as it left:

> I cannot think of any initiative as mind-numbing, well-being sapping and pointless as Assessing Pupil Progress (APP). This was a workload nightmare and literally drowned us in useless data. This was a freakish fad from the land of spreadsheets with built-in madness.

During the APP years, one of us asked a group of trainee teachers how they started the lesson-planning process, expecting the answer to be the National Curriculum, only to hear that they used the APP grid. The grid was meant to be used to assess work, but instead, teachers were identifying a place on the grid, teaching it and, if it was achieved, stamping the pupil's work with a number and letter. It took a while for schools to get away from the specific assessment culture of numbers and letters when government policy went to the other extreme with 'Assessment without Levels' (Gov.UK, 2015) where schools were told to not inform pupils of their grades and particularly, as wisely advised by Kohn (1994), to never grade students while they are still learning. This digression into assessment trends shows that education policy comes and goes and veers from one end of the spectrum to the next. You will have to turn learning into data, but we hope that you can do this at summative rather than formative stage. All learning is turned into examination results in the end, and you will need to reflect this. To turn learning into a number, you need a mark scheme which is fair and transparent, and which has criteria related to numbers.

One number which has become very important to schools since 2016 is eight. Attainment 8 is the average number gained at GCSE subjects by pupils across eight subjects: English and Maths (grades counts as double in the statistic), e-baccalaureate subjects (Science, Computing, Geography, History and Languages) and then a selection from the rest. This not only means that schools need to ensure that all pupils are taught the e-baccalaureate programme, but that the grades from English, Maths and the other subjects under this banner are of critical importance to schools, whereas the rest can be (and often are) side-lined. We have witnessed the sad decline in Drama, for example, since this mode of assessment was introduced. The Attainment 8 scores of all pupils are added up and divided by 10 (because English and Maths scores are doubled) and this gives the average grade. The profile of the pupils' intake matters as there is a 'value added' nature to this assessment, and the expectations of the pupil profiles against the actual results gives a Progress 8 score which goes on to determine where the school is in the league table (and as we are writing this, we are not at all sure whether a school should be treated in the same way as a football team, but here we are).

Reporting Progress to Parents

As teachers, we feel ourselves to be responsible for the pupils' education. As parents, we feel ourselves to be responsible for our children's education. The school becomes a surrogate parent to the pupils, yet also central to education are the actual mum and dad (or just mum, or just dad, or mum and mum, or dad and dad, or carer, or step-mum or grandma – it is complicated, like families). Meeting parents/carers is an important opportunity. It should never be seen as additional to what you do in school, but part of the triangle of support of: pupil-teacher-parent/carer. The partnership with parents/carers is something that Tom Bennett encourages:

> If you say, 'We both want the best for Daniel,' then you tacitly create rapport between you and the parents because it's something they can't disagree with. You do want the best for Daniel, right? (Bennett, 2011: 177–178)

Gaining this rapport is very important, but it must be carefully managed. The problem with this, and with Bennett's general approach, is that the parents might get 'wound-up' by being managed. Imagine that a parent/carer has been summoned to school because their child has been disruptive and you sit there with the following attitude:

- we're right;
- we're kind;
- we're thoughtful;
- we're reasonable;
- we have thought everything through; and
- we know what's best for your child.

What does this mean for the parent/carer? That they are the opposite of this? The teacher can sit behind a desk and speak at parents/carers, or sit beside them, listen and commu-nicate. The one who has the stance that, 'I know best and your child needs to do this' is, we think, not going to get far. Parents/carers do not want to be processed like sausages. Instead, they: 'want to be treated with respect and as equals when communicating with educators' (Graham-Clay, n.d.). We would be furious, as parents, if a teacher came and told us what is right for our children. If a teacher phoned up for advice, or to inform, or to support or to praise, then that would be fine – welcome, in fact.

When meeting with parents face-to-face skilled body language and meaningful content is crucial. To communicate the partnership nature of your relationship, you might try PARENT (Bright Futures, 2019), which gives general advice about meeting parents from experienced practitioners.

- Prepare: make sure you have records about the child and it is a good idea to have photos of the pupils by their names.
- Attainment: let the parent/carer know where their child is in relation to expectations and the class. It would be worth asking the parent/carer how they think their child is doing first.
- Respect: see the parent/carer as an equal.
- Engage: this is about listening as much as talking. Link to the parent/carer and do not launch into a speech. The other person is there in a con (con means 'with') versation.
- Noise level: be aware of the noise and distractions in the room, and try to minimise them so you can have a calm conversation.
- Timing: keep aware of the time you have for each parent/carer and try to stick to it. This is never easy and needs to be balanced between what the parent/carer needs and your schedule. Some parents/carers do not want to hang around too long and have had long, hard days themselves.

To add to PARENT, we would like to add WPGALFF (it will never catch on).

- Welcome.
- Positive body language: open body, nod and mirror. Mirroring is when you copy the pose of the parent/carer. Try it, as it gives an immediate bond if you are sitting in the same way as they are. Of course, if they are waving their fists at you, it does not work.
- 'Good news sandwich': start with the positive, give something negative and give something positive.
- Ask: how are they? How do they think their child is doing? Have they any concerns?
- Listen: to the answers and respond.
- Follow up: this meeting is the start of the links and the conversation. This is an invaluable point of contact to improve the way your pupil can achieve.
- Finish positively: if only to promise more contact.

In the real world of meetings with parents/carers, there is not much time, so we suggest as a quick-list of possible content the following: APEAT (we tried a bit harder with the acronym this time):

- Ask the parent how they think the pupil is doing.
- Progress details.
- Example of successful work.
- Attitude to learning
- Targets and how to achieve them.

You should prepare for how you might deal with different types of parents/carers.

- Deeply engaged: arrange a separate time to meet and discuss concerns privately and when there is more time. Sending home family activities/projects that go with a lesson is also a good way to keep parents/carers involved in student learning. They may not be responded to, but might satisfy them; alternatively, you will have formed a link to support the pupil that is worth its weight in gold.
- Bossy: do not respond in the same manner. You may need to refer them to the Senior Leadership Team (SLT) if they want further action.
- Chatty: best to schedule a meeting by phone or online, as the school policy dictates.
- Concerned you are pushing the child too hard: listen carefully to what the parent/ carer wants and respond. They could be right and they know their child much better than you do.
- Angry: have data available. Remind the parent/carer that you care. Empathy is a valuable teacher trait, not only with the disruptive child but also with their parents/carers. Try the 'look, repeat, acknowledge, understand' method where you engage the eyes, repeat their concern, make an emotional link to the concerns, and show that you realise why they are angry. Then, you can consider further action, which may involve SLT.

The short time you get with a parent/carer is never going to be enough and should only be part of the home communication process, which includes email, apps, website, blog, phone calls, letters, merits, homework book, newsletters and report cards. Try to keep the lines of communication open because you have an ally at home who wants the same outcome as you.

Conclusion

Assessment through pitching and marking comes with experience, which is why you are in schools on a placement. Make sure that you keep learning about your subject and the curriculum, and take as many opportunities as possible to encounter pupils and practise marking. Think about what you can control, which includes your ability to vary AfL and questioning, and the various ways of assessment, including an ipsative approach, and try to understand the factors that are likely to affect attainment, and how to mitigate them.

....**REFLECTION**

Think about what the following statistics from the Office for National Statistics mean for communication with parents/carers:

- Between 68 and 71 per cent of single parents/carers are at work, 9–5 p.m. every day (ONS, 2015).
- Twenty-eight per cent of parents/carers believe that their children's education is mainly or wholly their responsibility (Peters et al., 2007)
- Twenty-two per cent of parents/carers are unable to help children with homework because they don't understand the topic being learnt in class (Goodall and Vorhaus, 2011).

(Continued)

- Eighty-one per cent of parents/carers would welcome support and guidance on how best to support their child's learning at home (Education Scotland, 2018).
- Seventy-nine per cent of children reported that they would like their parents to know more about what they are learning in class so they can provide more support outside the classroom (Education Scotland, 2018).
- Eighty-four per cent of parents/carers reported that their child's school provided them with little or no resources to help support their child's learning at home (Education Scotland, 2018).
- Thirty-eight per cent of parents/carers do not understand their children's school work (Goodall and Vorhaus, 2011).
- Eighty thousand eight hundred and fifty pupils in England are Looked After Children (Gov.UK, 2021), which means that they will not be with their parents but in the care of the local authority, in a foster home, residential children's home, wider family or a secure unit.

Think about how it would feel, as a parent/carer, if you knew a school report had been written by Artificial Intelligence (AI). Is it good that teachers can spend their time on what might seem like more important matters or is the contact with the parent/carer something that should be human and personal? Consider your response, as it might allow you to think about how reports are often generated these days and the scripted nature of some online parents' evenings and what this might do to the pupil–parent/ carer–school partnership.

....

.... **ACTIONS**

- Observe as many lessons as you can and note the way the teacher evaluates the success of a lesson.
- Take part in standardisation and moderation processes to help you gauge the expected levels of work.
- Talk to pupils about the lessons and assessment and keep them informed about what is happening.
- Encourage pupils to self- and peer-assess.
- Assist your mentor in drafting reports to parents/carers.
- Take part in parents' evening.

....

Case Study 9

Arte Artemiou is a Special Education Needs (SEN) teacher in a small, independent, Social and Emotional Mental Health (SEMH) school, which he joined after he completed a Drama Post Graduate Certificate of Education (PGCE) in 2021 as a School Direct trainee. He is responsible for delivering Key Stage 3 Religious Education and enrichment Drama, as well as being a tutor for a Year 7/8 group. Because the school is not set up to run the Early Career Framework (ECF), he still has not completed two Early Career Teacher (ECT) years to get full Qualified Teacher Status (QTS). He is, though, continuing academic study by taking a Master's degree in special educational needs and inclusion, specialising in SEMH and trauma. Here, he presents a (fictional) reflective diary of a typical event at school in which he plays a card game with a pupil who finds it difficult to settle without activity. It shows that 'progress' is relative to the pupil. All names and scenarios are made up; the two diary entries are based on scenarios Arte might typically experience in school and consider not only the wider role of the teacher but also how parental discussions may not always be fruitful.

4 May 2024, evening

I had a breakthrough with James today. I've been keeping a log for the past three weeks on his energy, words, and actions in the morning before lessons during tutor time. He sometimes has low energy and at other times an almost frantic energy. He's become fixated on this card game I showed him last week, so we play this every morning. It's quite an easy way to touch base and see how he's doing. I've begun to make it a habit to ask three main questions: (1) How are you feeling this morning? (2) How did you sleep? and (3) What did you get up to last night? I ask these questions not in rapid succession but over the course of the card games. The three questions help me gauge where James is and how his morning is likely to go. The breakthrough has been this: when James comes into school in an almost frantic state he has probably either watched, listened to, or played something violent the night before. We know that those with SEMH needs will often replay these experiences in the following days through their words or their actions. It may be because his chronological age doesn't match his psychological age and he is struggling to process what he sees and hears, but when we play the card game, he will say things like, 'Kill me!' I keep a log of it as its helped me to find these patterns in his behaviour, and communicate with home what I've been seeing so that we can try to work together and address what he's watching, playing, and listening outside of school. I wish I could say that these conversations with home have been fruitful, but James's parents don't seem to see anything wrong with him engaging with media that is rated as his chronological age, even though I am witnessing what the result of that is.

Playing card games with James has also allowed me to see how he interacts with other students, as sometimes students come from the other groups to join in with us. When it's just James, his Teaching Assistant, and me playing games, James can express himself however he wants, whether he is frantic or not. When another student, Gavin, is in the room, James is visibly vigilant, becoming quieter, noticeably observing Gavin with a slight smile (a sign of awkwardness? Discomfort? Joy at seeing Gavin?) on his face and will either compliment him, or help him out in the card game. I'm not quite sure whether James wants to be Gavin's friend or wants to be like Gavin, but Gavin has an impact on James when he enters the room. Gavin has an impact on everyone when he enters the room in the morning as he is usually 'bouncing off the walls'. I remember a staff member saying to me that often in SEMH schools, staff focus on the emotional and mental health and forget the social. That has stuck with me, and it is now another lens through which I view students' actions and words. They sometimes just want friends and will do inappropriate or out of character things to try to be accepted. This is true of students in mainstream education, but especially true of some in special schools who have been removed from their peers and placed in an essentially isolated context. I've read some articles by researchers who have carried out studies on the feelings of exclusion by those in special schools and I'm convinced that we need to reintegrate special and mainstream schools so that those in mainstream can learn acceptance of diversity and those in special schools can learn to be accepted. I know it's not as simple as that, but I find it saddening that James's only consistent 'friends' at school seem to be myself and his Teaching Assistant. He struggles so much to make friends with the other students because his words and actions can be loud, random, and hard to bear.

12 May 2024, evening

James has been slowly building a friendship with a student named Joshua, but when another student is in the room, Joshua withdraws a little, and even joins in if there is any mocking of James. Students at school haven't yet usually cultivated compassion or filters and so they can say some mean things to James which I have to address. That's difficult, as some of them I haven't built up a relationship with yet, so I'm just going to be the guy that 'has words' with them, even though all I'm doing is trying to make sure James knows he matters to at least one member of staff and that he can rely on me as his tutor to be on his side. One of the students who comes and plays cards, David, came in the other day and said, sarcastically, 'I can smell the magnetism', referring to James and Joshua playing cards together. David tends to say quite mean things in the mornings when he hasn't taken his medication. I have the same mental diagnosis as David and we've had conversations about our condition before, so I feel able to pull him up on this. I've recently been trying to explain to David that although he is feeling a certain way, he doesn't have to be mean to others. Today he stayed after the other two had left to go to the dining hall and I was able to speak to him privately. He said that he wasn't going to be quiet in the mornings and I said that's not what I was asking. I repeated that we didn't need to be mean even if we were 'bouncing off the walls'. He seemed to accept this, but I know he'll forget it tomorrow. 'Incremental steps' are the only way to go here.

............................WHAT TOOLS ARE IN YOUR TOOKIT NOW?

- Reasons for assessment.
- Strategies for AfL.
- Ways of creating a dialogic classroom.
- The vocabulary of assessment: ipsative, 'value added', criterion-referenced and norm-referenced.
- Ways of communicating with parents/carers effectively.

Places to Get More Tools for Your Toolkit

Morgan, N. (2016) *Engaging Families in Schools: Practical Strategies to Improve Parental Involvement*. London: Routledge.

As the title informs, this book has practical steps to bring families into the life of the schools, some of it on an institutional basis, but plenty that involves the classroom teacher and comes with an impassioned plea for the benefits of parental/carer involvement.

Whitaker, T. and Fiore, D. (2016) *Dealing with Difficult Parents*. London: Routledge.

It is not all positive out there and some parents/carers will want to be in contact with the school, sometimes reasonably, sometimes unreasonably. This book gives advice on how these situations can be managed.

References

Alexander, R. (2017) *Towards Dialogic Teaching: Rethinking Classroom Talk*. Thirsk: Dialogos.

AQA (2019) *Grade Boundaries – June 2019 Exams*. Available from: https://filestore.aqa.org.uk/over/stat_pdf/AQA-GCSE-GDE-BDY-JUN-2019.PDF

Bennett, T. (2011) *Not Quite a Teacher*. London: Continuum.

Bright Futures (2019) *Parents' Evening*. Available from: www.allianceforlearning.co.uk/blog-parents-evening/

Broadfoot, P., Dougherty, R., Gardner, J, Harlen, W., James, M. and Stobart, G. (2002) *Assessment for Learning: 10 Principles*. Available from: www.stir.ac.uk/research/hub/publication/640252

Cowley, S. (2011) *Getting the Buggers to Write*. London: Bloomsbury.

Dabell, J. (2018) *Educational Super-fad: Assessing Pupil Progress*. Available from: www.teacher toolkit.co.uk/2018/04/22/educational-fad-2/

Education Scotland (2018) *Review of Learning at Home*. Available from: www.education.gov. scot/media/zk2mbwlt/par19-learning-at-home.pdf

Gershon, M. (n.d.) *AfL Toolkit*. Available from: www.tes.com/teaching-resource/assessingpupils-progress-app-in-english-6089433

Goodall, J. and Vorhaus, J. (2011) *Review of Best Practice in Parental Engagement*. Available from: www.assets.publishing.service.gov.uk/government/uploads/system/uploads/attachment_data/file/182508/DFE-RR156.pdf

Gov.UK (2015) *Final Report of the Commission on Assessment without Levels*. Available from: www.assets.publishing.service.gov.uk/government/uploads/system/uploads/attachment_data/file/483058/Commission_on_Assessment_Without_Levels_-_report.pdf

Gov.UK (2021) *Children Looked after in England Including Adoptions*. Available from: https://explore-education-statistics.service.gov.uk/find-statistics/children-looked-after-in-england-including-adoptions/2021

Graham-Clay, S. (n.d.) *Communicating with Parents: Strategies for Teachers*. Available from: www.adi.org/journal/ss05/graham-clay.pdf

Kellogg, R. (2008) Training writing skills: A cognitive developmental perspective, *Journal of Writing Research* 1(1): 1-26.

Kohn, A. (1994) Grading: The issue is not how but why. *Educational Leadership*, October, 1994.

McCormick Calkins, L. (1989) *The Art of Teaching Writing*. London: Heinemann.

ONS (2015) *Families and Households in the UK: 2015*. Available from: www.ons.gov.uk/peoplepopulationandcommunity/birthsdeathsandmarriages/families/bulletins/families andhouseholds/2015-11-05

Peters, M., Seeds, K., Goldstein, A. and Coleman, N. (2007) *Parental Involvement in Children's Education*. Available from: https://dera.ioe.ac.uk/8605/1/DCSF-RR034.pdf

QCDA (2010) *Assessing Pupils' Progress: Learners at the Heart of Assessment*. Available from: www.dera.ioe.ac.uk/10945/7/Assess_pupils_progress_webo_Redacted.pdf

Voice21 (2024) www.voice21.org/

Wright, T. (2009) *How to Be a Brilliant Teacher*. Abingdon: Routledge.

Wilkinson, A. (1970) The concept of Oracy, *English Journal* 59(1): 71-77.

10

The Complex Nature of Learning

What this chapter will cover

- Key Stages Two and Five
- Learning development

Introduction

In this chapter, we want to delve further into the idea of learning development. We examine the way it is currently often viewed as a movement upwards of a number, and the reasons that this view has come about. We also examine learning as something natural in children and adults and consider how trainee teachers might harness this need to their advantage. We stress the need for variety, emotional intelligence and for children to have fun while they learn. We start, though, with a warning about the required level of subject knowledge in secondary school. You need to understand what the wider curriculum expectations are beyond Key Stages 3 and 4, and to make sure that age-level learning can occur in your lessons.

Key Stages Two and Five

On a secondary teacher training course, you will be teaching Key Stage 3 and Key Stage 4. Your training course should also incorporate primary experience, which is Key Stages 1 and 2, and sixth form, which is Key Stage 5. Key Stages are age groups with Key Stage 3 being 11–14 years old and Key Stage 4 being 14–16 years old. There is a point, you notice, when they overlap and many schools move the curriculum onto GCSE teaching in Year 9 or even earlier. Sometimes, our trainee teachers create lesson plans for topics of learning that ought to have been covered in Key Stage 2. It is worthwhile checking the national (or local) curriculum for your subject at the levels below Key Stage 3; you will probably see that the expectations of your subject there are seem to be quite high. You can revise Key Stage 2 topics, of course, or develop them, but pick on a Key Stage topic of your own size when choosing what subjects to devote most lesson time to. We also think that you should, during your training course, experience your subject at Key Stage 5, whether this is at Advanced Level or a technical qualification. Positioning the Key Stages you teach within the earlier and later Key Stages will be invaluable to you.

Learning Development

The German author Johann von Goethe (1749–1832) once wrote: 'No-one is more enslaved than the man who believes himself to be free' (1994: 151) and paraphrasing Karl Marx, Zygmunt Bauman said that people are 'not under conditions of their choice' (Bauman, 2000). Conditions are the circumstances in which we work; teaching has, in the last few decades, had its conditions changed as it has been affected by the powerful social and economic force called neoliberalism. Neoliberalism is the New Liberal system that has dominated Western economies since the 1980s. Liberalism was the recommendation of economist and philosopher Adam Smith (1723–90), regarding a system that would benefit everyone. From observations of economies across Europe, Smith concluded that if individuals were given the freedom to pursue profit, it would benefit all:

> As every individual, therefore, endeavours as much as he can both to employ his capital in the support of domestic industry . . . He generally, indeed, neither intends to promote the public interest, nor knows how much he is promoting it. (Smith, 1827: 184)

Self-interest produces public good, in other words. Today, this system has been hypercharged to become neoliberalism where: 'What is private is necessarily good and what is public is necessarily bad' (Apple, 2004: 59). This is not good news for teachers, who tend to be employed in the public sector (no matter how much the government tries to move this sector to market economics). A neoliberalist way of thinking includes suspicion of those who act in the interest of others, as if they are hiding something or are not able to survive in the cut-and-thrust of the real world. Perhaps because of this suspicion of the idea of working for the good of others, neoliberalism has brought measures to monitor and control public sector workers. Teachers are increasingly monitored by data and their success is measured against whether their targets have been achieved.

A key feature of neoliberalism is the way employees are managed by individualised targets. At some point in the 20th century, much of the responsibility for learning moved from the pupils to the teacher. Perryman and Calvert's study (2019: 2) linked this high-stakes accountability to excessive burnout and teacher turnover, arguing that their participants expressed:

> a discourse of disappointment, the reality of teaching being worse than expected, and the nature (rather than the quantity) of the workload, linked to notions of performativity and accountability, being a crucial factor.

This idea that teachers were given scripts for how to perform, and monitored while they did it was addressed in the essay 'The teacher's soul and the terrors of performativity' by Stephen Ball. The title gives a clue to his views on the system, as does his 2016 paper, 'Neoliberal education, confronting the slouching beast'. For Ball:

> Teachers are no longer encouraged to have a rationale for practice, account of themselves in terms of a relationship to the meaningfulness of what they do, but are required to produce measurable and 'improving' outputs and performances; what is important is what works. (2003: 222)

Teachers are increasingly controlled by being instructed in fixed ways of working and monitored by a reward and sanction system. This is what is known as 'performativity' which

> requires individual practitioners to organize themselves as a response to targets, indicators and evaluations. To set aside personal beliefs and commitments and live an existence of calculation. The new performative worker is a promiscuous self, an enterprising self, with a passion for excellence. (Ball, 2010: 215)

Ball was addressing the way that progress is frequently based on numbers, so everything in schools is datafied – given a number and a target to achieve. The school has its Attainment 8 and Progress 8 scores to improve, and teachers are pressurised to ensure that certain grades are achieved by pupils. There is incentive from 'responsibility points' which are numbered

+1, +2 and so on for those who take on curriculum tasks such as Subject Lead. Performance-related pay allows progress up the pay-scale and is given to those who achieve their numbers, which incentivises compliance and goals.

All of this data can obscure a central point of school – it is where children go to learn. Education can be for education's sake; it is the same as 'art for art's sake', done for its own pleasure and rewards. Education does not have to 'do' anything; it is a natural aspect of being human. Concern that this natural disposition gets taken over by curriculum and progress are a concern can be traced back to Jean-Jacques Rousseau's (1712–1778) concerns for the 'freethinking child' being sent to school to learn by rote (being taught solely through instruction and memorisation). Over 100 years later, John Dewey (who worked alongside his less publicised daughter, Evelyn) critiqued explicit teaching:

> I believe that much of present education fails because. . .it conceives the school as a place where certain information is to be given, where certain lessons are to be learned, or where certain habits are to be formed. The value of these is conceived as lying largely in the remote future; the child must do these things for the sake of something else he is to do; they are mere preparation. As a result they do not become a part of the life experience of the child and so are not truly educative. (Dewey, 1897)

Step forward 30 years from the Deweys, and Maria Montessori (1870–1952) is writing on the same topic:

> Like a sponge these children absorb. It is marvellous, this mental power of the child. Only we cannot teach directly. It is necessary that the child teach himself, and then the success is great. (Montessori, 1964: 11)

Step forward 50 years from Maria Montessori, and John Holt was another voice in what he saw as the wilderness of the mainstream education system:

> Nobody starts off stupid. . .what happens , as we get older, to this extraordinary capacity for learning and intellectual growth? What happens is that it is destroyed. . .We destroy this capacity above all by making afraid, afraid of being wrong. . .afraid to gamble, afraid to experiment, afraid to try the difficult and the unknown. . .We destroy the. . .love of learning in children. . .by encouraging and compelling them to work for petty and contemptible rewards – gold stars or papers marked 100 and tacked to the wall or As in report cards. . .We encourage them to feel that the end and aim of all they do in school is nothing more than to get a good mark on a test. (Holt, 1990: 273–274)

Ken Robinson wrote similarly in the 2000s, Frank Furedi similarly in the 2010s: when school becomes a place dominated by the one-way transmission of knowledge, this can actually have a detrimental effect on learning, damaging the love of learning which is inherent in every child. A natural love of learning is replaced by what Dewey and Dewey (1915) called: 'a meaningless reflecting back of symbols with no understanding of the facts themselves' in tests and examinations. Rousseau was writing from a French perspective, Dewey and Holt American, Montessori Italian, Robinson British, and Furedi Canadian, so the concerns for education are not exclusive to one country or continent. Brazilian thinker Paolo Freire, called the nature of schooling 'oppression', when a forced curriculum is forced on children and a 'banking' system of deposits of knowledge put in place, as if learning is something that just gets delivered to pupils.

Most schools and teachers know that learning is more complex than a banking system. Teachers respond in individual creative ways to engender a love of learning their subject. While neither teacher, nor trainee teacher, can alter the system, practices can be put in place which focus on the natural desire of all humans, and especially children, to learn. These three recommendations are an adaptation of the ideas of Freire:

- Harness the passion they have for what they care about and move it to your subject.
- Give pupils a reason to learn, beyond an exam. A 12-year old is unlikely to be worrying about the weekend activities, let alone something that may happen in over three years' time. The immediate concerns of the day - pleasures, worries, next activities and possible actions - will be far more dominant than an exam which, anyway, may not be necessary anyway for the superstar trajectory they might have in mind.
- Be open to a classroom in which everyone learns from each other. You are not the only holder of knowledge, skills and understanding. Celebrate what each child brings.

Fun is not a compulsory factor in lessons and, for some, it is seen as a distraction from the business of cognitive development. But we are fans of it, and there is research which supports it (though to be honest, there is research that supports everything) including Ma (1997) who concluded that pupils' success in subjects was directly related to whether they considered the subject enjoyable. One thing we know is that a teacher droning on about a topic of no relation to their lives is about as welcome to teenagers as a frank and full talk about reproduction with their parents. We would go one step further than Freire who complained that: 'the teacher talks, and the students listen - meekly' (Freire, 2000: 54) because some of the time we are not even sure if they are listening. We sometimes observe underwhelming lessons tasked with a form we should be filling in ... and even we are drifting off. You are not the only source of learning in the room because pupils can learn from each other. Here, it is traditional to give a respectful 'nod' to Lev Vygotsky (1978) who stated that in order to learn more pupils must move into the Zone of Proximal Development - i.e. to have enough knowledge to be able to develop a step more. The person who can move them to the next stage of learning he called a More Knowledgeable Other (probably sounded better in Russian) and this can be another pupil, rather than you. Pairing or grouping pupils where one knows more than another can be done through a traffic light system - ask the class about their level of understanding of a topic; some might be green (strong) and others red (weak), and red and green - then 'buddy up'. You might use your seating plan to make sure that one person with a more advanced understanding in the class sits next to one who does not and then one pupil can support another. If you add an 'ask three before me' policy into your lesson, the pupils will not always see you as the 'holder of the knowledge' and they will learn to rely more on each other. There are many ways of grouping – pairs, threes, fours (five, in our experience results in the fifth person testing their chair's ability to stand upright on two legs, so is perhaps too many). The group can be given roles. A triad of pupils might have one pupil as speaker, another as the recorder of the speaker's ideas and a third as an envoy transmitting them to others. You could jigsaw the groups by giving groups of four pupils a number each and a separate aspect of the topic to discuss. You then move pupils onto mixed tables of all four numbers and each pupil gives the perspective of their first group to the rest.

You can also try working on the strengths of the pupils rather than addressing weaknesses. There are interesting studies into appreciative inquiry (such as Kadi-Hanifi et al., 2013) which poses the idea that if we move away from a deficit culture – where we are constantly finding the weaknesses and trying to fix them – everyone will be better off. This turns learning around from: 'I am good at A and not good at B so let's concentrate on B' to 'I am good at A but not good at B so let's concentrate on A'. Focus on what the pupil is good at, goes the theory, and they will learn that they can do it. B will come later but not until the pupil has enough self-belief to move to it.

One issue with the above methods of trying to engage pupils is that we still seem to be prioritising ways of getting prescribed curriculum knowledge into children. Perhaps instead we should try prioritising development of the happiness of the pupils or move to a more northern European concept of Bildung: 'the promotion of liberty and human dignity' (Prange, 2004: 502). Perhaps we can try to develop the pupils' 'inner-life of the human soul, mind and humanity' (Biesta, 2002: 378), or even try to change the world – 'teaching to transgress', along with the great bell hooks (1994). The educational thinker Dave Trotman has observed that when he cites these authors and ideas and advocates looking at learning and children holistically he often gets this sort of reply: 'Yes, this is lovely Dave. It's all very middle class, isn't it? People knocking around, pontificating. It's all lovely, lovely, lovely' (2020: 401). This kind of theory can be seen as coming from a privileged position from which the idealist stands by, decrying a state education system that in fact gives everyone, regardless of their background, a chance to achieve. Yet, at the same time, and equally, we should attend to the voices of those who believe that the school system takes a naturally learning human being and places them in a building where teachers impose forced topics at forced times, preventing rather than aiding learning.

There are many approaches to learning, and theories of learning offer a new 'tool in the toolkit', as does understanding of the 'isms': **behaviourism**, cognitivism and **humanism**. Each is a belief system about people. Behaviourism states that through external control by rewards and punishments and modelling, 'good' behaviour and learning become a norm in the classroom. Cognitivism/constructivism states that the human organises knowledge and that this organisation is reinforced by memorisation which changes the pupil's brain structure and gives new ways of thinking and understanding of the world. Humanism states that everyone creates their own sense of who they are and what the world is like. There is no one ideal way of doing this, so a pupil is free to develop at their own pace and to form their understanding of what things mean. Creativity and individualism are central to the process of becoming human. We cannot be, simultaneously, both manipulable non-beings (behaviourism) and individualised developers of the self (humanism) but each 'ism' has strengths in attempting to understand different facets of learning: humans can be controlled by the environment; learning is developed in stages; we strive to create and express our individuality.

Another 'ism' is elitism – the idea that some are inherently more academically able than others. Innate intelligence is an idea which never quite dies down, emerging over the years as a founding reason for grammar schools, Intelligence Quotient tests, the **Gifted and Talented** schemes, and remaining today in the phrases 'low ability' and 'high ability'. While we know that the genes carry some parts of a human's make-up and no one is born with a 'blank slate' brain (Pinker, 2003), the idea that some are more capable of learning than others is brought into question by every pupil who is a super-achiever until the age of 14 and who dive-bombs thereafter, and also by the child who does the reverse. Capacity to learn is not a fixed state and in our years in schools we have found no reason to believe that some children have it and others have not. Hans Eysenck, who was a firm believer in genetic intelligence and who until his death was the most cited living academic author, stands as a warning against both thinking intelligence is genetic and believing that a theory must be true if it is widely cited. His Intelligence Quotient (IQ) was a measure of brain power that purported to classify such individuals and he came to believe that some racial groups were less intelligent that others – his own, of course, being the most intelligent. In a fascinating account of interaction with Eysenck, Andrew Colman documented the change in a man who started out questioning his idea and ended with certainty:

> What starts out as a 'not unreasonable hypothesis', cautiously advanced by a writer who does not claim to know all the answers, is progressively transmogrified into a simple 'fact' of 'genetic inferiority' backed up by 'all the evidence to date'. (2016: 12)

Eysenck's certainty about a system that is widely suspect – as, apart from anything, you could improve your IQ score – should warn us all about theory. No matter how convincingly the argument is presented, or how widely quoted the author, it is always to be questioned.

In this section, we have discussed the terror of being managed in a neoliberal system through data. Matthew Clarke's study of Australian teachers 'Terror/enjoyment: performativity, resistance and the teacher's psyche' (Clarke, 2013) suggested that for all the 'terror' that Stephen Ball proposed, there can also be an enjoyment of the performance. Michel Foucault's understanding of people as game-players of all discourses is one that we can find comfort in – there is a knowingness in the performativity of the times, and a pleasure in both compliance and resistance. Schools often act against the ruling ideology, despite pressures from above. Faith schools are the most obvious places for resistance because the messages of capitalism and neoliberalism are counter to the 'we-culture' that religions and seekers of spirituality promote. Steiner schools, for example, are a world away from an ideology that promotes the acquisition of grades and goods:

> We should think: I must certainly do everything for the culture of soul and spirit but I will wait tranquilly until, by higher powers, I shall be found worthy of definite illumination. (Steiner, 1910)

Some Sikh schools have a period of kirtan or spiritual singing included in their day for a time of quiet reflection on life and God/Waheguru. Faith schools are not the only places where capitalism and neoliberalism can be tempered. All good schools have an ethos or a moral underpinning, shared by the management and teaching staff, guiding pupil attitudes and behaviour, and are run on an ethic of kindness and service, to make a positive difference in the world.

Graham Nuthall gave a very interesting speech reviewing his 50-year educational career in 2001 in which he described how he had moved from a researcher intending to perfect the process of teaching to one who understood more about the complexity of school life and learning. His early studies of lessons came to the stunning (at the time, and it still has some power to surprise) conclusion:

> there were no discernible differences between the experienced teachers and the beginning teachers in what they did or what their students learned. Being an experienced expert teacher apparently made no difference. (Nuthall, 2001)

In other words, you – as a trainee teacher – can teach as good a lesson as anyone experienced, partly because a lesson is often a performance in which the script has been written anyway. Nuthall (and his collaborators including Adrienne Alton-Lee) then set out to work out which of the routinised actions produced the best results, including what kinds of exchanges in the classroom. This was done in order to prescribe a script for teachers to use in lessons, based on what works best. But, Nuthall being a wise person, stopped himself:

> I began to realize that the end product of this kind of research would be an enormous list of experimentally validated dos and don'ts. If teachers could digest such a long list, it would turn them into robots. I realized I was following a path that satisfied the cultural rituals of the research community, but would be of little value, and probable harm, to teachers. (Nuthall, 2001)

This is an important stopping point, as giving teachers a list of what they have to do, and when, would result in identical lessons and teachers feeling devalued in their profession. He recalled how he and Alton-Lee observed that lessons were far more than the transmission of knowledge from teacher to pupil:

We...began to realize that students live in a personal and social world of their own in the classroom. They whisper to each other and pass notes. They spread rumours about girlfriends and boyfriends, they organize their after-school social life, continue arguments that started in the playground. They care more about how their peers evaluate their behaviour than they care about the teacher's judgement. (Nuthall, 2001)

The life of the classroom goes beyond the official content offered by the teacher and the classroom group exists as a separate entity; pupils make their own pleasure, learn what they want from each other (who likes whom, football facts, what someone's parents said last night, etc.). They also care about each other, more than they do the teacher. In terms of lesson content, Nuthall argued: 'What matters is the sense the student is making of the experience'. Here, we come across a 'thorny' problem for those who simply want to transmit knowledge into children: we are all different and we process information in unique ways. Nuthall (2001) posed the idea that some pupils are more equipped to learn than others because of their lives outside of school:

> those students whose backgrounds provide them with the cultural knowledge and skills to use the classroom and its activities for their own purposes, learn more than those who dutifully do what they are told but do not want, or know how, to create their own opportunities.

Nuthall (2001) concluded his review of his lifelong quest to understand teaching and learning with a final flourish:

> Knowledge is more like a continuous landscape rather than a set of discrete countable objects. It cannot be sensibly represented by numbers.

It cannot be sensibly represented by numbers, we agree – but it is. Numbers can also inform us about what the Initial Teacher Training and Early Career Framework (ITTECF) is most focused on: 61 mentions of 'knowledge'; 17 mentions of 'progress'; one mention of 'pedagogy'; and no mention of 'creativity'. It is up to you, the trainee teacher - to fill in the gaps of the curriculum you are presented with if it does not recognise learning in all of its wonderful complexity.

Conclusion

As an aspiring teacher, you are in the business of learning, so you should read all you can about it. Everything you read can give you more insights into what makes successful teaching. The founder of the counselling approach Cognitive Behavioural Therapy, Aaron Beck (1975), hit back at critics who stated that it does not solve mental illness – 'what can it cure?' – with, 'what can't it help?' We would argue the same - there is no 'Holy Grail' unifying learning theory that instructs all teachers in how they must act, and it is more fruitful to empower new teachers to explore and reflect on the nature of learning and teaching in different ways. There is even a danger with 'what works' approaches – in which a certain style of learning is seen to be preferable and all teachers must copy it – because they can result in pupils receiving 'identikit' lessons four, five, six, seven or even eight times a day and getting bored.

....**REFLECTION**

Think of the last time you learnt something from somebody else in a formal lesson or lecture. What triggered the desire to want to know? What was new about the learning? What did it do to your mind and how did you assimilate or accommodate it into your mind? What did the teacher do to help you to learn? Think back from the learning point and consider how the teacher worked from getting your attention, through to teaching you something new, and then helping to make sense of it in your life. Intentioned teaching can cause learning to happen, but it does not automatically follow.

....

.... **ACTIONS**

- Read the work of those who have gone before you. You would not try to fix a leaking tap without consulting someone, so why attempt the far more difficult task of engaging and teaching 30 or more teenagers without doing the same?
- Look out for inspiring practitioners in your school and seek to emulate what they do – how are they encouraging creativity, dialogue, fun and engagement?

....

Case Study 10

Sam McDonough was a stand-out trainee teacher because he managed to 'be himself' in the classroom. This normally takes time, but Sam quickly learnt that if he could form positive relations with the pupils while remaining the main centre of control in a lesson he could survive the challenging classes he had while training. With a mixture of calm control and a dry sense of humour, Sam treated each lesson as interaction with the pupils and picked up conversations and threads of interests while bringing each lesson back to its central point. Sam gained employment as a teacher straight after his training year of 2017–2018 and stayed at the same mixed-sex academy, completing his first two years in a school successfully and therefore gaining full Qualified Teacher Status (QTS). In 2024, he made his first move to a single sex state school, picking up a whole school responsibility for the first time. Here, he recounts his style of teaching.

> I think what is fundamental to successful lessons is relationships. They can be formed with something as minor as the posters in a room. I have posters of Maradona, Marvin Gaye, and George Best, which are nothing to do with the lesson but are fundamental in building rapport with some pupils as they always ask who they are and why they are there. I will bore them by telling them about a gig I went to

at the weekend and stop lessons so they have to listen. If you are going to take pupils anywhere, I think, they have to 'buy into' you. This is not to advocate basing your teaching life solely on charisma and certainly not ego, but a giving of parts of yourself to the class. My Year 11 in their closing lesson ran a quiz on me, because I had bled into the lessons my dislikes and enthusiasms. I think you have to trust them with parts of who you are; they do want to invest in you. I also think that you should not hide your character too much. I am very sarcastic and ironic and have a deadpan sense of humour and while I am careful with individuals, I can direct this at the whole class or topics in the lesson and it adds a perspective on it. I get to know the pupils who enjoy irony and am willing to 'take back' the sarcasm from them.

I also invest in them and try to find what I think of as an 'easy win' with difficult to reach pupils, by learning what they are interested in and including it in the lesson. It might be that they are interested in music or football or something that I can link my own interests to, but it has to be genuine. They would know, for example, if I tried to fake an interest in cinema. It is fundamental to know names and do so quickly but also to learn about their characters. One skill goes with another because if you listen to what they like, the names tend to get attached to this and it becomes easier. Mention of their interests in the lesson brings them 'on board' and engages so I move lesson content to their lives and worlds. It helps me to focus on diversity and making sure the texts I use are relevant to the students now. It does not take much to listen to what they want to talk about and move the lesson towards this.

I praise effort and application above achievement and celebrate successes beyond the examinations and tests by asking them what they had been doing outside of school and the lesson. Some pupils I teach have trouble at home but they come into school and I ask about their lives and achievements – perhaps about a game they are playing – and that gets the relationship right from the start. With my Year 11 class, I have just received some thank you cards and very often the pupils have written that I made them enjoy the subject. I think, perhaps, they enjoy the lessons because they are not all about numbers and progress but include space and time to listen to what they enjoy. You have to let lessons breathe and not be too concerned merely about curriculum coverage because lessons are an interaction not a function.

I want the pupils to leave the room looking forward to the next lesson. I never end a lesson with a sanction or any form of negativity and I certainly never start the lesson with any. I always tell them what they are going to be doing in the next lesson and that it will be the best lesson ever, and sometimes the class groan in unison and say that I always say that, but If I can be passionate about what I am teaching, they can be passionate about it. It is certainly the case that the reverse is true as if I did not care for my lesson, why should they? There is pressure of results, exams, data, and you want them to do well, but it is better to instil scholarship in them and a love of learning. I want them to learn about the subject when they have left school and, hopefully, one day, look back and see the origin of their passion in the classroom.

- Greater understanding of what 'progress' means in schools.
- Greater understanding of the system in which education operates.

....

Places to Get More Tools for Your Toolkit

Freire, P. (1970) *Pedagogy of the Oppressed.* New York: Herder and Herder.

Old-style pedagogy by a thinker from another age, which still resonates with teachers today who want to think about what learning really is.

Holt, J. (1967) *How Children Learn.* London: Penguin.

American commentator whose pedagogy was a voice for a more free education system. It didn't quite happen this way, but that does not mean it should not have done and perhaps one day it will.

hooks, b. (1994) *Teaching to Transgress.* London: Routledge.

Radical in the best possible way, bell hooks, from their lower case and non-gendered name onwards, reminds us of the need to think about gender, race and the forces that can dominate education.

References

Apple, M. (2004) *Ideology and Curriculum* (3rd edn). London: Routledge.

Ball, S. (2010) The teacher's soul and the terrors of performativity, *Journal of Education Policy* 18(2): 215–228.

Bauman, Z. (2000) *Liquid Modernity.* Cambridge: Polity Press.

Beck, A. (1975) *Cognitive Therapy and the Emotional Disorders.* Madison, CT: International Universities Press.

Biesta, G. (2002) Bildung and modernity: The future of bildung in a world of difference, *Studies in Philosophy and Education* 21: 343–351.

Colman, A. (2016) Race Differences in IQ: Hans Eysenck's contribution to the debate in the light of subsequent research, *Personality and Individual Differences* 103: 182–189.

Clarke, M. (2013) Terror/enjoyment: Performativity, resistance and the teacher's psyche. *London Review of Education*, 11(3): 229–238.

Calvert, G. (2019) What motivates people to teach, and why do they leave? Accountability, performativity and teacher retention. *British Journal of Educational Studies*, 68(1): 3–23.

Dewey, J. (1897) My pedagogic creed. *School Journal* 54. Available from: www.dewey.pragmatism.org/creed.htm-:~:text=I believe that much of,habits are to be formed

Dewey, J. and Dewey, E. (1915) *Schools of To-morrow.* Available from: www.gutenberg.org/files/48906/48906-h/48906-h.htm

Freire, P. (2000) *Pedagogy of the Oppressed.* London: Continuum.

Von Goethe, J. W. (1994) *Elective Affinities.* Oxford: Oxford University Press.

Holt, J. (1990) *How Children Fail.* London: Penguin.

hooks, b. (1994) *Teaching to Transgress*. London: Routledge.

Kadi-Hanifi, K. Dagman, O., Peters, J. Snell, E. and Wright, T. (2013) Engaging students and staff with educational development through Appreciative Inquiry, *Innovations in Education and Training International* 51(6): 584-594.

Ma, X. (1997) Reciprocal relationships between attitude towards mathematics and achievement in mathematics, *Journal of Educational Research* 90: 221-229.

Montessori, M. (1964) *Reconstruction in Education*. Madras: Theosophical Publishing House.

Nuthall, G. (2001) *The Jean Herbison Lecture: The Cultural Myths and the Realities of Teaching and Learning*. Available from: www.nzare.org.nz/assets/Uploads/Award-Citations-/Herbison-Lecture-/graham_nuthall_herbison2001.pdf

Pinker, S. (2003) *The Blank Slate: The Modern Denial of Human Nature*. London: Penguin.

Prange, K. (2004) Bildung: A Paradigm regained? *European Educational Research Journal*, 3(2): 501-509.

Smith, A. (1827) *The Wealth of Nations*. London: Thomas Nelson and Son.

Steiner, R. (1910) *The Way of Initiation*. Available from: www.gutenberg.org/files/39986/39986-h/39986-h.htm

Trotman, D. (2020) *Selected Papers on Education*. Birmingham: The Education Studies Press.

Vygotsky, L. S. (1978) *Mind in Society: The Development of the Higher Psychological Processes*. Cambridge: Harvard University Press.

11

Creating Your Professional Identity

What this chapter will cover

- Pedagogy
- The reflective trainee teacher

Introduction

This chapter aims to help you to future-think and future-proof. It examines the nature of being a teacher, including the mediated impression many people have of the job. It advises about the cultural and legal expectations of those in the profession. With practical advice about maintaining a career, there are details on progression and promotion and roles in schools as well as related career routes people take beyond teaching. The professional knowledge needed to be a working teacher who can adapt to changes in school, policy and role will be explored.

Pedagogy

Shakespeare wrote: 'To thine own self be true'. (*Hamlet*, Act 1, Scene 3). And at the entrance to the ancient temple of Delphi (Wilkins, 1917) this command was apparently inscribed: 'Know thyself'.

Despite being separated by centuries, the two go together well. They suggest that self-discovery is a worthwhile human endeavour but one which has to be worked at. We think that it is important that trainee teachers work out who they think they are, in order to navigate a placement. What is the fundamental pedagogical drive behind your decision to teach? It may be one of these.

- Altruistic – I want to help others.
- Vocational – I want to make sure all children achieve good results and go on to purposeful jobs; I want to address the needs of children who, like me, struggled at school.
- Love of the subject – to pass on the passion for a subject which sustained them through their school and university lives.

Personal pedagogy (what you think learning and teaching is for) is so central in teaching that the first question we ask those who want to train to be a teacher is: 'Why do you want to be a teacher?' Of course, it is a leading question because it presumes the person sitting in front of us actually does want to go into the profession. We have had a trainee teacher, in the middle of a university teaching session muse out loud: 'You know, I don't think I want to be a teacher'. One of us had a trainee teacher who, in the first week on placement asked his mentor: 'Can I pass this course without doing any teaching?' Understandably, neither trainee teacher walked away with Qualified Teacher Status (QTS). What is often missing from the answers of those who do want to teach is the satisfaction of self which teaching gives:

- Self-fulfilment – I want a sense of life purpose in my career.

What other job gives you the type of good stress that challenges you every hour of every day to make a difference in the lives of others? What other career gives such variety in a typical day? No two days are the same and your stories will build up about this pupil, this teacher, this meeting and this event. The scars will build up too, but they become medals of achievement as you went through it and came out the other side. One of our trainee teachers gave this as a reason for wanting to teach: 'Because I love the buzz'. It was a memorable response, and rare, as it recognises that there is an awful lot of fun to be had in the school building and that there are selfish reasons for wanting to be in there and take part in it. A milder and more common response linked to this idea is the pleasure when a pupil has a 'light bulb moment'. Here, there is recognition of the self-satisfaction of a job well done because a child has been helped to understand something they could not understand on their own.

The Reflective Trainee Teacher

The English language is a living, breathing system of communication that can forever contain new words because it reuses parts of old ones. The bound morpheme (part of a word that has meaning but cannot be used on its own) 're' is found in 'repeat' and 'recycle' and, if you ever had to revise to resit or re-take an exam, there too. The following words - 'reflection', **'refraction'** and 'reflexivity - all mean that something happens again. This is an important pausing point because to do them, you must make an active leap with your mind to change the way of thinking previously employed. Jenny Moon (2004) is a guru of reflective thought who advises us to rethink, reconstruct, and repurpose our thoughts and feelings about events. Reflection does not have to improve us, or your practice, and you do not have to 'go forward'. Instead, it is a cognitive act - a point when you actively change your way of thinking, and think again. Much, in the same way, as the young Dick Whittington who, on running away from London heard a voice saying: 'Turn again,' a voice in your head should say: 'Think again." If we are open and able to think of alternatives to our current way of thinking, that is the end product of reflection. Reflection is, 'the component of emotional intelligence that frees us from being a prisoner of our own feelings' (Goleman, 1996: 57). It does this because it enables us to experience an event that may have troubled us from different perspectives and offers up new ways of feeling and thinking. It gives us a valuable lesson that our thoughts and feelings are only one way of viewing a situation and we do not have to be trapped by them.

There are many useful models of reflection, including Kolb's (1984) cycle of reflection: from experience to reflection to trying something new, to new experience and round again. Tripp's (1993) work on critical incidents (events that make us rethink our practice) helps the trainee teacher to understand that we change according to key moments in our lives. Brookfield's (1995) model offers 'four lenses of the teacher' through which we can view a situation, and think again:

- Self: consider alternative ways of thinking about an event.
- Peer: ask others what they think about how you responded to an event.
- Expert: read the work of others who have experienced teaching and consider their advice.
- Theory: read the theory of psychology and sociology in order to understand how humans act and respond.

Brookfield (1995) gave many reasons to reflect, including the need to 'ground yourself'. This is a good way of seeing a purpose of reflection – it brings us, including our emotional state, to a level of balance that means we can start afresh in the classroom each day. Although there are lots of models of reflection, we feel that the market is ready for one more – CASP. It is just another model of reflection and probably not even the best, but here goes. Imagine that you have experienced a disturbing incident in a school:

1. Circumstance – where were you, when was it and what else was going on for you and others involved? Ask yourself, or those affected, what happened before, during and after the event.
2. Ask – others (friends, family, fellow trainee teachers and mentor) about how they think and feel about the event, and ask for honesty. If your event concerns a pupil, why not ask them, if appropriate, what they thought about the event?
3. Self-analyse – try to see whether there is something in your past that may have made you react, think and feel this way. Go over the event and the people it involved and think about whether there was anything that might have triggered an old memory or reminded you of something.
4. Pattern – think about whether this event or these feelings are recurring. Remember when you have acted, felt and thought like this before.

The process of reflection is not to come to other conclusions, but to allow the possibility of other conclusions. Importantly, you do not have to change yourself, and do not have to agree with any other viewpoints. This process opens you up to dialogic thought – a range of possible views on the same situation – which includes your analysis of how you are thinking and feeling, and why. Here is an example. Imagine that you set homework and half of the pupils did not hand it in, leading to you telling the whole class off and ending up with complaints from those pupils who had done it. The following is a possible CASP reflection on this incident:

1. Circumstance – the homework was set in a rush at the end of the lesson and some did not write it down properly. It was a boring activity and you knew that.
2. Ask – a teacher in another school said that they do not set any homework for some classes, as it gets done badly or not at all and ends up with an unnecessary battle. You spoke to a pupil who did not do the work and she said that she just forgot because she had not written it down.
3. Self-analyse – the experience of collecting up only half of the homework made you feel foolish. You remember getting embarrassed while collecting it and 'hot under the collar'. It reminded you that you are not succeeding to 'winning over' this class and you are worried about this, especially as your mentor keeps mentioning it. You could not give sanctions to half of the class as it would be noticed on the homework record and that would trigger issues for you with senior managers at the school. You knew you should not complain to the whole class but did it anyway, because you were starting to feel hopeless about the situation. This event also links in to how you felt in your own

schooldays when you were the only one to do the homework and other pupils laughed at you, and reminded you of a similar sense of shame.

4. Pattern – you have now told off a whole class three times on this placement, and you are disappointed with your actions. You have found no pattern in terms of handing in homework, as some pupils did hand it in in this lesson, and in other lessons the whole class do.

What has come of going through this CASP process? Perhaps nothing. Probably, only the self-analysis stage gave some insight, because this event could be reconfigured as:

If I set homework, I feel like a fool; I feel shame.

In which case, this does not seem a good enough reason to stop doing something that helps half of the class, and if we were on the end of this analysis we would conclude that its value is worth the personal pain.

Alongside reflection, we 'refract' government and school policy, and even the instructions from our mentors. This is a subversive practice as it is doing what we are not supposed to – but this does not mean that we are consciously being rebellious. The phenomenon was wisely noticed by Ivor Goodson in his studies of teachers' practice. He found that they often take a government or school policy and reinterpret it according to their own pedagogy or views on how teaching and education work. They may have misinterpreted what they have been told to do, not really taken it in at all, or rationalised why the policy or instruction does not apply to them. Goodson visualised this process as like passing policy through a 'membrane' (2010: 770) where the teacher's 'own trajectories, life histories and professional identities. . . mediate policies and negate the effects of ideology and power' (Goodson, 2015: 37). Refraction happens when there are, 'motivations behind practice that appears at odds with predominant waves of reform' (Rudd and Goodson, 2016: 101). Teachers do not always support the waves of prevailing political and ideological systems in which they work, but they often remain teaching quite happily for decades. They generally manage to do so by coping with unwanted expectations through a process of altering what these expectations mean. Having reinterpreted the policy or instructed way of acting, they lead themselves into thinking that they are obeying it, but they have changed the reality of their unwanted situation. Both in the doing and in the not doing, the teacher resists aspects of the system that are not agreed with. This is not an act of willful rebellion but a new reading of policy or initiative which may allow the teacher to think that they are conforming while, in practice, they are not. Refraction of light is often symbolised by a pyramid of glass which receives a single white light and transmits a rainbow of colour. This image is a good one, as it visualises how we make sense of a sometimes cold reality of government and school policy and turn it into a rainbow of individual practice.

Reflexivity is an in-the-moment awareness of ourselves and our environment and the ability to respond accordingly. The reflexive teacher responds well to the class; they can feel the mood shifts and adapt. A reflex is something that seems to happen involuntarily and a reflexive teacher has the ability to change something automatically rather than stick to a fixed script. One of the issues, which is a perennial for teacher trainers like us, is the problem of lesson timing. Rather than having to adhere to a lesson plan's timing, for example, a teacher develops an in-the-moment responsiveness to the pace and responses of the class. A reflexive teacher notices that the class has not understood the instructions, stops the class and gives them again. Reflexivity is reflection-in-action (Schön, 1991) – the ability to rethink the lesson while it is happening. The trainee teacher who can see that a lesson is not working and start again has an advantage over the one who cannot sense the lack of understanding or engagement of the class and ploughs on regardless. Questioning is a good example of reflexivity because it has its own built-in dialogue with responses from the pupils that have to be reacted to in-the-moment. Like reflection and refraction, being reflexive is a thinking skill that needs to be exercised in order to get better. The processes of reflexive thinking are part of our mental gym and they need a regular workout.

Conclusion

Do you need an adrenaline, 'buzz', an 'ego rush', the need to 'think on your feet' and/or do you need to get everything right? If so, this may well be driving you through your placement. Whatever you are like, we know that some thoughts can be unhelpful and do not always reflect how we want to think and feel, or who we want to be. In order to 'know thyself' and be true to yourself, we recommend that you become a reflective trainee and work on the cognitive skills which allow you to rethink yourself and your experiences. We also recommend that you become more aware of the way that you 'refract' your reality in school and how other teachers do the same. Also, develop reflexivity – you will need it to respond to the pupils. Your principles may not be ours and we both may not share those of the government or your school. Understanding the prismatic way an institutional belief, ethos or standpoint gets altered by the individual teacher is important, as is the ability to reflect on what we are being asked to do and why. A key to success is not so much that you have a particular type of pedagogy, but that you know what yours is and why you have it. This is the drive that will sustain you on a day-to-day and year-to-year basis, and it may even (probably will) change over time. Teaching is often all-consuming, but what a pleasure it is to be in a job that engages the whole being in a meaningful purpose.

.... **REFLECTIONS**

There are many pedagogies of teaching, but the one you hold should should be capable of sustaining you personally. Why do you think education is important? Why did you come into the profession? We are not unaware that for some trainee teachers, the answer is that they could not find another graduate job, or they wandered onto the course because they could not think what else to do. If this is the case for you, teaching is likely to be a difficult route to paying your bills. If you can do the job well, that is what matters. You do not have to have a self-sacrificial heart to be a teacher but, we think, you do need the honesty and openness with yourself which comes from the practice of reflection.

Do you refract the school, the system and the 'best practice' models offered by others? Where are the spaces in which you say 'no' to ideas and those spaces in which you say 'yes'? By naming these spaces, you will be able to better realise your pedagogy, the reasons which instruct your teaching. It can be hard to see refraction because you have given your own interpretation of how the school and system works and, in your own mind, are conforming to it. Look at the ways other teachers operate and see the differences and become part of the rainbow of practice in a school.

How are your thoughts? Do you think that they give a true picture of who you are and want to be? The idea that our thoughts are not us is a big realisation and can free you up from your current state of mind and actions. Try talking back to your thoughts and feelings as if they were from another person, and take them through a process of rethinking, either the CASP one we propose, or Brookfield's or Kolb's.

....

.... **ACTIONS**

Build reflective dialogue into your routine. Think about the day, then rethink about the day. The ongoing dialogue with yourself is a key to success in teaching; otherwise you are likely to find that your mind finds other ways of dealing with stress and new situations.

....

Case Study 11

Naima Begum was one of our trainee teachers who was placed in a very strict school which had a no-tolerance regime for staff and pupils. It was managed through data and from the top down. During her training year, Naima wrote an essay which revealed her response to the school and therefore her pedagogy. We present it here as an example of how political thought can inform an approach to teaching. This extract also shows the value of researching into your profession in order to 'arm' yourself, protect your sense of self and justify your pedagogy by reference to others who support it. After completing her Post Graduate Certificate of Education (PGCE) year in 2018, Naima worked in an inner-city mixed sex academy in the West Midlands before leaving in 2024 to relocate back home in the North of England, and join a new school there.

> Recent Ofsted research has shown that headteachers found that teachers are too
> 'focused' on exams rather than 'developing a more rounded curriculum knowledge'
> (Ofsted, 2011). This is despite the National Curriculum stating that pupils should be
> taught how to communicate their 'ideas and emotions ... to develop culturally ...
> socially and spiritually' (DfE, 2013). The problem with our education culture is that
> it is centred around the idea of 'competitive performativity', based on targets
> (Ball, 2010). This is apparent in my second placement (School A) where I was first
> introduced to the pupils through their data, which included their target grades. They
> were not presented as children, just numbers that needed to be matched to other

numbers and education is the most 'noticeable domains affected by datafication' (Jarke and Breiter, 2019). Data is used everywhere and will shape the way 'future generations construct reality' (Jarke and Breiter, 2019). Pupils are now like 'objects' that are used to generate data (like Ofsted reports etc.), which are stripping them of their basic human rights (Lupton and Williamson, 2017). It is the government that puts the pressure on teachers to 'work faster, harder, and longer' (Stevenson, 2017), which causes teachers to change their practice and why so many teachers quit the profession.

Data has become 'increasingly detached from supporting learning' and has more to do with a teacher's 'performance' (Stevenson, 2017). Moreover, the data is used for measurement and comparison (Stevenson, 2017). However, all of this data is being 'generated and processed' at an unrivalled level (Selwyn, 2014) which might lead to civilians becoming overwhelmed (Selwyn, 2014). Furthermore, surveillance, or 'dataveillance', is increasing in schools through CCTV, online monitoring and biometric tagging (2017). Not only that, but young people are growing up in an era that 'track their thoughts, movements and actions' (Taylor and Rooney, 2017) since birth their movements are tracked. Arnold (2010, quoted in Taylor and Rooney, 2017) argued that children are being 'denied personhood by being reduced to digits.' This loss of identity may be linked with pupils' ability to 'engage' with their education (McCune, 2009) because identity is a main concept of a learner's participation in the 'community of practice' or the classroom (Farnsworth et al., 2016). For example, a student's identity can be linked with their 'enthusiasm' and what is 'meaningful' to them in a subject (McCune, 2009). In addition, belonging is 'a crucial source of personal identity for the people' (Rodriguez and Fortier, 2007). Learners are not presented with these reasons when they ask, 'why do we need to read this book?' instead, teachers respond with, 'for the exam'. I have often found myself replying, 'you need to study this for your GCSEs' when really I wanted to go and find one more interesting.

In School A, my mentor often reminded me that I was responsible for the pupils' marking and making sure they achieve their target grades through the assessments. Once I was trying to help a Year 10 pupil, however, she snapped, 'You're not going to be in the exam with me, I have to do this on my own!' Learning should prepare pupils to function as members of society (Ofsted, 2011), not just to sit in and worry over an exam.

A question proposed by Michael Apple is, 'Are schools 'strongly determined' by ideological, economic, and cultural forces outside of them or do they have a significant degree of autonomy?' (Apple, 2004: 1). The school I am in is governed by outside forces, and neoliberal ideology. There are new ideological concepts, such as 'new managerialism', for example, where heads of departments end up focusing not on education but on the business side of the school (Deem and Brehony, 2007). Neoliberalism has 'incorporated ... the way we interpret, live in, and understand the world ... swept across the world like a vast tidal wave of institutional reform and discursive adjustment'. (Harvey, 2007). However, it has not always entailed a positive 'reform' (Harvey, 2007). It has not been 'effective at revitalising global capital accumulation, but it has succeeded in restoring class power' (Harvey, 2007). The difference in 'class power' (Harvey, 2007) is encouraged 'between individuals so that competition ... becomes an integral social features (Lauder et al., 2006 quoted in lngleby, 2015). Pupils are forced to make choices that will benefit them in 'future employment' rather than pursuing their 'interests or talents' (Grealy and Laurie, 2017).

·····················WHAT TOOLS ARE IN YOUR TOOLKIT NOW

- The language and process of reflection, refraction and reflexivity – ways of thinking that will act as psychological armour for the year.
- Permission to question the structures you find yourself in.
- Permission to admit to mistakes and see human fallibility in you and your colleagues.
- Encouragement to act on your thoughts and feelings rather than be a victim of them.

···

Places to Get More Tools for Your Toolkit

Buckler, S. (2021) *How to Challenge the System and Become a Better Teacher*.
    London: SAGE.

A working teacher and one who 'tells it like it is'. Scott Buckler is a highly thoughtful practitioner who advises on which voices to listen to in teaching and how to challenge the system from within.

Robinson, K. (2022) *Imagine If.* ... London: Penguin

Imagine if Ken Robinson had been responsible for the direction of UK education. Robinson gives a call to think about thinking skills and creativity rather than memory and repetition.

References

Apple, M. (2004) *Ideology and Curriculum*. New York: Routledge-Falmer.
Ball, S. (2010) The teacher's soul and the terrors of performativity, *Journal of Education Policy* 18(2): 215-228.
Brookfield, S. (1995) *Becoming a Critically Reflective Teacher*. San Francisco: Jossey-Bass.
Deem, R. and Brehony, K. (2007) Management as ideology: The case of 'new managerialism in higher education, *Oxford Review of Education* 31(2): 217-235.
DfE (2013) *English Programmes of Study: Key Stage 3*. Available from: https://assets.publishing. service.gov.uk/media/5a7b8761ed915d4147620f6b/SECONDARY_national_curriculum_-_English2.pdf
Farnsworth, V., Kleanthous, I. and Wenger-Traynor, E. (2016) Communities of practice as a social theory of learning: A conversation with Etienne Wenger. *British Journal of Educational Studies* 64(2): 139-160.

Goleman, D. (1996) *Emotional Intelligence: Why It Can Matter More than IQ*. London: Bloomsbury.

Goodson, I. (2015). The five Rs of educational research, *Power and Education* 7(1): 34-38.

Grealy, L. and Laurie, T. (2017) Higher degree research by numbers: Beyond the critiques of neoliberalism, *Higher Education Research and Development* 36(3): 458-471.

Harvey, D. (2007) *Neoliberalism as Creative Destruction*. Available from: https://justassociates.org/wp-content/uploads/2022/02/neo-liberalism-as-creative-destruction-david-harvey.pdf

Jarke, J. and Breiter, A. (2019) Editorial: The datafication of education, *Learning, Media and Technology*, 44: 1-6.

Kolb, D. (1984) *Experiential Learning. Experience as the Source of Learning and Development*. New Jersey: Prentice Hall.

Ingleby, E. (2015) The house that Jack Nuilt: Neoliberalism, teaching in higher education and the moral objections, *Teaching in Higher Education* 20(5): 518-529.

Lupton, D. and Williamson, B. (2017) The datafied child: The dataveillance of children and implications for their rights, *New Media & Society*, 19(5).

McCune, V. (2009) Final year biosciences students' Willingness to engage: Teaching-learning environments, authentic learning experiences and identities. *Studies in Higher Education* 3: 347-361.

Moon, J. (2004) *A Handbook for Reflective and Experiential Learning*. Abingdon: Routledge-Falmer.

Ofsted (2011) *Removing Barriers to Literacy*. Available from: https://assets.publishing.service.gov.uk/media/5a748327e5274a7f9c58694b/Removing_barriers_to_literacy.pdf

Rodriguez, J. and Fortier, T. (2007) *Cultural Memory: Resistance, Faith and Identity*. Austin: University of Texas Press.

Rudd, T. and Goodson, I. (2016) Refraction as a tool for understanding action and educational orthodoxy and transgression, *Revista Tempos e Espacos em Educacao* 9 (18): 99-110.

Schön, D. (1991) *The Reflective Practitioner*. Aldershot: Ashgate Publishing.

Selwyn, N. (2014) Data entry: Towards the critical study of digital data and education, *Learning, Media and Technology* 40(1): 780-794.

Stevenson, H. (2017) The datafication of teaching: Can teachers speak back to the numbers? *Peabody Journal of Education* 92(4): 537-557.

Taylor, E. and Rooney, T. (2017) *Surveillance futures: Social and Ethical Implications of New Technologies for Children and Young People*. London: Routledge.

Tripp, D. (1993) *Critical incidents in teaching: Developing Professional Judgement*. London: Routledge.

Wilkins, E. (1917). *Know Thyself in Greek and Latin Literature*. Chicago: The University of Chicago.

12

Looking Towards the Future

What this chapter will cover

- Interviews and jobs
- Building a career

Introduction

A school training programme will include two placements in schools which ought to vary in their styles, pupil demographics and ethos. This chapter will explain the reasons for this and give advice about adaptability and dealing with change. Giving practical advice about applying for jobs – where, when and why – this chapter will guide the trainee teacher about their next steps. This chapter will move towards the subject of the final chapter, the need to become 'future-proof' and towards consideration of the long-term prospect of working in the education system.

Interviews and Jobs

The process for applying for a job may be forestalled by your placement school wanting to keep you. Many schools take on trainee teachers for placements intending them to be extended interviews. This makes sense because the school has given time and effort getting the trainee teacher ready to teach. If the school is not for you or you are not for them (which might simply be because they have no jobs), you will need to apply for jobs on the open market. This can be done at any stage in the year, but there will be a surge of vacancies after 31st May. On this date, anyone who wishes to leave their teaching job and wants to be paid until the last possible day before the new term (31st August) gives three months' notice to terminate their contract. The school is only then legally able to advertise their post. There are multiple sites where jobs are advertised but the government has tried to simplify the process by offering a centralised online search engine. If you see a job you like on there, you will have to go through two stages: written application and interview day.

The first stage is application, and this is the main way that the school will assess whether you are the right person for the job. For most teaching posts, you will be required to complete an application form specific to the school and provide a supporting letter of application that includes a personal statement. For each job, there are 'job specifications' and 'person specifications'. If there is an 'essential' specification for the person – for example, a degree in the teaching subject – and you do not have it, do not apply because, if nothing else, you will be wasting the world's resources through the unnecessary use of electricity. Once you are sure that you fulfil the essential person specifications, you can tell the school how, and provide evidence. We advise trainee teachers to write their applications as a boxer would behave in a boxing ring: each point made as to why the applicant should be chosen is like another punch. Did you get top grades for one of your placements? Pow! Are you the student representative on the Post Graduate Certificate of Education (PGCE) course? Pow! Did you teach in Dubai for a year before coming to train in the United Kingdom? Pow! Try to answer interview questions in three-part answers. Three is a magic number in rhetoric or persuasive speech as in: 'We cannot dedicate, we cannot consecrate, we cannot hallow this ground' (Abraham Lincoln, 1863). Or in Martin Luther King's (1963) majestic *I have a Dream* speech when he spoke: 'Free at last! Free at last! Thank God Almighty, we are free at last!', words you might echo at the end of a difficult placement.

In the interview, do not presume that the members of the panel have read your application form – it was used to get you there, but the members often have it printed out in front of them on the day for the first time. There will be a list of your achievements on this form, and these should form the basis of the answers to their questions. If they ask how to deal with an unruly pupil, for example, you could relate how as a deputy manager of a shop you not only had to deal with the pupils from the local school but their parents (Pow!) and when you were a Teaching Assistant you were placed to calm the most disruptive pupils (Pow!) and how you got called 'outstanding' by a member of the Senior Leadership Team (SLT) for the way you dealt with the challenging behaviour in a lesson they observed (knockout!). In this way, you are ready for questions because you already know what you want to include in your answers.

In interviews, there are typical questions, so you can rehearse them. For example:

- 'Why do you want to work at this school?': (1) strong Ofsted report; (2) geography so can settle in the community; and (3) your commitment to the pupils as shown by the amount of extra-curricular groups you have (you can see that a little flattery is often a winning formula).
- 'What do you understand about safeguarding?': (1) prime role of a teacher and school; (2) Keeping Children Safe in Education details including reporting to the Designated Safeguarding Lead; and (3) an example of when you have safeguarded a pupil.

If they ask you a question about your weaknesses, rather than telling them that you spend your weekends playing computer games in your pyjamas and that your main weakness is that the crisps you keep eating make your hands go all slippery, take a key area of practice that you would like to develop. Do not be too self-critical. So, perhaps you need to broaden the range of the subject topics being taught or to have more opportunities to work with more challenging pupils because your experience to date has been limited. There is a typical question in interviews about where you see yourself in five years; we have been asked many times. The first time, one of us recalls thinking: 'I haven't even planned my weekend, yet'. On being asked it in a second interview, we thought: 'Not here!' In the end, the more interviews we did, the better we got at answering questions. So, we learnt not to reply that we wanted to be Head of Department and therefore take over the job of the person who was interviewing us; instead that we would be looking to: (1) take responsibility for an aspect of the curriculum; (2) be responsible for a thriving after-school club, but above all, (3) keep improving as a teacher in the classroom.

On an interview panel, there should be a representative from Human Resources, a member of the Senior Leadership Team, and someone from your subject area – probably the head of subject. Each will have a particular question to ask related to their area of responsibility. There will also probably be someone from the Special Educational Needs and Disabilities (SEND) team as well. There may be a governor who brings outside expertise and is concerned with the running and reputation of the school.

Job interviews have to be transparent and equitable, so the same questions are asked to all candidates in the same manner. If you are not the first to go in to be interviewed, you may even get the 'heads-up' on the questions being asked, if there is a very kind person in front of you. There is often a number system to rate the quality of the answers you give (in case there is a legal challenge and there is an accusation of discrimination), so make each answer detailed and try to get the points on offer. On being questioned, take your time before answering. Even if you know the answer, pause and gather your thoughts. Realise that in stressful situations, your mind goes faster, as does your voice, so you have to consciously slow down as the other person is writing down your response. It is hard to control voice speed, so consciously breathe at the end of sentences to allow the panel a chance to catch up and write down your answer. When you get a question:

- pause,
- think,
- look at the questioner, and
- answer.

Look at your questioner only. One of us remembers being at a school interview with 11 interviewers, not knowing this strategy, and ending up with neck-ache as well as no job.

One question you will probably be asked is: 'If we offered you the job would you take it?' Your answer (unless you are entirely convinced otherwise) has to be a fulsome 'yes'. Even feign surprise that you might say 'no', if you are a good actor. This is how they make sure you want the job. If you really do not want the job, you can put your reservations in here – and you might as well do so. It will probably mean the 'end of the road', but is necessary, if you would only really take the job if the salary was raised or you were allowed to get in at 8.30 am rather than the expected 8.15 am. You might turn this into a pitch for the job if you were to tell them that you would take the job but would need to teach RE as well as Science – if you find out they are looking for someone who would be able to do both. One of us deliberately tried to fail an interview in this manner by telling the panel that they would accept the job only on these conditions: no cover duty and no break-time supervision. To our surprise and consternation, the school acceded to these demands and on shaking hands, sensing our misgivings, reminded us that 'a verbal contract is binding'. As for this, there is a good saying: 'verbal contracts are not worth the paper they are not written on'. We have sometimes been contacted by trainee teachers who have accepted a job and wanted to see if they could get out of it. Our advice to our trainee teachers that they really should go through with the position on legal and moral grounds. Our trainee teachers do not always heed our advice, which is fair enough; after all, we are not the ones who have to go in and work there. The school could take legal action against the trainee teacher (and vice versa if a school withdraws a verbal contract), but we have not experienced anyone actually doing so. It is not good publicity to sue a trainee teacher for breach of contract, as it advertises that someone does really not want to work in that school and it also costs money the school does not have. We have also witnessed schools threaten to withdraw job offers to trainee teachers; and actually to do so. If a trainee teacher has accepted a job at a placement school and then their performance 'takes a dip', mentors and senior leaders may well put the trainee teacher's new job offer 'on the line' and subject to improvement. Such threats might be veiled (intimations that the job may be readvertised) or sometimes explicit (delivered orally which makes them easier to deny). One of our trainee teachers walked away from both a placement and a job because the school told her that if she did not work in the half-term holidays, they would rescind the job offer. Realising the kind of school she would be subjecting themself to, she made the brave decision to quit the placement and completed the course during the following year, finding a much better school to work in. If you have accepted a job at your placement school, but genuinely feel that you cannot go through with it, we would advise that you approach the head teacher honestly and apologetically, and state the reasons why you have doubts about accepting a job. In some cases, we have known this to provide both parties an amicable way out. If it does not, you will have to absorb the disapproval and it is best to do this at the end of the placement. It is also likely to mean that you will not be selected for any future post in the school for as long as the head teacher's memory lasts. Teachers talk, and there is a web of social media commu-nication between schools, so be aware that how you act may well find its way to the next school. Act professionally, honestly, nobly even, if you can. Integrity is a quality we could all do with more of. If you show it, the web of communication starts to get spinned in your favour.

From our experience of being on the other side of the desk as interviewers, if anyone shows reluctance to do any aspect of the job (or all of it!), it sets off 'warning bells' and these are usually attended to in the final decision. If you want the job, 'don't look down' is our advice. Always be positive about the job and communicate that you want it. One strategy is to look the panel members in the eyes when they ask if there are any more questions and tell them how much you hope to work at the school. A clear message that this is the school for you cannot guarantee you the job, but it sends a powerful emotional signal to those who have to choose. All of the candidates that you are up against are as qualified as you or they would not be there; the school would theoretically employ everybody there who has applied. Generally, if there are six people for an interview, then the odds are the same as rolling a dice and hoping for a four. It is worth remembering that if you get rejection after rejection, you have to roll the dice six times until the odds are with you. In the past, feedback we have received following unsuccessful interviews has included observations that we were too serious (what did they want us to do, wear a revolving bow tie?) and that we looked too young at the time (should we have worn a false grey beard?). In other words, there was no good reason, but the chosen candidate just had something extra which happened to be that they were looking for. We have known the strongest candidate for a job to be rejected because the panel could not see them fitting in with the rest of the department. The awkward period where you have to meet the department is part of the interview process and while it is best not to be 'pushy' or transform into a Saturday night 'turn' at the local social club, be sociable, and take this advice: listen to others. Ask them a question about the school and listen to the answers. Try to get them to talk. It is a strange phenomenon that if you do not say much about yourself but listen to what others have to say they tend to find you very interesting. Try this out before an interview by just asking and listening and see the effect it has on the listener. Try it out anyway on other occasions!

In most interviews that we have been involved in there is a 'preferred candidate', a back-up and what might be called 'an outside chance'. One of our trainee teachers overheard the Head of English say loudly: 'my preferred candidate is. . .'. It was not the trainee teacher's name and they did not go on to get the job. We write this fully realising that we have often been 'an outside chance' many times in the past. In an interview one of us went to, we noticed the other candidate arrived from an office next door to the interviewer's room, so was evidently already working there and going for a more permanent position; we even recall that they were wearing slippers, but this detail was probably the result of an uncomfortable dream, as interviews often end up seeming to be. You must persevere on the interview circuit, no matter how demoralising it can be. On the third interview of the same week, one of us was being interviewed at a school along with five other candidates. The day had started in reception at 8.30 am; there had been an interview, a lesson to teach, lunch with the staff, awkward conversations in the staffroom, and a second round of interviews. At 6 pm, the head teacher said: "We cannot decide but" (pointing in our direction) "You can go". At this, point one of us had to trudge shamefacedly out of the room while the other five stayed. Next week, two job offers were made on the same day meaning that one of us was unexpectedly now in the position to reject a school. Hang on in there and do not take the interview process personally. As well as the school interviewing you to see if you suit it, you are, in a sense, interviewing the school and need to make a decision whether you would be comfortable working there for, ideally, a couple of years at least. Ask yourself the following questions:

- How does the school feel? – you can usually get a sense of the school's ethos quite quickly.
- Did you enjoy the lesson? – if you did not enjoy teaching this hand-picked group of pupils, you are unlikely to want to work there.
- How do you feel about your potential future colleagues? – think whether they are the kinds of people you want to spend time with.
- Is the job what I thought it was? – consider whether the job that they are explaining in the interview is the same as the one you applied for. If they have added another subject or altered it, you have to rethink whether you would have applied for it in the form offered.

You will most likely be asked to teach a sample lesson to pupils. The pupils you teach will be involved in the decision, so be warm and friendly, and try to learn some names quickly. You might do this with name stickers at the start although they may invent all kinds of names so, perhaps, ask for a class list of names and then use this. The interview will want you to explain why you acted in the way you did, so think ahead for actions and reasons. A school is probably not going to choose a difficult class to teach, because this would put the candidate off, and there should be enough teachers and managers in the room to ensure an orderly environment so you can get on and teach. Adapt a lesson you have done successfully before and avoid an overreliance on technology, which can (and will) always go wrong. Have an analogue back-up plan which does not rely on computers and screens.

On dealing with interview nerves, some advice we have read about is to think of the panel members as toothbrushes, naked or in underwear, but we are not quite convinced that this advice helps, especially as it may affect your facial expression when you look at them. For nerves, do not catastrophise because this school does not have to be the only one for you. You have absolutely nothing to lose by attending an interview. You come in without the job and if you leave without it, you will leave exactly the same. You can walk out of that interview day at any time and, if you do so politely, with no consequences. Desperation is never an appealing quality so try to avoid this. Go in, give it your best shot and if you get it, you get it. If not, act graciously and thank them for the experience and move on to your next interview. To paraphrase the poet George Herbert and the author F Scott Fitzgerald, the best revenge is always to live well. The next school will be offered your dedication and skill.

Building a Career

Once Qualified Teacher Status (QTS) has been awarded and you have been successful in finding a teaching job, you will become an ECT – Early Career Teacher. This title replaced the old ones of NQT (Newly Qualified Teacher in the first year of teaching) and RQT (Recently Qualified Teacher in the second year of teaching). The Early Career Framework (ECF) launched in September 2021 (DfE, 2021) made the induction, or probation, period a two-year process and formalised a training programme for new teachers in schools. This meant a mindshift in the way that early teachers were to be seen – not as a finished article by the award of QTS, but a third of the way through training. You have to start as an ECT at a school which is set up to run the induction programme, undergo further training and be judged against the Teachers' Standards at certain intervals. After two years, all being well, the Teaching Regulation Agency will be informed that you have successfully completed the induction period. If you do not successfully complete this, then you will no longer be able to act as a qualified teacher (although academies and independent schools can still employ you as an unqualified one). You cannot 'fail' your ECT years; you just do not satisfactorily complete the induction period. There is no time limit on when you have to complete the two years and you can work in a school without starting the process. If registered as an ECT and struggling, you can move schools during the process. You will still undergo training as well as mentoring. The training courses are directly funded by the Department for Education (DfE) and cover the following topics:

- behaviour management,
- pedagogy,
- curriculum,
- assessment, and
- professional behaviours.

After two years' worth of additional training at the end of this course, you will be equipped with the qualities of perseverance, bravery, initiative, work ethic, reliability, trustworthiness, dedication and every other positive adjective there is. Today's employment world calls on us to be: 'entrepreneurs of . . .self' (Foucault, 2008: 226). In this marketplace of portfolio careers (where you may be employed in a number of different jobs and can package them up by the qualities they share), we are very much our own projects and the qualities which being a teacher instils are values for life.

You might be thinking about career progression after you have completed the ECT years. There are two main careers pathways in teaching: pastoral leadership and subject leadership. Beyond these, there will also be opportunities to take on whole school leadership work for particular areas of work, for example the role of Special Educational Needs Coordinator (SENCo), coordinating enrichment activities, or leading on 'stretch and challenge'. We have even known a school appoint a 'Director of Fun' to improve the well-being and morale of pupils and staff. Imagine that as your job title! We would encourage you to explore what is involved in these areas of work through staffroom conversations and work shadowing to find out the route you prefer. You can also offer to assist in these roles – on an unpaid basis of course – to gain useful experience for your next steps. You might also find it reinvigorating to move to new types of school or new education sectors. We both made the move into the university sector and found this as a way to keep doing what we love – teaching – in a new sector with new challenges. Had you asked us, when we were school teachers, if we would be comfortable in front of 100 people and we would have shrunk from the challenge but as our experience built we became ready for it. You can also create a fulfilling career without any formal responsibility roles, and there are currently progression options that come from demonstrating excellence in classroom teaching that access upper pay spines. Teaching remains a fulfilling career for as long as it sustains and rewards you. Seek out your niche in this world.

·· **REFLECTION**

Think about your many achievements and jot down everything you have won, every certificate you have gained, every prize, and then consider the social achievements of family and friend relationships, the economic achievements of being able to afford a car or a house, the emotional achievements of overcoming adversity, the health achievements of coping with any physical suffering. Consider other aspects where you have helped and supported others, and overcome the odds, and you will be in a good position to face an application and interview process with the a positive mindset: they will be lucky to have you.
··

·· **ACTIONS**

Prepare your answers, identifying three points for the following questions, you might get asked in an interview:

- Why do you want to work at this school?
- What qualities can you bring to the school and department?
- What are your strengths and weaknesses as a teacher?

- Describe the worst or best lesson, state why it was or was not successful and what you would do differently if you taught it again.
- How do you ensure the progress of pupils in your subject?
- How do you assess the progress of pupils in your subject?
- If we visited your classroom, what could we expect to see?
- Where do you see yourself in five years?
- What do you understand by the word 'safeguarding' and how have you ensured it in your teaching practice? (You will definitely be asked a question on safeguarding which may include a scenario to respond to.)

Case Study 12

Evie Booton-Ford graduated with a degree in English Literature with History at the age of 21, took on a PGCE at Keele University in 2017, had her first teaching job in 2018 and within nine months was working as the whole school literacy coordinator. Alongside this, she started a part-time Master's at the University of Cambridge, studying Advanced Subject Teaching. A year later, Evie was second in department and a whole school Teaching and Learning Coach. By the time she was 25, she had become Head of Department then Head of Faculty. She now works in this position at a girls' grammar school. Here, she reflects on the nature of career progression.

Within education, the word "money" can often be seen as something dirty – yet why? Though many of us do feel a desire or calling to teach, ultimately, we go to work to pay our bills. Seeking promotions is something that many of you will likely do within your first few years of teaching, and with promotions comes higher pay. It also gives you the opportunity to have impact over a wider range of students, supporting them either pastorally or academically, even if you do not personally teach them. Perhaps because it is seen as rather unsavoury, how to get these promotions is rarely spoken about. Teaching is moving away from "the person who stays the latest gets the job". We live in a world where (thankfully) flexible working and wellbeing are being prioritised more than ever. Those who can be the most effective, efficient and reliable are those that will be most likely to get these promotions. Teaching is an incredibly time-poor profession. Teachers and leaders who can efficiently and effectively reactive to problems and proactively works to prevent them are highly valued.

Here is my advice about how to seek promotion:

1. Decide what path you want to take. Are you more interested in a pastoral or academic role? Everything you do should be geared towards that goal. See if there is anyone who you might look up to as a role model – what do they do well? How are

they successful? Why do people look up to them? Speak to them about their work and find out what can you learn from them.

2. Invest in yourself through Continuing Professional Development (CPD). Consider whether you might be interested in a Master's degree, a National Professional Qualification or a Chartered Management Institute (CMI) qualification or a course. You can ask your school to pay or contribute from their CPD budget, though this support is not guaranteed.

3. Consider taking on some responsibility without pay for a short period of time to gain more experience. I took on the role of whole school literacy coordinator for a year unpaid, and every subsequent job I had has had some connection to this role. Gaining promotions and climbing the ladder is something akin to following dominos - everything leads to something else.

4. Do not be afraid to move schools. Often, you will climb faster if you do so. It is a good idea to remain at a school for at least two years, but ultimately, if you see a job that you would be passionate about, it is worth asking for a tour and a meeting with the headteacher to discuss it.

5. Ensure you record your data 'highlights' year on year. Interviewers want to know specifics - your data can be excellent to refer to in an interview and a cover letter. Here's an example from a cover letter of my own:

During my NQT year, 90.9% of my mixed ability Year 11 class made progress following their English Language mocks in February in comparison to their final grades. Ultimately, this Year 11 class completed their English GCSEs with a Progress 8 score of +0.14. In my first year at School X, 93.3% of my class either reached or exceeded their English Language target grades, with 40% of all of these grades being 7+.

It important to record as much data as possible, from progress made from mocks or baseline assessments, to final Progress 8 scores for Year 11 students: this is evidence of your impact. You should also be able to detail what you specifically do to help students achieve the grades that they did.

6. Be positive. Leaders want staff to come to them with ideas to fix issues, as they may deal with at least five problems per hour themselves!

7. Be flexible - the ideal staff member is able to adapt. Schools are dynamic. Circumstances are constantly changing, and, thus, school leaders must make quick decisions and be willing to change their plans at the drop of a hat to react to issues.

8. Come to your interview day extremely prepared. You should have read the school's Ofsted reports, websites, social media pages and curriculum documents. You should be aware of the exams boards within the subject area(s) you seek to teach. If you know who is on the interview panel, research them on LinkedIn. I always appreciate it when applicants are knowledgeable about the school on the day as it shows a good

level of enthusiasm. It is especially important during pupil panels. There is often the question of 'What do you like most about our school?' My least favourite answer I have heard was 'I like the building' which they had just toured. Be ready with knowledge such as 'I really like how many competitions you run. It must be really good for inter-house rivalry and getting students engaged with extra-curriculars! I saw on social media about the House Drama competition you ran last week and how Raleigh House won. What do you think – was it a close competition?' Show the students and staff that you care and will be invested in the school community.

9. As someone who interviews candidates, I like to see a clear understanding of Ofsted terminology such as 'intent, implementation and impact' or 'know more and do more', as well as key terms such as 'attainment' and 'progress'. Questions like 'what does progress look like to you?' in the classroom are rarely answered well, in my experience. Ensure that your answer shows you know the definition of this, and that you can clearly translate this to your own practice. For example:

To me, progress in the classroom exists on many levels – students must make progress on a micro-level, such as during individual moments within the classroom such as during hinge point questioning. They must walk out of every lesson knowing more than they did previously. Progress also exists on that macro-level, where we can see gains in data over a longer period of data, from one data point to the next, or even from one year to the next. Essentially, progress is that invisible process where students show that they know more and can do more than they did before. A good example is my Year 11 class from last year. As a bottom set, their Year 10 data was the weakest in the year, with an average point score in Maths of 4.8 at the end of Year 10. However, by the end of Year 11, their average point school was 5.9. I was really proud of this progress, as it was better than the previous year's bottom set, and showed that the intervention strategies I put in place allowed them to make further progress than we'd initially expected.

This answer demonstrates an understanding of what progress is, as well as evidence of Ofsted terminology and a real life example that uses data to back it up. Remember – practice makes perfect, so it's a good idea to rehearse answering these kinds of questions as interviews for leadership positions are often 45 minutes or more and are quite challenging.

10. Know your worth. Excellent teachers are incredible resources. They are hard to both find and to retain. Recruitment is getting more and more challenging, especially in subjects such as Science, Technology, Engineering and Mathematics (STEM) or Languages. Do not be afraid to negotiate, but do so with grace, after proving yourself on an interview day.

This advice, and putting it into action, can serve you well on your journey to seeking promotions. Be confident, be brave, and be self-reflective and you will be well on your way to making fantastic impact over even more students than you can as a classroom teacher.

.... **WHAT TOOLS ARE IN YOUR TOOLKIT NOW?**

- Tips on applying for jobs.
- Tips on succeeding at interview.
- Greater understanding of the teacher interview process.
- Greater understanding of the way promotion works in schools.

....

Places to Get More Tools for Your Toolkit

Petty, G. (2014) *Teaching Today.* Oxford: Oxford University Press.

Measured, excellent advice from an experienced and wise professional, on how to thrive in the teaching profession.

References

DfE (2021) *Early Career Framework.* Available from: www.gov.uk/government/collections/early-career-framework-reforms

Foucault, M. (2008) *The Birth of Biopolitics: Lectures at the Collège de France, 1978–79.* New York: Palgrave Macmillan.

King, M. L. (August 28, 1963) I have a dream. In *March on Washington for Jobs and Freedom.* Washington DC: Lincoln Memorial.

Lincoln, A. (1863) *Gettysburg Address.* Available from: https://www.loc.gov/exhibits/gettysburgaddress/ext/trans-nicolay-inscribed.html

13

Classroom Enquiry, Critical Engagement and Going Beyond

What this chapter will cover

- Research-informed practice
- Future-proofing your practice
- Contributing to the world of knowledge about teaching and learning

Introduction

In this chapter, we advise that you ask critical questions about education theory – in other words, to ask not just 'what works' but when it works, and why it doesn't always work. We also encourage you to engage in further academic study in your chosen subject and profession.

Research-Informed Practice

Research-Informed Practice (RIP) brings the initialism RIP and we hope that it will signals that the age of thinking that some education theory is 'true' and some not will Rest in Peace. Instead of a 'what works' approach – the idea that a theoretical approach to education can always be put into practice and be successful – we come from the 'whatever works' field of education theory. If what you are doing in the classroom with the pupils is successful, keep on doing it! Do more of it, in fact. We take our pedagogies with us through changing educational fashions; as the educational landscape changes – and change is the only constant in this business – we interpret it and respond.

There is no excuse, though, for not continuing to learn more about your profession and using the research literature (a term which encompasses all of the forms of communication you can learn from, including newspapers, blogs, journal articles and so on). One common frustration we have in our jobs is when a trainee teacher selects an essay title and then tells us there is not much research on it. We then go to the university library site and find five hundred books, ten thousand journal articles and 50 billion websites on the topic. The problem is that there is too much research literature. It is also hard to find the 'good stuff' as there is certainly a lot of nonsense out there that will stream your way on the internet. To pick an easy target, according to Wikipedia (at the time of writing), Edmund Hillary, the first recorded person from Europe to climb Everest, stated that he did it: 'Because it was there'. George Leigh Mallory (Britannica, 2024) actually said it and he had a much sadder fate, dying while climbing Everest. Similarly, if numerous internet memes are to be believed, Mark Twain stated that: 'A person who won't read has no advantage over one who can't read'. It was actually the Virginian State Superintendent of Public Instruction who stated this in a publication called 'The Southern Workman' (1910) in support of libraries (QI, 2012). All of this epistemological chasing of tails may not matter. We can still be inspired by Hillary's so-called words of endeavour and take heed of those reportedly by Twain: we do things because they challenge us, and we read to help us be so. To extend this idea, no-one would climb Everest without preparation, and surviving placements is your Everest; you are able to read (after all, you are reading this), so read and learn from research literature. We think it is not only important to learn from others but also to think about what you read including who wrote it, when and why. If the government wants us to do something in education, we have the right to question it because the government is motivated by ideological reasons which may not be in the best interests of schools or children. We should, in other words, not only 'stand on the shoulders of giants' (as Robert Hook wrote to Isaac Newton, quoting 12th-century philosopher Barnard of Chartres who no doubt got it from someone else, lost in the mists of time) but we should also think about whose shoulders we choose to stand on and why.

Research literature includes the work of experts (those who have gone before you into the world of teaching and want to share their experience and knowledge), government-based reports, and social science research which informs us about the psychology and sociology of learning. Education studies is in the social science branch of education, which can be a shock, and a disadvantage, to anyone who comes from a different discipline. The best social science can give us is insight. You may not have a social science background; its main disciplines are not National Curriculum subjects. If you have this background and managed to do a subject converter course you will find the assignments easier because the mode of study, the way ideas get synthesised and presented as an argument, along with the style of extended writing and form of case-making will be 'second nature' to you.

A PGCE course often comes with 60 or 90 credits at Master's degree level. If you pass at this level, explore completing the full MA award with a dissertation component in order to study a body of literature in depth. You should be able to complete a piece of your own research and contribute to the body of knowledge about education. If you do not want to take further formal academic study, there are lots of opportunities in Continuing Professional Development sessions. Become part of your subject community by joining in with local or national bodies. You can engage with national bodies such as the Educational Endowment Foundation, the Chartered College of Teaching, ResearchED, and Teach Meets. When you become a teacher, you join in with other professionals and build knowledge together. The conclusion of your studies on a teacher training course is not the end but the beginning of your learning about your chosen profession.

Future-Proofing Your Practice

For some trainee teachers, theory is seen as a luxury that they cannot afford to spend time engaging with. If this is the case, it is to their detriment, because they become trained in the system as it is, without the understanding that it was not always so and will not always be so. It does not future-proof to learn about and replicate current practice in schools. It is even more dangerous, we feel, to keep changing your practice, responding to the pressures from school and government policy without thinking, judging and negotiating the messages received about what supposedly works. Your personal pedagogy matters. You may still have to work in schools that hold other, possibly contradictory, views but what you care about will still illuminate your lessons. When the fashions for education change, or when you move to another school, you should find more of a match with your pedagogy. Your training year is a time to try out different environments and look for the place where you are a best fit. Stay in the same place in teaching and you are likely to find yourself in what is effectively a different school within a few years, anyway. External pressures will change schools; new heads do the same; people with 'visions' come along. We sit with former German Chancellor Helmut Kohl on this point: 'people with visions should go to see a doctor' (FT, 2021). Visions come and they go, and the person who had them in the first place and tried to impose it on an unwilling staff leaves before long. It is sometimes worthwhile pausing on new initiatives and visions in school and waiting to see if they 'stick'. If they do, you can attend to them more fully but pausing first is not a bad idea, as is standing back and watching others try to implement them, and learning from this too.

Conclusion

As a teacher, you have to remain a learner. We often visit staff rooms and see teachers who have valiantly remained in post for decades but not spent the time developing their career and their knowledge. It is a good idea to keep the momentum of learning going, realising that 'research-informed practice' and 'research literature' are terms which encompass the many sources from which you can learn. You learn from the colleagues, mentors, books, experts, media clips and more often than not, your pupils.

....**REFLECTION**

As you are on your training year, consider the value of learning. You will probably be asked to keep a reflective diary, so you can use this to document the sources of learning. This can be from journal articles, books, and other published sources, but equally from experience.
....

.... **ACTIONS**

Observe successful teachers, and you should see that they are always engaging with further study. Talk to these teachers about their sources of learning, and you will be able to add some of this magic to your practice.
....

Case Study 13

Barwago Ismail first worked in a mixed-sex secondary school in Birmingham for two years, then moved to Qatar, teaching English to second-language learners at a private British curriculum school. Within two years of her contract, she became a pastoral lead for a Year 10 cohort. After two years in Qatar, she returned to the United Kingdom to undertake a PhD in Education, examining the way Character Education is implemented in Birmingham secondary schools, whilst also continuing to work as an English teacher. Here, she recounts her reasons for studying alongside teaching. Her future plans are to carry on teaching, but in the Higher Education sector.

The reason I undertook doctoral research is because I rediscovered research-informed practice in my teaching. I could see how the more I learned, the more effective I became and arrived at the amazing realisation that theory is not just 'over there' but can change pupils' lives when put into practice. I would have done this while working in school but the pressures of time and the need to plan, teach and mark means that I lost a sense of curiosity and reflexivity so I needed to take a break to be able to think about and explore my pedagogy.

I chose to study for a PhD in education with a focus on Character Education. Character Education occurs in the teaching of values such as curiosity, kindness, respect, honesty, etcetera. Schools within the UK, in some shape or form, teach character in their curriculum, some more overtly than others. Having worked in the UK, I taught Character Education as a form tutor, in assemblies and lessons whilst also embodying the virtues through my own conduct. I wanted to understand more about what it means and how to focus on the child, holistically, rather than just cramming for examinations. I see the role of the teacher as one which is about developing the whole child and value the moral, cultural and spiritual role given to teachers by the government. Through observations and interviews, I have so far discovered the importance of political, religious and historical factors which affect character, and these have become what I call the 'golden threads' or key ideas within my research. The more I study, the more I grow in expertise about one particular topic and can pass on this through conferences and development days in school.

.... WHAT TOOLS ARE IN YOUR TOOLKIT NOW?

- A greater understanding of what 'research literature' is.
- Some ways of contributing to the world of knowledge about teaching.

Places to Get More Tools for Your Toolkit

Mullin, S. (2019) *What They Didn't Teach Me on My PGCE: and Other Routes into Teaching*. Ontario: Word and Deed.

Each short chapter, written by a practising teacher or senior leader, gives a first-hand account of what it is like to be working in the profession, alongside invaluable advice for new teachers.

References

Britannica (2024) *George Mallory*. Available from: www.britannica.com/biography/George-Mallory

FT (2021) *Financial Times Letter: Recalling Schmidt's Quip about Leaders with Vision*. Available from: www.ft.com/content/eeedbd06-6fab-4ad1-8919-79e5c9e7f28d

QI (2012) *The Man Who Does Not Read Has No Advantage over the Man Who Cannot Read*. Available from: www.quoteinvestigator.com/2012/12/11/cannot-read/#:~:text=Dear%20Quote%20Investigator%3A%20Mark%20Twain,one%20who%20can't%20read

Conclusion

Standing in a foot of water in a cellar with a screwdriver in one hand and a torch, trying to fix an electric light, one of us had a timely reminder of the ancient advice to practitioners of medicine: 'First, do no harm'. In teaching, your first responsibility is to ensure the safety of children, and your second responsibility is to yourself. Make sure that you are coping and doing no damage to your mental and physical health. This book has tried to give you the tools of safety. These tools include providing support, offering advice and positioning you within a community of trainee teachers sharing their reflections. All of this is intended to show you that you are neither alone in your quest nor with the troubles and triumphs you have found.

We have not offered you 'solutions' to your teaching problems. In teaching, advice is often offered in this way: 'Do this and it will work. If you do not do it and then encounter problems in the classroom, it must be because you didn't take my advice. And if you do take my advice, but it does not work, then it must be because you not doing it correctly'. This is the twisted logic of those who believe in 'solutions' to teaching problems. Managing behaviour, for example, may be taught as a step-by-step guide to success. If you try the steps but they do not work for you and your pupils, the person giving the steps may have such faith in them that it is your practice that is questioned. Actually, the steps do not work – or do not work for you, or with this class, or they would work for you and with this class at another time and day. This book has tried to make one particular point clear: there are tools for your toolkit but every 'job' is different and requires a particular skill at a particular time. We have refrained from suggesting 'solutions,' in favour of tools which may empower you.

We have tried to stress that you cannot force children to learn but you can encourage them (and some teachers may resort to cajoling, bribing and begging). The poet Kahil Gibran (1883-1931) perfectly expressed this truth about teaching children: 'You can give them your love but not your thoughts/For they have their own thoughts' (Gibran, 1923). Love is such a tricky consideration when it comes to school and the professional boundaries we need to keep, but we suspect that good teaching sometimes comes down to the love of your subject, of learning, and of the pupils just being there with you and their peers, and the dynamic energy that you can all generate in a room. What makes this positive dynamic happen? The trainee teacher, the pupils, the school, the time of day, the classroom layout, the events which occurred before the lesson, or are being anticipated... and just that 'something' that happens when people are together enjoying each other's company and purposefully working towards a common goal.

While writing this toolkit we were aware of how much we have had to miss out. Teaching is such a complex multi-nuanced activity, and we only know so much. The more we learn, the more we learn how little we know. But in the end, like all human endeavours, this book has had to be abandoned rather than finished, and will have to stand as it is, for all of its limitations and its flaws. The exciting part is not which are written here, anyway, but what you do with them. A toolkit alone can never make a successful lesson, but we hope that one or more of the given tools will be useful to you. We also hope that you are helped by being given permission to question, and that you will see that you are not alone in your experiences. We have seen hundreds of trainee teachers come through our doors and it has been our job to care for them while they were with us, as best as we could, knowing that we were modelling what we wanted from them in the classroom. It is also our job to become redundant. This is an unusual aim – but it is essential that we are no longer needed by our trainees by the end of the course. When your pupils no longer look to you to know how to behave, or how to learn, you too will be redundant – your job will be finished. But there will always be others who need you, so turn to them. The beauties of your chosen career in teaching are that there is always more work to do, and always more to learn.

.... **ACTIONS**

- Do your best.
- Be kind to yourself.
- Be a great teacher – while you are doing your best and being kind to yourself.

....

Reference

Gibran, K. (1923) *The Prophet*. New York: Albert Knopf.

Glossary

Apprenticeship: School-based training route to Qualified Teacher Status, also known as Post Graduate Teacher Apprenticeship.

Assessing Pupils' Progress: A scheme run from 2008 to 2011 which broke down the skills, knowledge and understanding in core school subjects to specific stages with numbers and letters, in order to label the pupils with their level of progress.

Assessment for Learning: Checking the knowledge, skills and understanding of pupils in the lesson.

Assessment Objective: The desired learning knowledge, skills or understanding. The government creates these for each subject and they inform the content of examinations.

Assessment of Learning: A test or examination that allows monitoring of pupils' current level of understanding, knowledge and skills.

Assessment only Route: A way to get Qualified Teacher Status without further study for those who have worked in schools for years.

Autism: A neurological variation that affects communication and interaction.

Behaviourism: A theory that human behaviour can be controlled by external forces.

Board of Education: UK national governing body for schools from 1899 to 1944.

British Values: Set of personal qualities essential for teachers practising in British schools, including a belief in democracy, upholding the rule of law, promotion of individual liberty, and a tolerant attitude towards those with different faiths and beliefs.

Bursary: Sum of money given to support education and training.

Carer: An adult who is not the biological parent of a child but responsible for their maintenance and support.

Character Education: Focus on the moral values and a positive learning attitude towards learning and others rather than academic success.

Coaching: Practical form of mentoring that works more to improve actions rather than understand reasoning and feelings.

Cognitive Load Theory: Theory of learning which states that brain development is optimised by ensuring that new knowledge is made accessible to the learner.

Cognitivism: The branch of psychology that studies how humans learn, remember and think.

Continuing Professional Development: Courses and training for practising teachers.

Core: Name used for university-led teacher training.

Core Content Framework: Framework given by the government to teacher training providers, around which they can design a curriculum for training teachers.

Credits: A university value that indicates how much teaching time and work is required for a part of a course.

Department for Children, Schools and Families: The name for the Department for Education from 2007 to 2010.

Department for Education: Current name for the government branch responsible for education.

Department for Employment and Education: The name for the Department for Education from 1995 to 2001.

Department for Education and Science: The name for the Department for Education from 1964 to 1992.

Department for Education and Skills: The name for the Department for Education from 2001 to 2007.

Diagnostic assessment: Method of finding out what the current level of knowledge skills and understanding is.

Differentiation: Changing the lesson content, pace and resources for individual pupils, including those with special needs.

Dyscalculia: A neurological variation that affects the processing of numbers by the brain.

Dyslexia: A neurological variation that affects the processing of language by the brain.

Early Career Framework: The curriculum that must be followed by training teachers during their first two years.

Education Act: Laws that are often updated and give the rules for schools, teachers, pupils and parents/carers.

Education Endowment Fund: Organisation that receives funds from the Department for Education for its work to improve the educational outcomes of children from lower income groups.

Education Reform Act: 1988 law which introduced a National Curriculum and moved schools away from local authority control.

English as an Additional Language: Term used in UK schools when a child's parents or first language is not English.

Equality Act: Law which makes it illegal for anyone to act in a discriminatory manner because of age, disability, gender reassignment, marriage and civil partnership, pregnancy and maternity, race, religion or belief, sex and sexual orientation.

Every Child Matters: Government initiative in the early 2000s to ensure individualised treatment of children in the classroom and multi-agency support for those who need it.

Extracurricular: Additional activities in school that are not part of the taught subjects.

Fixed mindset: Negative way of viewing learning as something that you can or cannot do naturally.

Formative assessment: Method of checking pupil learning during the lesson.

Forster Act: First UK laws requiring provision for, and attendance at school.

Gifted and Talented: A term used in schools to define those with advanced academic or physical skills.

Growth mindset: A way of thinking about learning which sees attitude rather than results as a sign of success.

Humanism: Belief that people are thinking, moral, active beings who make their own choices based on individual reasoning.

Inclusion: All children learning together and being supported to allow equal progress.

Induction: The first two years of teaching which must be successfully completed or the teacher cannot be employed in local authority-run schools.

Information technology: Computer-based systems used to communicate.

Initial Teacher Training and Early Career Framework: Due to be launched in 2025, amalgamating the Core Content and the Early Career frameworks which inform what Training Providers should be teaching in their curricula.

Keeping Children Safe in Education: Regularly updated policy guidance document for schools about safeguarding children.

Key Stage: Age range that determines which subjects, knowledge, skills and understanding will be taught and learnt in schools.

Level 7: Postgraduate academic standard which may lead to a Master's degree.

Literacy: The ability to read, write and speak with developed skills.

Looked-after Child: A child who is in the care of the local authority, foster home, residential care or secure unit.

Maintenance loan: Money for living expenses which will eventually have to be paid back.

Master's degree: Qualification which is above and comes after an undergraduate or Bachelor's degree.

McNair Report: Government study into teacher training published in 1944.

Ministry of Education: The name for the Department for Education from 1944 to 1964.

NASUWT: Second largest teachers' union in the United Kingdom, the National Association of Schoolmasters and Union of Women Teachers.

National Curriculum: A set of subjects and standards that schools run by English local authorities must abide by.

NEU: Largest teachers' union in the United Kingdom, the National Education Union.

Neoliberalism: Political, economic and social belief system that human behaviour should be given the conditions that allow them to pursue individualised goals, lifestyles and economic ends without state intervention or collective organisations.

Neurodiversity: The recognition that differences in brain make-up are natural variations in how people think and act should be part of our understanding of being human.

Non-salaried: School Direct route into teaching that comes with tuition fees which can be paid for by a student loan – also known as Training.

Numeracy: The ability to understand how numbers can be used to solve problems and create understanding.

Ofsted: Department for Education-funded organisation which checks and regulates the quality of schools, colleges and teacher training organisations.

Pedagogy: Methods and practices of teaching.

Post Graduate Certificate in Education (PGCE): The academic part of a teacher training course.

Pitching: Changing the content, learning materials and approach to suit the age and prior achievement of the class.

Qualified Teacher Status: Position which shows that the legal standards to teach in local authority-run schools have been met.

Reflection: A rethinking process that takes the original thoughts and feelings about a situation or event and considers alternative positions.

Reflexivity: An in-the-moment ability to consider what is being thought and done and how to respond to a situation.

Refraction: The way an idea, policy, document or instruction is reinterpreted by the teacher to fit their pedagogical views.

Regulatory: Controlling powers who use rules or laws.

Salaried: School Direct route which has fees paid, payment for work and the legal status of an unqualified teacher.

Scaffolding: The process of making sure that new learning is accessible to pupils and fits their current level of understanding.

Schema: A model or visualisation of the way the brain organises knowledge and skills.

Secretary of State for Education: Government minister responsible for the Department for Education.

Special Education Needs and Disabilities: Term used as a catch-all for those who need additional support to access school and curriculum activities.

Spiral curriculum: Approach to teaching which introduces the topic at any level of complexity and then keeps returning to it with the view that reinforced ideas that are gradually learnt.

Statutory: Required by law.

Stretch and challenge: Term used to describe learning activities that extend pupils' knowledge and skills beyond the expected level.

Summative assessment: Examination or test that can give a grade and allow a staged check on progress.

Teach First: A teacher training provider set up to provide graduates with direct access to the classrooms of schools in economically deprived areas.

Teacher Regulation Agency: Department for Education run organisation which oversees the official registration of teachers and their right to practise.

Teachers' Standards: Set of legal requirements that teachers must fulfil to qualify and continue to practise as a professional.

Teacher Training Agency: Governing body for teacher training providers from 1994 to 2005 when it became the Training and Development Agency for Schools.

TES: Times Educational Supplement, a newspaper and online site dedicated to school matters.

The Pupil Premium: Funding provided to schools to give extra support for those from economically disadvantaged backgrounds.

Training Provider: Organisation which has been given the legal right to guide training teachers through their initial year and gain Qualified Teacher Status.

Unqualified Teacher: Someone teaching in a school who does not have Qualified Teacher Status.

Virtual Learning Environment: The online computerised communication system used by teachers, pupils and parents/carers.

Initialisms and Acronyms

ADHD: Attention-Deficit Hyperactive Disorder

AfL: Assessment for Learning

AI: Artificial Intelligence

AoL: Assessment of Learning

AO: Assessment Objective

APP: Assessing Pupils' Progress

AQA: Assessment and Qualifications Alliance

ASC: Autistic Spectrum Condition

BAGM: Black Asian Global Majority

BAME: Black Asian and Minority Ethnic

BBC: British Broadcasting Corporation

BICS: Basic Interpersonal Communicative Skills

CALP: Cognitive and Academic Language Proficiency

CCF: Core Content Framework

CMA: Competitions and Markets Authority

CoP: Community of Practice

CPD: Continuing Professional Development

CRE: Commission for Racial Equality

DAB: Degree Awarding Body

DfE: Department for Education

DfEE: Department for Employment and Education

DfES: Department for Education and Skills

DNA: Do Now Activity

EAL: English as an Additional Language

ECF: Early Career Framework

ECT: Early Career Teacher

EEF: Education Endowment Foundation

GCSE: General Certificate in Secondary Education

GMS: Grant Maintained School

GPT: Generative Pre-trained Transformer

GRT: Gypsy, Romany, Traveller

GTP: Graduate Teacher Programme

HE: Higher Education

ICM: Instructional Coaching Model

ICT: Information Communication Technology

IQ: Intelligence Quotient

IT: Information Technology

ITT: Initial Teacher Training

ITTECF: Initial Teacher Training and Early Career Framework

KCSiE: Keeping Children Safe in Education

LLM: Large Language Model

LSA: Learning Support Assistant

MAT: Multi-academy Trust

NASUWT: National Association of Schoolmasters and Union of Women Teachers

NATE: National Association for the Teaching of English

NATRE: National Association of Teachers of Religious Education

NEU: National Education Union

NQT: Newly Qualified Teacher

OECD: Organisation for Economic Co-operation and Development

OIA: Office of the Independent Adjudicator

Ofqual: Office for Qualifications

Ofsted: The Office for Standards in Education

PGCE: Post Graduate Certificate of Education

PGDE: Post Graduate Diploma in Education

PGTA: Post Graduate Teaching Apprenticeships

PhD: Doctor of Philosophy

PISA: Programme of International Student Assessment

PP: Pupil Premium

PP+: Pupil Premium Plus

PRT: Provisionally Registered Teachers

PRU: Pupil Referral Unit

PSHE: Personal Social Health and Economic

QTS: Qualified Teacher Status

RPI: Rules, Praise and Ignore

RQT: Recently Qualified Teacher

RSE: Relationship and Sex Education

SACRE: Standing Advisory Council for Religious Education

SCITT: School-centred Initial Teacher Training

SD: School Direct

SEMH: Social, Emotional and Mental Health

SENCo: Special Educational Needs Coordinator

SENDCo: Special Education Needs and Disabilities Coordinator

SEND: Special Educational Needs and Disabilities

SKE: Subject Knowledge Enhancement

SLT: Senior Leadership Team

SoW: Scheme of Work

SpLD: Specific Learning Difficulties

TA: Teaching Assistant

TES: Times Educational Supplement
TLR: Teaching and Learning responsibility
TRA: Teacher Regulation Agency
TTA: Teacher Training Agency
UNESCO: United Nation's Educational, Scientific and Cultural Organization

Index